Struggle for the American Mediterranean

Struggle for the American Mediterranean

United States—European Rivalry in the Gulf-Caribbean, 1776–1904

Lester D. Langley

The University of Georgia Press
Athens

Library of Congress Catalog Card Number: 74−84527
International Standard Book Number: 0−8203−0364−X

The University of Georgia Press, Athens 30602

Set in 10 on 13 pt. Mergenthaler Baskerville
Printed in the United States of America

for
Lowell H. Harrison,
Raymond G. O'Connor,
and
George L. Anderson (d. 1971)

Contents

Preface

Though several earlier works focus on the history of the Caribbean and United States policy toward that region, few explore the United States–European relationship in the Caribbean periphery in the nineteenth century. This study concentrates on that subject, using the American Revolution and the establishment of the Dominican Republic customs receivership in 1905 as boundary lines.

The earliest expansionist impulses of an independent United States were directed southwestward and southward toward Louisiana and Florida. In the nineteenth century the American people moved westward to the Pacific (and looked beyond to Asia), yet they never forgot about the European presence in the Gulf-Caribbean world. They annexed the Texas republic in order to undermine European diplomatic maneuvering along the Gulf littoral. In Central America the United States sought equality of opportunity with British trade and capital, until such time as it became necessary to extend over the isthmian region a political paternalism. The European colonies of the Caribbean posed a different problem. There the United States accepted European colonialism as a necessary evil preventing the eruption of slave insurrection. For years the horrifying example of the Haitian revolt convinced a generation of political leaders that it would be folly to allow the revolutionary spark to ignite the Caribbean world. Thus the perpetuation of Spanish colonialism in Cuba and Puerto Rico continued until the last decade of the century when the American people decided to intervene on the grounds that they could bring to ravaged Cuba the measure of humanitarianism and progress the Caribbean world so desperately needed. Where European colonialism had failed, it was argued, American paternalism would succeed. The Dominican troubles of 1904 demonstrated to Europe that it must operate in the Gulf-Caribbean periphery under American "rules," and I have chosen to end this work with an account of that episode.

In recounting the history of United States–European rivalry in this region, any historian encounters a number of problems. The first is terminology. I have used the term *Gulf-Caribbean*, admittedly an awkward phrase, to show more precisely two regions—the Gulf area, bordered on the north by the United States, on the west by Mexico, and on the south by Cuba; and the Caribbean, marked on the north by Cuba, on the west by Central America and Panama, on the south by Venezuela, Colombia, and the Guianas (one of which is now Guyana), and on the east by the Lesser Antilles. The phrase *American Mediterranean* refers to turn-of-the-century usage after the Spanish-American War, when many Americans came to think of the Gulf-Caribbean as their "Mediterranean." The term was popularized in the protectorate era of the early twentieth century, when Americans looked naturally upon themselves as the carriers of civilization to backward peoples. The journalist Stephan Bonsal, father of the last American ambassador to Cuba, employed the term in the title of a popular historical account, *The American Mediterranean.*

Also, it would seem appropriate to use the terms *England* and *English* when referring to matters occurring before the American Revolution. Most references to post-1783 events employ the words *Britain* and *British.* Another difficulty arises with *Hispaniola,* the island named *Española* by Spain. France called its colony *Saint-Domingue.* In 1844 the eastern, Spanish-speaking portion declared its independence from the Haitian republic and became the Dominican Republic with its capital of Santo Domingo.

A second difficulty in writing a general history of American-European rivalry in the Caribbean is the abundance of both published and unpublished material in English, French, and Spanish. I have relied mostly on printed sources, though in some instances I have used archival material, especially where it related closely to the general theme of the rise of American power in the Caribbean world. Probably the greatest difficulty has been the danger of being sidetracked into the fascinating history of the Caribbean people, particularly Haitian history, or of being lured into more detail in the accounts of United States relations with individual countries.

In researching and writing this book I have incurred debts to dozens of colleagues, librarians, and students. Some of them are Lydia Pulsipher, J. Milton Nance, Donald Warner, Charles McCann, Cornelius Gillam, Robert Krebs, Bernard Martin, Earl Glauert, Floyd Rodine, Burton J. Williams, Beverly Heckart, J. Chal Vinson, Charles E. Wynes, and Wanda Langley.

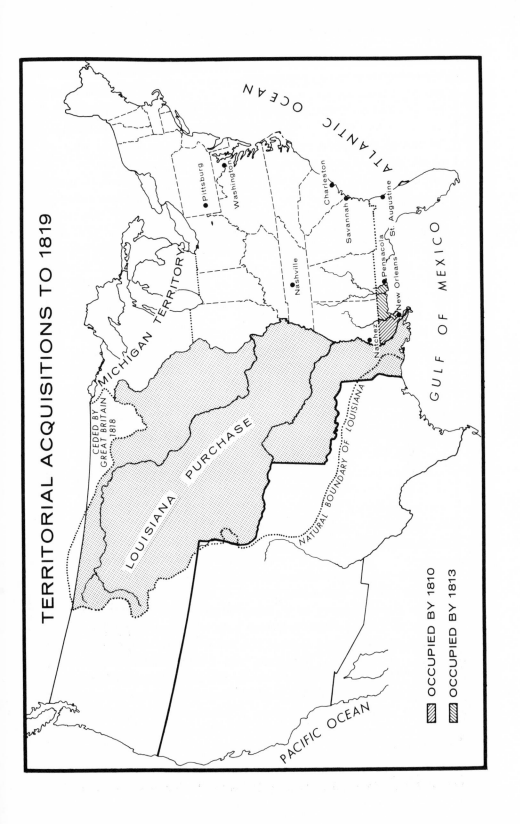

TERRITORIAL ACQUISITIONS TO 1819

ATLANTIC OCEAN

GULF OF MEXICO

PACIFIC OCEAN

MICHIGAN TERRITORY

LOUISIANA PURCHASE

CEDED BY GREAT BRITAIN 1818

NATURAL BOUNDARY OF LOUISIANA

Pittsburg

Washington

Nashville

Charleston

Savannah

Pensacola

St. Augustine

New Orleans

Natchez

OCCUPIED BY 1810

OCCUPIED BY 1813

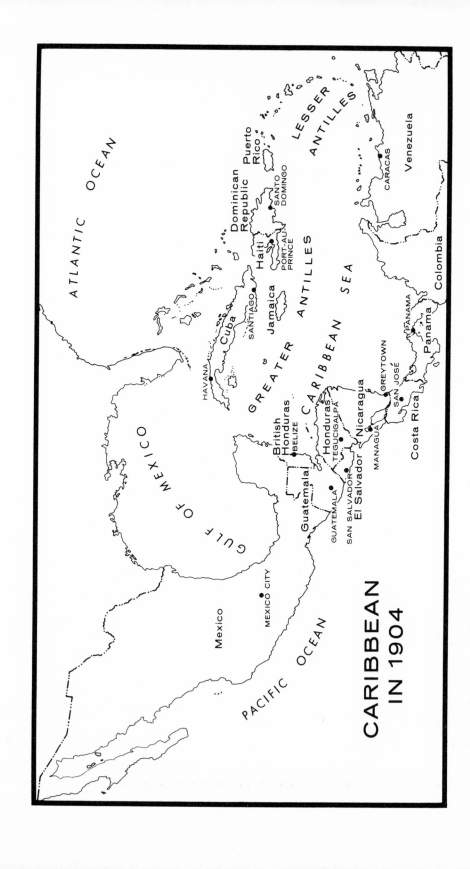

CARIBBEAN
IN 1904

Struggle for the American Mediterranean

1 • The Southward Drive to the Gulf

The Gulf-Caribbean world the American people confronted in 1783 had been the scene of nearly three centuries of European rivalry. Within a decade of Columbus's first voyage to the New World, the Spanish ordered the construction of carracks to hunt down French corsairs and in 1513 sent out a decree to guard Cuba's coastline. By 1520 French ships were operating regularly along the Spanish Main. Until mid-century they were Spain's most feared opponents in the Caribbean. Their successors, the English privateers, indoctrinated with the virulently anti-Spanish attitudes of Elizabethan England, became the scourge of the Spanish Main. Two of them, John Hawkins and Francis Drake, combined a Protestant zeal with free trade notions in their attacks on Spanish mercantilism. To the English the concept of a closed empire in the New World was anathema. From the 1560s on Drake conducted an intermittent crusade against the Spanish, capturing precious metals dug out of Mexico or Peru and demoralizing Spanish defenses. In countless towns on the Spanish Main the populace prayed for deliverance from the Protestant scourge "Draques."

Though the French, English, and later on the Dutch intruded in Spain's Caribbean world, these countries did not conquer much territory unless one counts the colonies they acquired over the years in the Lesser Antilles. In 1655, for example, England held Barbados, Nevis, Antigua, Montserrat, Jamaica, Bermuda, and a portion of Saint Christopher. France claimed the other part of Saint Christopher and Martinique, Guadeloupe, Desirade, Marie-Galante, Grenada, and Saint Lucia. The Dutch were lodged in Aruba, Saint Eustatius, Bonaire, Saba, and Curaçao. For the most part these were not conquests but acquired because Spain chose to concentrate on the mainland.

In 1670 Spain signed the famous Treaty of Madrid and extended de facto recognition to English colonies in the Caribbean in return for an English pledge to terminate the illegal trade between Spanish and English settlements and to withdraw support from the privateers. Thus the principle of ownership by right of occupation gained some legal recognition among societies that still exalted the divine right of kings. More than a century later the American people would apply such a concept to buttress their doctrine of continentalism, their belief that Spain was unfit to rule in Louisiana and Florida. Similarly the old idea of "forcing a trade" in the Spanish Caribbean survived and flourished later in the American determination to overcome the bureaucratic barriers of Spanish mercantilism in New Orleans and Havana.

But it was the eighteenth century that left the most significant imprint on the American mind in this three-hundred-year rivalry. From 1700 until independence in 1783 the American people witnessed the rise and fall of French Louisiana, intermittent warfare along the southern frontier between English Savannah and Spanish Saint Augustine, English conquest of Havana in 1762, and termination of the second Hundred Years' War the next year, in which Spain inherited the western portion of French Louisiana and England acquired Florida, Canada, and Louisiana east of the Mississippi. The French were left with the economically prosperous and strategically valuable sugar isles of Martinique and Guadeloupe.

The following years witnessed both protest and revolt against English colonialism in the New World. From the first those who conspired against England knew well the political advantages to be gained by exploiting European diplomacy, and the American rebels gained an alliance from the French and covert aid from the Spanish. Spain supplied money and materiel to the revolutionists from New Orleans and Havana and reconquered Florida. The aims of Madrid during the Revolution were self-serving. No effort was made to promote a cordial political relationship, and the American proposals for a formal alliance with this old world power were rejected. The momentary union with Spain against the English Empire left no spirit of friendship and camaraderie, as it did in the Franco-American bond. Instead Spain and the United States departed from the peace conference of 1783 mutually suspicious, distrustful, and antagonistic.

Toward the close of the American Revolution, a perhaps apocryphal observation was rendered by one of the more cynical—and some would add, one of the abler—Spanish diplomats, the Count of Aranda. The fledgling United States, its antimonarchical revolution safeguarded by the European balance of power, Aranda remarked, would one day menace its benefactors. In the case of Spain and Spanish policy in the New World, conflicting policies had already appeared before 1783. Spanish rejection of an alliance with the American colonies and the obvious contempt for revolutionary processes which their diplomats held long after American independence aroused deep suspicion. Of all the European powers that retained territorial interests in the New World, and especially in North America, Spain appeared to be the most sinister and dangerous. With Spain the United States possessed a common boundary, from the mouth of the Saint Mary's to the Mississippi, and with that nation the American people shared the common use of the most important waterway on the continent for most of its distance. It was not so much the presence of Spain but Spanish potential for capricious action on the frontier and on the river that alarmed a generation of Americans.[1]

From the perspective of New Orleans, or even Mexico City, the outlook was gloomy. At no time in the 1780s did the Articles of Confederation government maintain any significant force near the Spanish border nor did the United States possess the naval power to encroach upon Spanish authority on the Gulf. Frontiersmen to the north were looked upon as landed freebooters, wild and unmanageable, who might "invade" the king's dominion in their collective rage. Hunter, trader, and land speculator, the frontier "settler" was more often a transient than a domiciled yeoman. His concept of property rights derived logically from a curious amalgam of "natural law" and the "law of occupation." The divine right of kings, insofar as it applied to the Spanish Bourbon Empire, was a reprehensible principle. In political thought, the frontiersman was very much the product of a tradition that has been labeled "particularism," a defiance of central authority and a determination to erect and run communities on the basis of local customs or needs. In economic thought, the frontier settler was highly independent, resentful of any restraints upon his speculative inclinations. Any kind of imperial or central regulation of territorial domain he regarded as the embodiment of tryanny.

Nevertheless, the economic existence of the trans-Appalachian migrants was at the sufferance of New Orleans, and this made them politically vulnerable. The westward migration into the Ohio and Kentucky regions was accompanied by a corresponding decline in the fur trade, the growth of permanent settlements, and an increasing dependence on an export-import trade with the outside. Transportation, especially cheap transportation, meant survival, and prosperity came only from shipping the bulky produce of Kentucky, which could not be sent profitably across the mountains, down the river to the entrepôt of New Orleans.[2]

Lacking a direct economic link over the mountains, the frontier people sensed the precariousness of their position, and they were alarmed at the proposals of New England politicians to negotiate a trade treaty with Spain at the expense of the "right of navigation" on the Mississippi. The Jay-Gardoquí treaty, which very nearly became law in the mid-1780s, was defeated only by a sense of nationalism that prompted Congress to retain its claims to navigation of the river, even at the loss of a desperately needed commercial agreement. In the final months of politicking Gardoquí employed every means to win a victory and in fact tried to bribe some congressmen, particularly southerners, into changing their minds. The treaty failed.

This was only a battle, not the war. Spanish diplomacy now shifted to the frontier itself, where malcontents could be suborned and manipulated by the crown. One such man was James Wilkinson, a notorious plotter, who exploited the fears of Kentuckians afraid of being sold out by the Articles of Confederation government and earned himself a subsidy from New Orleans. The possibility of a separate western state under a Spanish protectorate was an attractive idea in New Orleans and remained a goal until the signing of Pinckney's Treaty in 1795.

The diplomatic background of this important treaty was intertwined with Anglo-American negotiations, which culminated in Jay's Treaty of 1794, and a growing disillusionment in Madrid about the New Orleans–based policy of frontier intrigue. Whether the Spanish foresaw an inevitable historical process in the admission of Kentucky into the union in 1792 and decided to cease their

overtures to the frontier settlements or whether the fear of an Anglo-American alliance promoted them to conciliate the Americans
has been the subject of extensive historiographical debate. In Madrid the view of the frontier was changing. In New Orleans, the Baron de Carondelet held steadfastly to the older conviction that
frontier alliances with the Kentuckians were a profitable venture.
That failing, the next course of action was incitement of the Indians to attack the outlying settlements. The republished accounts of
these years contain letters from Americans appealing to Carondelet
to intercede on their behalf in order to stop the Indian depreda-
tions. Carondelet saw in the westward migration from the older
eastern regions to the Ohio Valley a weakening of the United
States. No American would risk war with Spain. He was convinced
that the frontier people would be abandoned by the eastern seaboard in the event of hostilities. Spain must promote the creation
of an independent West that would be politically and economically
subservient to New Orleans.[3]

So compelling was Carondelet's argument that the debate went
on within the Spanish government while the negotiations for a
Spanish-American treaty were underway. As late as February 1795
the Council of State, the supreme policy-making body in the government, thrashed out the implications of his plan, which called for
economic power as a means of undermining American authority in
the West. Already Spain was preparing to launch a flotilla of war
galleys on the Mississippi, principally for protection of Louisiana,
but possibly for offensive action.[4]

In any event the timing was favorable to the Americans, for Jay
had just negotiated a treaty with Great Britain, and in Madrid the
devil theory of history occupied a lofty place in Spanish diplomatic
reasoning. The Spanish may have looked upon Jay's treaty as an
Anglo-American alliance and thus sought to woo the Americans
with concessions on the frontier. The right (or privilege, as Spain
claimed) of deposit at New Orleans for three years, the thirty-first
parallel for the boundary of Florida, and a promise to restrain the
Indians were important concessions. Certainly the vicissitudes of
the European war operated in favor of the United States, at least
where frontier questions were concerned, because American diplo-

mats were able to play their European antagonists against one another. But an important factor was the pressure of the frontier people themselves and the clash of cultures on the frontier.

In 1779 the French minister in Philadelphia received petitions imploring his government to recover Louisiana. A decade later, on receiving the news of revolution in France, New Orleans theater audiences demanded the playing of the "Marseillaise." In the early 1790s a secret New Orleans Jacobin Club was formed, and already a delegation from the colony had appeared before the National Assembly to demand reunion with France.[5]

A cursory survey of French memoranda on Louisiana in the first half of the decade illustrates the contours of bureaucratic thought on the possibility of retrocession. The pessimism that was characteristic of pre-1763 commentary on Louisiana—that backward and underpopulated province—was no longer present in the official observations of the 1790s. A stagnant region under Spain, Louisiana under French rule could be rejuvenated as an agricultural success, and the proximity to the Antilles enhanced its commercial possibilities. The political implications of an Anglo-American alliance, whereby the British would guarantee the integrity of the western country in any Spanish-American confrontation, offered compelling reasons for a reassertion of French authority on the North American continent. By 1795 the more determined French imperialists were ready to press Spain into retroceding the province by negotiation. Failing success through diplomatic channels, the best course of action would be to harass commerce at the mouth of the Mississippi, demonstrating to the western Americans and the Spanish alike their vulnerability to French power.[6]

The normally lethargic Spanish overseers required a great deal of persuasion. The first gesture of submission came in September 1795 in the Treaty of Basle, by which Spain forsook the anti-French coalition and atoned for her misdeeds by ceding to France the Spanish portion of Hispaniola. At the time Spanish diplomacy operated on the fallacy that France might trade its portion of Hispaniola for all of Spanish Louisiana, but the French wanted both. With all of Hispaniola as a supply depot French Louisiana made

more sense as a colonial venture. The year after Basle the overtures were renewed, this time in a spirit of cordiality and Latin
"union" reminiscent of the atmosphere of the Family Compact.[7]

Napoleon applied the decisive pressure. His dreams of New
World empire were shaped by the immediate French past, particularly the shame of 1763, when Louisiana was lost, a year that he
viewed as humiliating in the annals of French diplomacy. Louisiana
meant not only an extension of empire but a revival of French glory. He was sustained in his reverie by the minister of foreign affairs, Talleyrand, the link with the Ancien Régime, who
contemplated the broad sweep of French domain from the Antilles
to the Great Lakes, the re-creation of an empire to rival that of
Spain. In Madrid Spanish officials were already making the necessary psychological preparations for the next ultimatum by convincing themselves that Louisiana was, after all, not worth its cost of
upkeep and certainly not worth a fight. France was not a very adept colonizer anyway, and an underdeveloped French Louisiana
would still serve as an effective barrier in keeping the roaming
Americans away from the doors of Mexico. The final act was completed on 1 October 1800 in the Treaty of San Ildefonso, the
French obtaining a Spanish commitment to the anti-British alliance,
six warships, and Louisiana. On 30 September in Paris, Napoleon's
ministers had signed a convention with the United States, terminating the Franco-American alliance of 1778.[8]

Louisiana, the Antilles, possibly Florida—the French manipulation of Spanish politics opened up new possibilities for French power in the Gulf-Caribbean. Paris joined Madrid as a decisive force in
the Antilles. From the center of the empire, Saint Domingue,
French power radiated outward to Cayenne in the Guianas, to New
Orleans and beyond. The resurrected empire, Napoleon was convinced, would eventually rival that of Carthage on the Mediterranean, with arsenals and bases strategically placed in the Antilles
and Louisiana, and with the sugar wealth of the West Indies fulfilling the mercantilist dream. The extension of military power adapt-
ed to Napoleon's military preconceptions about the battle against
Britain, for France now could successfully challenge the enemy
with a French variation of the worldwide empire. He failed to rec-

ognize that the British Empire he sought to emulate was a protectionist empire rapidly disappearing. The economic philosophy he studied was not that of Adam Smith's *Wealth of Nations* but that of the Navigation Acts of the pre-1763 generation. Protectionism was to be the core of his colonial policy for the New World, and Saint Domingue and Louisiana were now committed to the old mercantilistic game—economic subservience to the *mèrepatrie*.[9]

As a political idea, the reborn French Empire was one thing; as a working operation, however, it was a long way from reality in 1801. The difficulties in applying such concepts apparently caused no hesitation, for no sooner had the first consul affixed his signature to the Louisiana retrocession agreement than he began to ponder the advantages of a French Florida. Its geographical relationship to Louisiana and the Gulf offered compelling arguments for further aggrandizement of French power. Established in Louisiana and the Floridas, in the Antilles, and on the northern coast of South America, French influence would be paramount in the New World Mediterranean.[10]

The retrocession produced political shock waves in two other capitals. When the transfer of Louisiana was broached in a conference between Rufus King, the United States minister, and Lord Hawkesbury, secretary for foreign affairs, in London in May 1801, Hawkesbury candidly spoke of the implications of French rule for British interests in Canada. The achievements of the French and Indian War would be undone, and in the Antilles the French would threaten island trade and perhaps lay the foundation for a military invasion of British possessions. By similar logic, the United States too was an enemy of British interests in these places, but the threat did not appear so imminent. Until the last moments, when it was known that Napoleon's dreams had vanished and that Louisiana would be sold to the United States, the official British view was still the pessimistic one: France would not relinquish a prize like New Orleans unless defeated militarily; the United States coveted the city and would resort to forceful means to acquire it. Britain should champion the American cause, the British minister in Washington observed, and thereby "attach still more of this country to our interests, and derive all the advantage possible from the intercourse with that important part of the world."[11]

Similar considerations, of course, were already circulating among the Jeffersonians, who were now apprehensive about France as an immediate threat to American expansion. In 1790, as secretary of state, Jefferson had looked with horror at the prospect of "encirclement" if the British possessed Louisiana and the Floridas. The trade of the interior would fall under British domination. With Louisiana in French hands, the Jeffersonians faced a quandary; if they applied the same logic to French Louisiana, they would be leaning heavily on current Federalist arguments. In 1801 the Federalist opposition argued strongly for an Anglo-American alliance on the credible grounds that it was the only way to contain the French threat in the lower Mississippi region. If Jefferson's party were headed in this direction, it was with reluctance, and its leaders contemplated an alliance only as a last resort.[12]

Two of the more compelling reasons for the French sale of Louisiana were the disaster of French military activities in Saint Domingue, which will be considered at length in the next chapter, and Napoleon's fear of an Anglo-American alliance. Doubtless, in the final consideration in Paris, these issues had a great deal of weight in the French decision.

Pressure of a different kind also worked against the success of French Louisiana. In the Treaty of San Lorenzo, signed in 1795, the United States and Spain had laid the basis for settling the Mississippi question by rectifying the Florida boundary, by agreeing on the Indian problem, and most importantly by coming to an understanding on the question of deposit at New Orleans. In the intervening years between San Lorenzo and the retrocession the economic prospects for the frontier brightened considerably. Trade on the Mississippi, for instance, increased dramatically from 1797 to 1798, when a number of Spanish administrative judgments opened up New Orleans and the West Indies to American produce. Sugar, flour, and cotton now flowed into New Orleans for eventual sale in the war markets of the West Indies. New Orleans, Saint Louis, and Pittsburgh prospered.

The impact of the West on Louisiana was more than commercial; it was social and cultural as well. In 1802 five hundred fifty vessels from the western country docked in New Orleans, and more than 50 percent of the ships in the harbor flew the flag of the United

States. Already the flour market of New Orleans was American-dominated, and countless Spanish products were exported from the colony on American ships. Thus, in the Louisiana negotiations the United States capitalized on the reality of the American presence in New Orleans. In 1785 when John Jay very nearly "sold out" the western country for a Spanish trade treaty the economic future of the trans-Appalachian region was unclear; in 1803 it was of decisive national importance.[13]

The public announcements of the sale in Louisiana were styled in grandiloquent language: the menace of renewed European war dictated a new direction to French policy, and Louisiana was ceded to the United States. To the Spanish, Napoleon's action seemed the ultimate in the art of caprice. Having faithfully promised Spain in 1800 that Louisiana would remain French, he now broke his word. In all fairness to the first consul, it must be pointed out that he considered the *totality* of the French enterprise in the New World—Saint Domingue, Louisiana, and a possible absorption of the Floridas—and, perceiving the failure of the whole, resolved to give up the component parts. The initial American overtures concentrated on the sale of the Isle of Orleans, but there is little evidence to show that Napoleon ever thought of selling Louisiana in bits and pieces, though it might have been more profitable. He wished to get out of the Mississippi Valley altogether, and the retention of a part of Louisiana would have served only as a magnet for future colonial ventures. By relinquishing all of the colony, by pulling back completely from Saint Domingue, the transformation in his new anti-British strategy, in which there was no place for an extensive New World French domain, would be complete. Faced with the prospect of a steady drain on French resources in Louisiana and Saint Domingue and inevitable American pressures, he chose instead to concentrate on the European battleground.[14]

Americans of Jefferson's age viewed Florida and Louisiana as complementary issues. The fact that Jefferson directed his greater efforts toward the Louisiana question derived from the simple logic that French power was more menacing than Spanish and that the

possession of the Isle of Orleans had become by 1803 an economic
necessity. Louisiana annexed, Florida now became the nation's primary territorial pursuit.

Doubtless the Spanish government sensed already that its future
in Florida was limited. For more than a century, since the founding
of the Carolinas, *La Florida* had been subjected to gradual erosion.
In 1670 the crown had been compelled to recognize English settlements in Charleston, and as a result of James Oglethorpe's Georgia
venture, had relinquished claims to the land north of the Saint
Mary's River. Following a local conflict with the French in
1718–1719, the Spanish yielded to French rule eastward to the
Perdido River. The twenty-year British possession (1763–1783) was
essentially a blow to pride, and the Spanish vindicated their honor
during the American Revolution in their military campaigns in the
colony.[15] Spanish Florida of the seventeenth century was never restored; instead the Spanish confronted a determined adversary that
increasingly became more contemptuous of Spanish rule.

A few officials recognized the precariousness of Spanish Florida.
With Louisiana incorporated into the United States, the frontier
people would turn their attention to Florida, especially West Florida, wrote the diplomat Casa Irujo, and in the event of war would
invade it. The population "southwest of the Appalachian Mountains" had increased in thirty years to approximately 950,000. West
Florida was a bridge between the Isle of Orleans and the Southwest; its rivers were secondary "Mississippis," reaching into the interior, and were crucial to economic life. Thus, warned another
Spanish official, the United States would probably attempt the acquisition of West Florida "at almost any costs and risks." For the
defense of West Florida, Spain possessed pitifully small resources, a
condition that invited attack. Ensconced in West Florida, Americans
would transform Mobile and Pensacola into centers for contraband
trade with Mexico and Cuba. The crucial consideration in the loss
of Louisiana or the possible loss of Florida, Casa Irujo wrote, was
not the acreage, for Louisiana had never been a profitable colony,
but the steady encroachment of a hostile population toward the
Spanish Empire in Mexico.[16]

Jefferson tried to use the Napoleonic war as a lever to obtain Florida. He saw the embargo, for instance, as a weapon; the United States would appear to be joining Napoleon's Continental System, and in his gratefulness he would compel the Spanish to cede Florida. This logic Jefferson inferred from a report out of Paris that if the United States joined France in an anti-British alliance Napoleon would look the other way while Jefferson meddled in Spanish-American affairs. In this fashion, Jefferson believed, France would be underwriting American claims to the Floridas. In the end it was Napoleon who tricked the American government by levying even greater restrictions on American commerce.[17]

While engaged in these machinations Jefferson continued his professions of friendship to the Spanish crown. To carry his expressions to the Spanish he selected none other than James Wilkinson, who at one time had been in the pay of Madrid. Wilkinson believed that only an Anglo-American alliance could preserve the New World from the menace of Napoleon and his dupe, the king of Spain. Using the British fleet the United States must occupy the Floridas, invade Cuba, and liberate Mexico. Wilkinson was of course giving full vent to his own personal convictions, but the fact that he was the president's chosen envoy to the Spanish reveals some gross inconsistencies in Jefferson's behavior. He was ready to settle commercial differences with Napoleon if the emperor would press his Spanish underlings into ceding Florida—and Cuba too—but simultaneously he considered projects to subsidize Spanish American revolts, with Florida as the reward.[18]

An important element of Jefferson's Florida policy concerned West Florida. In West Florida, that portion of the colony from the Apalachicola to the Mississippi, American pressure from 1801 was intense and unrelenting. Sensing the mood of the administration, Congress responded in 1804 with the Mobile Act, extending American jurisdiction into Mobile Bay. When Spain protested the patent illegality of the act Jefferson in turn tried to press the Spanish into recognizing West Florida to the Perdido River, which emptied into the Gulf at Pensacola, as American territory, and accepting an offer for East Florida. Spain refused.

In West Florida especially the United States pursued dual courses to achieve the ultimate objective of annexation. One was legalistic and focused on the question of Louisiana's eastern boundaries. The French had once possessed the area known as West Florida, they had established settlements at Mobile and Biloxi, and their authority once prevailed on the Perdido. But English rule between 1763 and 1783 clearly extended westward to the Mississippi, and from 1783 the Spanish treated the territory of West Florida (from the Suwannee to the Mississippi) as a part of the Florida colony. Actually the debate rested primarily on the wording of the San Ildefonso Treaty of 1800, for the pertinent clause stated clearly that "Spain cedes to France the province of Louisiana with the same extension that it now has in the hands of Spain, that it had when France possessed it." Left alone, the statement would seem to support the American claim, inasmuch as French power did extend eastward into the disputed territory. But Spain rightly pointed out a qualifying clause, whereby subsequent treaties (i.e., after 1763) also applied to the boundary. Thus the Spanish conquest of West Florida during the American Revolution validated the claims of Madrid. The fact that the American negotiators did not insist upon an official statement from France designating the Louisiana boundary, as Albert Gallatin admitted in a letter to Jefferson in 1805, weakened the case of the United States.[19]

Whatever the legal merits of the American position the decisive factor in West Florida's absorption was the pressure of population. Among the first to admit the realities of West Florida's dependence on American settlements in Louisiana were local Spanish officials, who were torn between their duty to uphold the sanctity of Spanish mercantilism and their recognition that Spanish subjects in West Florida would suffer if they did. By 1808 the older restrictions on trade in Spanish bottoms only had largely given way to a policy of permissiveness to American commercial agents who sought the navigation of West Florida rivers. That such penetration was inevitable and even recognized by Spanish officials was clear to the frontier residents, but the agitation of the legal issue—the historical limits of Louisiana—by successive administrations served only to confuse matters. To Americans living near Spanish territory, the diplomatic debate over boundaries clouded the crucial problem posed by a neighboring territory desperately requiring political stability and economic development. Ultimately, as a leading student of this problem has observed, it was the frontier people who decided the fate of West Florida, and they accomplished their task largely by peaceful processes, systematically undermining the political stand of the diplomat and compelling him to act.[20]

When an official statement of occupation of West Florida was issued in 1810 it merely validated what had already taken place. To the French and British governments the Madison administration sent explanations of its decision, resting its argument essentially on the grounds that (1) the penetration of American settlers into the region at a time of upheaval within the Spanish empire created "a great uncertainty . . . in that quarter," and (2) the nation had an obligation to protect itself by preventing another foreign power from encroaching into Florida. In his letter to Paris the secretary of state was quick to point out that the occupancy was "merely a change of possession and not a change of right" and emanated from "the natural consequence of a state of things, which the American government could neither foresee nor prevent."[21]

Given the expansionist temper on the frontier, the outbreak of war with Great Britain, Spain's European ally, seemed like a godsend. More than a year before the declaration of hostilities the attitude of the administration grew increasingly belligerent toward Spanish Florida, and certainly a significant element in the population looked upon the crisis as an excuse to overthrow Spanish authority. To be sure, the justification for invading Florida was often founded on the perfectly acceptable reason that the colony might be employed as a base for British fleets and armies. Andrew Jackson's posttreaty victory at New Orleans provided some evidence for the existence of a British "southern" strategy. In this view the occupation of Florida was a necessary act of self-defense.[22]

Another factor of equal importance was responsible for the official pressure to incorporate Florida: the revolutions in Spanish America. Secretary of State Robert Smith observed in 1810 that the future of the Floridas was clearly American, not only for geographical but also for legal reasons, for the United States contended that its claim to West Florida rested on the Louisiana treaty. Fearful of

British action in the wake of the Spanish-American revolts, Smith believed it proper to warn London that the United States would view British moves in Florida as "unjust and unfriendly, leading to collisions, which must be the interests of both nations to avoid."[23]

Here Smith anticipated the "no-transfer" axiom, which was sanctified and applied by the Congress in 1811 specifically to the Florida question. Originating during the Revolutionary War, particularly in colonial opposition to French recovery of Canada, the "no-transfer" principle had conveniently served the Federalists in their arguments against the reinstitution of French Louisiana in 1800. Its application to Florida was inevitable. Principally it was directed against British policy, which might exploit the revolutionary situation in Spain's hemispheric empire to establish a commercial base on the northern Gulf shore. As a matter of fact British reaction to these statements warned the United States about any hostilities against the Spanish colony.[24]

By the time war was officially declared in June 1812 any possibility that the Spanish might hold back the dike in West Florida was of course out of the question, but East Florida was a different matter. Congress had already provided in a secret act of January 1811 that East Florida might be occupied if local officials agreed or if a foreign power threatened the territory. The "invasion" was captained by a former governor of Georgia, George Mathews, who doubtless saw himself as the military legacy of Oglethorpe. From his account Mathews possessed a secret agreement with James Monroe, the secretary of state, thus providing some official sanction to his plot. Mathew's plotting was incredibly crude and essentially rested on the frontier concept of the law of occupation. "Anglo-American" residents of East Florida, the plan noted, would conduct a "mock" revolution with the assistance of their brethren across the border. In later accounts written to Monroe, Mathews elaborated on his scheme, providing a detailed summary of his actions; but the final letter went unanswered. (Monroe never admitted receiving such plans.) Undaunted, and concluding that silence meant consent, Mathews moved his volunteers, mostly militiamen and hangers-on, into action. On 18 March 1812 the revolutionary liberators raised the flag at Fernandina on Amelia Island and from there set out to take

Saint Augustine. By this time Mathews's movements had become a source of embarrassment in Washington, and on 4 April the Georgian finally got his reply from the secretary of state, a note of dismissal. The invading force remained in the province under a new command, principally on the grounds that a British expedition was preparing to land troops.[25]

The aspirations of the frontier residents and official policy now diverged. The argument of the frontier was reaffirmation of the "natural right" of occupation of contiguous territory; within the administration the prevailing logic was still the "foreign-power bogey." To the commissioners negotiating peace in Ghent, Monroe sent reminders of the no-transfer resolution with the admonition that the intent of American policy in Florida should remain uppermost in the minds of the negotiators. The fact that aggressive action toward one of Britain's allies was detrimental to the negotiations was not lost on Gallatin, one of the American commissioners at Ghent, who wisely pointed out that (1) the United States could take possession of Florida whenever it pleased, and (2) hostile movements against Spanish Florida were in effect a warlike act and impeded a peaceful solution of Anglo-American difficulties. The occupation of Mobile particularly was a source of mental torment for him, for the post had been taken on the supposition of British intervention in the colony, thus making American actions imprudent, impolitic, and dangerous. Much of the difficulty, he observed, lay in the aggressive habits of the southerners living near the Spanish colony.[26]

The fear of an Anglo-Spanish "deal" lingered. But in the peace discussions at Ghent the British signatories did little more than make a perfunctory protest of United States designs on Florida. The overture was largely a Spanish one, and the effort was renewed at the Congress of Vienna. Briefly, the idea of retroceding Florida was linked to the concept of British occupation of Louisiana until the boundaries of the province could be ascertained. On paper the Spanish plan was unbelievably inept; after Jackson's victory at New Orleans in January 1815 it would have been militarily foolhardy. Viewed in this respect Jackson's triumph was hardly to be scoffed at, for had the British force won the battle their government might have repudiated the Ghent settlement, declared the Louisiana Purchase a fraud, and reclaimed New Orleans. The crusade against the Creeks, the seizing of Mobile and Pensacola, and most importantly the holding of New Orleans thus safeguarded the Louisiana territory.[27]

Jackson's feat at New Orleans virtually guaranteed him a niche in the ranks of national heroes. To the frontiersmen who lived within the shadow of Spanish territory, he epitomized the reckless spirit that frontier residents believed necessary to combat a wicked and perfidious foe. Jackson was forty-eight years old when he triumphed over the British, and he had come a long way since that day in 1788 when he rode into Jonesboro, in what later became Tennessee, with his fine horses, guns, saddlebags, and foxhounds. He had once tried schoolteaching but gave it up to study law. Tennesseans were most impressed with Jackson's appearance, his tall, straight body which, though appearing somewhat emaciated, carried an imposing head dominated by stiffly erect hair, high forehead, firm jaw, long teeth, and beady blue eyes that according to tradition kindled fire. They knew him as the landholding aristocratic westerner who had gotten his social education not in tea parlors but from horse racing, cock fighting, and carousing. And they also knew his temper and spirit and that he had once killed a man in a duel after taking his opponent's bullet in the chest. His feelings were absolute: he loved his friends and hated his enemies.

If in the minds of American diplomats the crucial consideration was Florida's place in the balance of power on the North American continent, for Jackson and his followers the issue of Spanish Florida was clear-cut and one-sided. Spain claimed land it refused to develop, supervised Indian tribes it could not control, and regulated vital waterways that reached into American territory.

As Spanish policy ventured in the direction of acceptance of Florida's cession, Spain demanded simultaneously that the United States pursue a policy of strict neutrality toward the revolutions of Spanish America. This meant in effect a toning down of the harsher phrases of official statements concerning Florida. The new American strategy, fashioned largely by Secretary of State John

Quincy Adams, was that Spain would eventually yield Florida if the United States maintained a steady diplomatic pressure and convinced the Spanish government that it did not intend to throw the weight of American arms into the struggle raging in her empire.

Adams's style contrasted sharply with Jackson's, but the two shared a few things in political beliefs and habits. Like Jackson, Adams went after his opponents with such ferocity that he was often looked upon as pugnacious, and with his Tennessee political enemy he possessed an unquestioned devotion to the Union. One reason he refused to censure Jackson for the 1818 Florida raid was his passionate nationalism. He could not bring himself to condemn publicly the actions of a fellow American against America's enemy Spain. He abominated Jackson personally. While the one was sowing his wild oats in the Carolinas the other was polishing his French in European courts. Even after Jackson became president and acquired some respect and following in New England, Adams could not bear to witness "his darling Harvard" grant at commencement in 1833 an honorary degree to that "barbarian and savage who could scarcely spell his own name."

A policy of "watchful waiting" was particularly exasperating for those who believed that Spain should be forcibly evicted from Florida. In the early history of Georgia the conflict between crown and colony concerning the Spanish menace had sparked a similar debate, not about ultimate goals but over tactics. On that occasion Oglethorpe and his associates had opted for the direct assault as a means of putting an end to what they considered a perpetual threat. The same logic pervaded the frontier in the years after Ghent, and the greatest disappointment was that Jackson and his men had not been allowed to eradicate Spanish power during the war.

It would be misleading to suggest that the Monroe administration repudiated the brazen raids carried out while the government negotiated with Spain. The repudiation was official, as were the apologies, but cabinet members disagreed over the utility of frontier raiding. An excellent illustration was the raid of 1817 against Amelia Island led by the Scottish adventurer Gregor McGregor. Failing to obtain official American or British sanction for his proposal, Mc-

Gregor allied with disaffected Spaniards resident in the United States, and set sail from Charleston, where he had been entertained in lavish fashion. Along the route he put in at Savannah, picked up more volunteers and collected, it was reported, "investments" in his expedition, to be redeemed by the sale of conquered lands. McGregor's goal was the fort on Amelia Island, which Mathews had seized several years earlier, and which now was taken with little trouble. The raiders turned Amelia into a sanctuary for smugglers, and their activity brought Spanish protests. In his December 1817 message to Congress Monroe dutifully condemned the seizure, although he seemed more concerned about the transformation of Amelia into a smuggling enterprise than about McGregor's violation of neutrality. Monroe's response to the problem came in the form of a contingent of troops dispatched to Amelia to clear out the smugglers. This action in itself was highly questionable and in the cabinet it led to heated debate. Adams and Secretary of War John C. Calhoun argued that the troops should remain pending negotiations with the Spanish. To Adams the issue was patently clear: Spain had failed to fulfill the pledge made in the Treaty of 1795 to police the Floridas. The retention of Amelia was necessary to safeguard American settlements from Indian attacks.[28]

Compared with the episodes of 1818 the Amelia Island affair was only a minor irritant. In early January Jackson, who had been granted the command of United States forces on the border, wrote a letter to his superior in which he promised, if given some kind of authorization from the president, to fulfill one of his lifetime goals, the seizure of Florida. Adams warned that the United States would have no alternative but to occupy the colony if the Spanish could not pacify the Indians in accordance with the treaty stipulations of 1795. During the fall of 1817 settlers and Indians had fought by the Apalachicola River near the border. Following one such incident, in which fifty-one Americans perished, Jackson received his charge with an order of 26 December to deal with the Indians.

To what extent the administration "authorized" Jackson's 1818 forays has been debatable ever since. One thing is certain: Jackson's actions fitted perfectly the frontier concept of justice. In March his force entered Spanish domain and headed toward Saint Marks, where he learned the Indians were gathering. There his superior force won a quick surrender from the Spanish garrison and took a prisoner, Alexander Arbuthnot, a Scotsman, who earned his living by trading with the Indians. The Indians had already departed, and Jackson now set out after them in hot pursuit. A hundred miles deeper into foreign territory at an Indian village on the Suwannee the contingent captured another British subject, Robert C. Ambrister, also an Indian trader. Once more Jackson's quarry had eluded him. On the return march to Saint Marks he vengefully ordered the destruction of villages along the way. Arriving at Saint Marks late in April, he commenced the famous courts-martial of Ambrister and Arbuthnot. Jackson's officers composed the tribunal. The evidence against Arbuthnot was flimsy; at worst his crime had been to warn the Indians, allowing them to escape. The fact that they had eluded their pursuers was a damaging factor. Ambrister readily confessed to the misdeed of having led the Indians in war. Here, apparently, the voting was very close, for one officer changed his mind, thus altering the punishment from death to fifty lashes. But Jackson overruled this gesture of clemency, and on 29 April both men were executed, Ambrister by a firing squad, Arbuthnot by the rope.[29]

The legal implication of the "trials" and sentences—the punishment of two British subjects by Americans on Spanish soil—was incredibly baffling. Many Britishers were convinced that Tennessee frontiersmen had been allowed to make a mockery of international law, but the evidence Jackson used against the two was relayed to London and presented to Lord Castlereagh, who did not refute it. Within the cabinet the raid occasioned a now famous debate over Jackson's conduct, with everyone except John Quincy Adams, according to himself, taking the position that the general must be repudiated. A few such as William Crawford wanted to undermine Jackson's political future. Adam's argument was a compelling one: Jackson acted rashly but he was authorized to cross into Spanish territory in pursuit of the Indian foe. To Onís, Adams defended Jackson's raids on the inability of the Spanish to pacify the Indian settlements, as promised in Pinckney's Treaty.[30]

Adams's logic was not a defense of Jackson nor a defense of

Jackson's tactics. The Florida raids provided the secretary of state with compelling evidence to convince the Spanish, with whom he had been negotiating since Monroe's inauguration, that Spain could not police Florida.

The Spanish government had come to a similar conclusion in the aftermath of the War of 1812 when Don Luis de Onís proposed to cede Florida to the British in return for a guarantee of the Isle of Orleans and Spanish Louisiana to Spain. Onís's superiors in the Council of the Indies shied away from his plan, principally because it would have meant war with the United States and because the British would have nothing to do with the idea. Thus when Onís began his negotiations with Adams Spain had already lost the one real bargaining lever, British power, that could have checked the American penetration at the thirty-first parallel. It was simply a matter of time until diplomatic pressure from Washington and the more dangerous frontier pressure drove the Spanish southward to Havana.

It was not the trademark of Spanish diplomacy to accept diplomatic defeat gracefully. Florida may have been only a northern buffer for the Spanish Empire, but for the United States it was a territorial necessity. So Onís reasoned that if he held firm and demanded favorable boundaries, claims settlements, and most importantly an American pledge to uphold strict neutrality in the wars of Spanish America, the United States would pay his price for the Florida cession. His duty was to procrastinate. Of all European diplomats resident in the United States none was his equal in grinding out verbose dispatches and memoranda summing up his determined opposition to change. In his obstinacy he merely carried out the instructions of Madrid, and if Monroe and Adams became irritated with Onís's intellectually tortuous arguments, it was because the man was a symbol of uncompromising standpattism. Little wonder that after a year of diplomatic sparring, Adams saw the Jackson raids as a decisive element in his case.[31]

Both Adams and Jackson looked upon the absorption of Florida as the supreme moment of their careers, although their tactics necessarily differed greatly. Adams saw the Florida question as a part of the larger issue of American security, which meant the gradual but inevitable eradication of the balance of power from the North American continent. It was not the addition of extra territory so much as the addition of territory lying on the Gulf that made the difference. His case against the Spanish failure to maintain order in Florida was couched in legalisms; Spain had failed to fulfill its pledges in the Treaty of San Lorenzo. Here his charges coincided with those of the frontier residents, intermittently plagued with Indian troubles, and for him as for Jackson and his militiamen the choice for Spain was a simple one:

> Spain must immediately make her selection, either to place a force in Florida adequate at once to the protection of her territory, and to the fulfillment of her engagements, or cede to the United States a province, of which she retains nothing but the nominal possession, but which is, in fact, a derelict open to the occupancy of every enemy, civilized or savage, of the United States, and serving no other earthly purpose than as a post of annoyance to them.[32]

Throughout the summer and into the fall and winter of 1818 the impact of Jackson's foray, the unceasing pressure of Adams, and the reluctance of any European power to intervene on Spain's behalf worked steadily to break Spanish resistance. Backcountry editorialists condemned Spanish intransigence and indifference to the near unanimous public demand that Florida become United States territory. In the Congress anti-Spanish feeling made great headway, especially in the speeches of Henry Clay, whose philippics against royalist atrocities in the mainland revolutions echoed the cries of anguish from the public press, which sought to satisfy the ravenous appetites of its readers by reprinting gory tales from the Spanish Inquisition. If Madrid was alarmed by the rhetorical onslaught it was even more alarmed by the reality of Jackson's escapade, which had among other things made a mockery of royal rule in the Florida colony. Onís was now instructed to drop the unattainable goals of diplomacy—absolute guarantees that the rebels of Spain's colonies would not be abetted or recognized—and instead was ordered to get a settlement that was compatible with Spanish needs. This meant essentially the drawing of a boundary line in the West that was not so patently absurd as Onís's first proposals, in which he had questioned the validity of the Louisiana Purchase.[33]

In the courts of Europe too Jackson's actions tended to hurt rather than help the Spanish position. Gallatin, writing from his Paris post in August 1818, saw clearly that in only one capital, London, would Spain be able to obtain more than the expected sympathy meted out to a harassed monarchy. And the British were fairly outspoken in their attitude that they preferred at least East Florida in the control of Spain, principally because Spanish Florida served as a buffer between the United States and the British West Indies. But if Castlereagh had been determined to intervene on behalf of Spain, the most propitious occasion would certainly have been in the few weeks after the summary executions of Arbuthnot and Ambrister. Instead the course of British policy remained unwavering where Florida was concerned, and Castlereagh continued to cultivate the American minister Richard Rush and to deny the persistent rumors that Britain was prepared to annex Cuba to block the United States in the Gulf of Mexico.[34]

On 22 February 1819 Adams and Onís signed the final draft of the treaty, now transformed into a document encompassing not only the Florida question but the entire United States boundary in the Southwest. In the future these boundary stipulations would spawn a host of controversies, but for the moment the quest to dominate the northern shore of the New World Mediterranean was fulfilled. Adams was effusive in self-congratulation for goals attained; the application of frontier justice to the anarchy of Spanish rule in Florida had been vindicated, and the public awaited the final solution of the Indian question.[35]

2 • The Era of the Monroe Doctrine— Revolution and Reaction

The American Revolution provided an ideological support for the historical movements to rid the hemisphere of all European rule. In the formulation of its diplomatic principles, the United States accepted the idea of rejection of Europe as hallowed doctrine. Thomas Paine in *Common Sense*, the most famous of the Revolutionary political tracts, had argued persuasively for political *and* commercial freedom; he saw in an independent United States the center of democratic, antimercantilistic thought. Its government would naturally follow by making America a port for the trade of all nations.[1]

The wars for Latin American independence began in 1808 as a protest against Napoleon's usurpation of the Spanish throne, but by 1810 the movements became openly defiant of Spanish rule. In Florida Spain's power was weakened by the withdrawal of forces to the European conflict and by territorial pressures from the United States. In Mexico the Spanish confronted a revolutionary opposition led by a sixty-year-old parish priest steeped in French culture, Miguel Hidalgo; in Buenos Aires they faced a junta composed of creoles—full-blooded Spaniards born in the New World—who audaciously announced they were exercising power in the name of King Ferdinand, whom Napoleon had thrown into prison and replaced with Joseph Bonaparte. When the *gachupines*—Spaniards who migrated from the old country to gain positions in the Spanish Empire—refused to live with the pronouncements of the creole juntas, war ensued. Except in Mexico, where the creole and gachupine became allies against Hidalgo's Indians and mestizos (those of Spanish and Indian parents), these wars for independence were conflicts between two groups of social aristocracy. In this respect the creole revolutionaries enjoyed a certain similarity of background with the leadership of the American Revolution.

Unfortunately the Latin American independence movement lasted so long—from 1810 to 1825—that the outcome was in doubt for more than a decade. Confronted with a threat to its neutral rights on the high seas, the United States gave less attention to the Latin American wars than it otherwise might have, though it did mark out the broad lines of policy toward the revolution in 1808. What interfered with a more detailed assessment was the War of 1812, the second war of American independence, and the related territorial questions of British Canada and Spanish Florida. Political expediency dictated a settlement of the Florida question while Spain was tied down in Europe and the rest of the hemisphere. Thus, as José de San Martín, the Argentine revolutionary of aristocratic bearing, crossed the Andes to liberate Chile in 1817, the United States prepared its final diplomatic assault on Spanish colonialism in Florida. As Simón Bolívar the creole revolutionary pursued victory in northern South America, American leaders still debated the question of recognition. Though Washington was the first capital to extend formal acceptance of a revolutionary government, the anger at United States delay in diplomatic recognition of kindred revolutionary societies and at the later American opposition to a meaningful hemispheric union had already appeared.

It is inaccurate to claim that the United States failed to develop a coherent hemispheric policy before the 1820s. At the beginning of the Napoleonic war the southern continent was still largely unknown to most Americans. Within the next fifteen years American merchants, such as the diplomat-trader William Shaler, ventured into Spanish dominions, clandestinely spreading the heretical teachings of free trade and independence. By 1808 Thomas Jefferson had projected certain broad principles of a Latin American policy: the continent should be kept free from European influence; Cuba, Florida, and Mexico must not be transferred to another European power.

Several forces undermined Jefferson's intentions. The Napoleonic war compelled the Republicans to forsake their "large policy" of 1808, the grandiose commercial design for Spanish America that had emanated from Jefferson's cabinet in the final year of his presidency. Instead Madison yielded to economic pressures, particularly the lure of the peninsular grain trade, and promoted commerce with Spain. Territorial pursuits associated with the War of 1812 distracted Americans from the struggles against colonial authority in Spanish America. In 1815 the cause of the Spanish-American revolutionaries appeared doomed—Bolívar journeyed from the South American continent to the Antilles; San Martín had yet to make his famous migration across the Andes to Chile; and in Mexico, where the "grito de Dolores" had launched a mass protest and eventual revolution against Spain, the insurrection's leaders had been jailed or killed.

In the years from the peace of Ghent to Monroe's message of 1823 American policy toward mainland Spanish America evolved from a position of nonbelligerency to recognition of revolutionary governments and eventually to official declaration of opposition to future European colonization of the Western hemisphere. Between 1815 and 1820 Americans became more aware of Spanish America, their information derived in part from the activities of naval officers sent to protect American commerce off the South American coast and from special agents dispatched to reconnoiter the political situation. Until the Florida title passed into American hands, there was no recognition of revolutionary governments, though in the Congress Clay waged a war of oratory against the policy of a republican government that wavered in its acceptance of fellow republicans to the south. Actually the Clay proposal for recognition of the new republics involved something more complex than the timing of official recognition; it concerned also the fundamental relationship between the United States and Latin America, by which both Clay and Adams meant *mainland* Latin America. In their famous oratorical displays of 1821 (when Clay gave one of several "retirement from public life" discourses to his political followers, and Adams one of his Fourth of July masterpieces), both men spoke to the question of the future of the inter-American relationship. Here the debate concerned mostly political and economic questions such as Anglo-American commercial competition in Latin American trade or the prospects of a closer political identification with the new republics. In a sense this debate lingered into the intervening years, overshadowed by the cabinet discussions of European intervention in Latin America in 1823 but reappeared in 1825–1826 as the government shaped its policy toward the first hemispheric conference, called by Bolívar to meet in 1826.[2]

Later observers exaggerated the Adams-Clay dispute over United States policy toward Latin America. After all, Clay's role in pressing the Monroe administration for early recognition and his 1821 call for a closer identification with Latin America contrasted sharply with the expressed attitudes of Adams, who justified the delay by pointing out numerous differences in the political and social climate of the United States and South America. The seemingly divergent proposals were in fact going through a process of reconciliation as early as 1822, when a dying Manuel Torres, who waited for years in the United States pleading for Colombian recognition, was finally summoned to a formal audience with Monroe and informed that Colombia would be the first of the revolutionary Latin American governments to be honored with American recognition. When Clay became secretary of state in 1825, his position was much more closely attuned to Adams's and together they formulated American policy.

A more significant characteristic of American policy was the general agreement among political leaders about the Caribbean, where United States policies sought the preservation of colonial structures, as the alternative of upheaval was frightening. In the Caribbean world the prospect of revolution created only fear in the American mind. The mainland liberators, who were for the most part social conservatives, were kindred spirits whose principal goal was to sever the colonial relationship with their European masters. In Europe's insular empire the implications of revolution were not only political—a struggle against colonialism—but social and economic, a war against class society. Americans had already witnessed what they considered a spectacle and a bloodbath—the Haitian revolution.

French intrusion into the western third of Hispaniola began in the buccaneering age of the sixteenth century, when the raiders of the Spanish Main discovered that isolated spots on the island made convenient bases. By the mid-seventeenth century, Haiti possessed a more permanent population, but the English portion of the buccaneering residents had been absorbed into a French-dominated enterprise. The Spanish from the eastern part were beaten back, and in 1697 Spain extended de facto recognition to France's claims in western Hispaniola. In the next century Haiti boomed as an economic miracle, producing sugar, coffee, indigo, cocoa, and cotton. In time the export-import trade reached 140 million dollars, a sum exceeding the productive wealth of the thirteen English colonies and greater than the production of Spanish America. Labor shortages were erased by the importation of African slaves, and the sugar planters settled into a life of ease. From the port cities they constructed a network of roads that reached to palatial plantation houses.

The wars of the eighteenth century considerably enhanced Saint Domingue's strategic value. In Môle Saint-Nicolas the French dreamed of a future Gibraltar in the Western hemisphere, and in their treaty of alliance with the revolting English colonies in 1778 they obtained a military guarantee for the colony. Already Saint Domingue was a crucial supply base for secret shipments of munitions to the Americans, who used them effectively at the battle of Saratoga, October 1777. It was a French fleet out of Saint Domingue that bottled up Cornwallis's army at Yorktown in 1781.[3]

In 1789 the colony manifested all the criteria of colonial stability. The plantation aristocracy, intensely proud of its French origin, presided over eight thousand plantations rich in agricultural production. The population was reckoned at forty-two thousand whites, thirty-eight thousand free blacks, and five hundred thousand black slaves. Cuba was Spain's "pearl of the Antilles"; Saint Domingue was the "queen of the Antilles."

Seventeen eighty-nine was a year of revolution in France. When the French in Saint Domingue heard about the call for a national assembly, they joyously paraded and wore the tricolored cockade. The next year whites began to assume more local control by convening an assembly and declaring that any French law concerned with internal matters of the colony was void unless approved by Saint Domingue's representatives. In Paris the national assembly declared this action illegal, but a trend had begun, and it was not to be stopped so easily. As the Jacobins gained ground in the mother country, colonial legislation became more tolerant of local attitudes, and in 1792 the French national assembly decreed that all free men were equal. At the same time, it underwrote the legal position of Saint Domingue's slave system. French strategists predicted war between France and Britain with the likelihood of Spanish participation against France. The Caribbean would become, as in the past, a crucial theater of war. The French admiralty considered plans for an expedition, with some six thousand black troops, for an attack from Saint Domingue against Spanish possessions in Mexico, northern South America, and Louisiana.

The plan failed to materialize in 1792. In Europe the war erupted in March 1793, and on the Spanish portion of Hispaniola the militia began to organize for an assault against French towns. By now all of Saint Domingue was in a state of unrest. Royalists had fled to the hills and there, ironically, had won the political allegiance of a sizable number of their slaves, who were also disgruntled with the revolutionary policy in Paris. Sensing the possibilities of the situation, the Spanish made overtures to a few of the black leaders and provided them with commissions in the Spanish army. One who received a Spanish commission was Toussaint L'Ouverture.

Toussaint was not to be in Spanish pay for long. In 1794 Saint Domingue slipped into total disarray. No central authority commanding the loyalty of all existed, and in June 1794 a British force seized a few port cities, including Port-au-Prince. Toussaint now calculated that the interests of the blacks would be furthered if he changed sides and rejoined the French effort, for only he possessed sufficiently widespread allegiance to raise an army of resistance against the British. In 1797 Parisian authorities recognized him as the supreme military leader of the colony.[4]

None of these concessions was able to stem an irresistible tide of black liberation. The French Revolution and its democratic principles had percolated to Saint Domingue's plantation society, but the blacks quickly learned that their masters were determined to preserve the institution of slavery. An opportunity for slaves to win their freedom appeared when a liberal-conservative split developed in the contest for local power. Sporadic outbursts in 1790–1791 brought severe repression, but on 7 September 1791 the planters were compelled to sign an agreement accepting legislation favoring freemen adopted by the national assembly in Paris. In the back-country black leaders had already led raids on plantation houses in their efforts to spark a revolt against a slaveholding society. Out-numbered, the planters were forced to flee.[5]

The presence of British troops on the island after 1793 offered the whites a chance to maintain the old social structure, reinstitute slavery, and quell the revolt of the blacks in the interior. Dissension among black leaders created a situation ready for exploitation. For-tunately for the revolutionary chieftains frustrations and dissension among their enemies were even greater. In July 1795 Spain was forced to terminate her anti-French policy by ceding to France the eastern two-thirds of Hispaniola. Spanish forces on the island were in a state of desperation; the British, who had landed two years be-fore to the cheers of the planters, were irritated with their local supporters. They had believed that the slaves could be forced back to the plantation, that the economy would be revived, and that the riches would erase all their expenses. Instead the next year wit-nessed a severe drain on British manpower and finances in a loss of eight thousand men, mostly to yellow fever, and the expenditure of 2.6 million pounds.[6]

The attitude of the United States toward the Saint Domingue dis-ruption and the British expedition was at first ambivalent. Econom-ically, American merchants stood to lose if the British were successful in gaining control of the island and bringing its trade under the jurisdiction of the navigation laws. Politically both were in agreement in a vigorous opposition to a black republic that would stand as a symbol of liberation to slaves in the British West Indies and in the United States. By 1798 British efforts on the is-land had reached a dead end. Toussaint had extricated himself from French rule, and the British could not defeat him. In this year a young British officer, Thomas Maitland, who had taken com-mand of forces on the island, resolved to withdraw his troops to two fortified positions, Môle Saint-Nicolas and Jeremie. Without authorization he struck a bargain with Toussaint whereby all Bri-tish troops would leave if the black leader promised not to lead a revolt against Jamaica. In London Rufus King, the American minis-ter, got wind of the agreement, which the cabinet tried to keep secret, and pressed the British for a clarification of Toussaint's status in British assessments of the revolt. Did Maitland's agreement constitute recognition of an independent Saint Domingue? In the resulting conversations both sides eventually agreed to share a trade with Toussaint, but neither he nor a third power might carry commerce to or from Saint Domingue. To prevent the exodus of a slave-liberating expedition, no native of the island, except for Toussaint or his representatives, would be allowed to depart. American merchants won their trade, and the exportation of black revolution to other hemispheric slave societies was prevented. Left unchecked, John Adams wrote to Secretary of the Navy Benjamin Stoddert, a black-ruled Saint Domingue would become a lure to Europe's worst elements who would employ the island as a base for piracy. The most venerated principles of morality, religion, and government would be swept away from all the West Indies if the islands gained independence.[7] Adams spoke as president, but he also expressed a view about revolution in the Caribbean where slavery formed the basis of the social structure. Whatever emotional commitment he felt toward the idea of revolution and independence for the Western hemisphere, it was a commitment far outweighed by a passionate fear of social upheaval.

Fear of a black republic provided a convenient emotional link between the Federalism of Adams and the Republicanism of Jefferson. In its twilight days the Adams administration ended the undeclared naval war with France, which had been going on since 1798, and terminated the alliance of 1778. The treaty was signed on 30 September 1800, and following the proclamation the navy department dispatched orders to American officers in the Caribbean to refrain from aiding Toussaint's forces, then struggling to conquer the eastern part of Hispaniola. In France Napoleon correctly inferred that the United States feared black republicanism in the Indies much more than the return of French power to the Caribbean. With the Louisiana retrocession firmly in his grasp the only military obstacle was the British navy. Happily the situation in Europe improved in October 1801 with the signing of the Peace of Amiens preliminaries. Jefferson, a Virginia slaveholder, was president, and the French believed that now the Americans would be grateful to Napoleon for suppressing a slave uprising on Saint Domingue. At the same time Napoleon was committed to the economic unification of Louisiana with France's Antillean domain of Martinique and Guadeloupe. The Louisiana venture so frightened Jefferson that he was willing, or so he stated, to run into the arms of the British to prevent the resurrection of French power on the Gulf coast, but he was unwilling to ally American power with Saint Domingue's black revolutionaries, who ultimately proved decisive in destroying Napoleon's Western hemispheric design. Saint Domingue's troubles brought out some grim observations from this philosophical statesman who had written often on the nature of man, who held respected positions in learned societies, who knew French, Italian, Spanish, Greek, and Latin, and who patronized the arts. Toussaint was no black Washington, Jefferson believed, and the country should have little to do with him. To publicize the revolution or to identify with its cause—even in political self-interest—would be a perilous course. In 1799 the Congress moved to open trade with Toussaint, and the sage of Monticello observed to Madison: "We may expect therefore black crews, and supercargoes and missionaries thence into the Southern states. . . .If this combustion can be introduced among us under any veil whatever, we have to fear it."[8]

Toussaint L'Ouverture never schemed to advance the interests of the United States in its designs on French Louisiana. After signing the retrocession treaty with Spain in October 1800 Napoleon made preparations to subdue Toussaint, who still possessed official status within the French Saint Domingue bureaucracy. His brother-in-law Victor Leclerc arrived in Port-au-Prince in 1801 at the head of an initial contingent of twenty thousand with plans for monthly reinforcements from France. Spain and Holland agreed to transport men to the island, and Britain committed supplies from Jamaica, believing, perhaps, that where Maitland had failed Leclerc would succeed. The force sent to put down Toussaint was international in support if almost completely French in makeup, and that it was dispatched in time of European antagonisms demonstrated that the black revolution on Saint Domingue was considered a malignancy to be removed from the Western hemisphere.

In 1801 Toussaint had perhaps overcome many of the emotional handicaps about whites that confound a man who was a slave for forty-seven of his fifty-nine years. He still looked for some under-standing with Napoleon and his military emissary. Toussaint would have willingly exercised power as Napoleon's subordinate if the first consul had given adequate assurances against slavery. Indeed, in messages from Napoleon Toussaint had been promised that the rights of the blacks would not be suppressed, though in private cor-respondence to Leclerc Napoleon set forth a plan whereby the French general was to escalate gradually his demands on Toussaint until the moment arrived when the latter would be in chains on a ship bound for France.

How Toussaint came to be captured is an involved story that would require a book to explain its intricacies. Leclerc exploited to advantage the jealousies of Toussaint's lieutenants Dessalines and Henri Christophe. Toussaint himself, though seemingly at the height of his military glory, trusted too much in his counterparts in the French command and was induced to come in person to discuss matters. On 7 June 1802 he rode into a French command head-quarters accompanied only by an aide-de-camp and was arrested. The French produced evidence based on letters allegedly written by Toussaint who, his enemies claimed, planned the subjugation of the island and eradication of the French.

En route to Europe, separated from his family, Toussaint main-tained a curious fidelity to France, writing to Napoleon that his ser-vice as a Frenchman now seemed to matter for little and that his skin color prompted the wretched treatment meted out to him and his family. He felt a certain pride in the fact that his sons had been educated in France and displayed a lingering optimism that the French legal system would free him. Leclerc warned that a trial would inflame the Haitian blacks, making subjugation even more difficult. So Toussaint was transported directly to the Fort de Joux, a fortress adorning a mountain near the Swiss border. Toussaint, accustomed to the tropics, now found himself in what must have been for him an iceberg prison, where winter temperatures fell below zero and even summer warmth rarely dispelled the chill in the air.

He lasted six months. His room looked more like a burial vault than a prisoner's quarters. All his military clothing, everything on his person signifying some former lofty status, was removed, though he retained some gold pieces, two letters, and his watch. In the clammy atmosphere of the prison his health declined rapidly, and he was constantly in need of medical attention. Despite a small fire, he stayed cold all the time, and an aide-de-camp of Napoleon, dispatched to interview Toussaint, reported a difficulty in speaking. Over a period of time the prisoner was gradually allowed greater privileges. Napoleon wanted to know about the arrangements made with Maitland in 1798, about hidden money and jewelry, about secret treaties with other powers and, most importantly, wanted Toussaint's confession that the Haitian intended to become another George Washington. Throughout Toussaint maintained his loyalty to France. Angered, Napoleon ordered the jailers to seize all of Toussaint's personal belongings and to deny him any visitors. At night the fort commandant would awaken Toussaint and remove him to another room while his quarters were searched. The Haitian complained of pains throughout his body, particularly in the stomach, and developed a dry, hacking cough, though in the last weeks he did not ask for a doctor. In early April 1803 the commandant left on business, assigning no subordinate to Toussaint. The guard noticed some slight improvement in the prisoner, who rose daily from the bed and made a fire. One day, he placed a chair by the wall near the fireplace, sat down, and fixed his eye on the flame.

Toussaint L'Ouverture's death in a lonely French prison thousands of miles from the Caribbean of his birth did not eradicate the Haitian problem. Leclerc failed to subdue the island and his soldiers perished from the fever. Napoleon sold Louisiana to the Americans, thus postponing for two generations the French dream of another New World empire. In 1804 Haiti became an independent republic. In the eyes of European and especially American leaders it remained a malignancy, its existence proof of the evils of Caribbean revolution.[9]

Toussaint's death and the birth of the Haitian republic did not alter significantly the politically conservative policy of the United States toward the Caribbean. Louisiana came under the American Flag, but the Floridas were still within the Spanish Empire. This fact alone served to make American overtures to the Latin American revolutionaries less daring and was one reason for the delay in recognition of the new republics.

Yet if by some miracle Florida had become American territory at the same time as Louisiana, the Caribbean policy of the United States would not have changed very much. The story of the black revolt in Haiti, real and imagined, left such a lingering horror in the minds of American policymakers that they saw no alternative to the political structure of the Antilles.

But Americans did want a change in Europe's commercial policies in the Caribbean. The Anglo-American trade agreement on Saint Domingue of 1798 had illustrated well just how much Americans wanted to participate in the economic benefits of European colonialism in the West Indies. John Adams had speculated as early as 1775 that the pronounced French affection for the thirteen colonies emanated as much from a determination to preserve France's West Indian colonies from British domination as from envy of British power. Indeed, the Franco-American alliance of 1778 had been prompted in part by a prevalent French fear that an Anglo-American reconciliation might possibly lead to an attack against French Haiti. In the treaty the United States guaranteed the integrity of France in its West Indian possessions.

Adams's reflections on the West Indies, moreover, were more than momentary political considerations. The trade of the area was bound by natural economic laws to the commerce of the United States. Neither element could exist economically without the other. Such devices as the British Navigation Acts or parliamentary legislation designed to suffocate the American–West Indian trade were shortsighted artificial barriers and would inevitably fail. The French mercantilistic system, which called for tightening regulations against foreign trade after 1783, was detrimental to the natural economic bounds between New England and Guadeloupe and Martinique. In the carrying trade with the islands the United States stood on the threshold of a new economic era, and Adams saw a direct relationship between the movement of American ships and the impact of American power in the Caribbean.[10]

In the 1780s the amount of United States–Caribbean trade had been heavily restricted, but the outbreak of the European war in

1793 compelled a greater reliance on neutral carriers. The issue of neutral trade, or more precisely the "rights" of neutrals in wartime, became the dominant theme in United States—European relations, and neutral rights dominated the presidential justification for war in 1812. In the Caribbean the United States had become very sensitive to fluctuations in trade. From 1790 to 1814 Caribbean commerce accounted for one-third of United States exports, and among certain merchants and cities the carrying trade with this region occupied a sizable portion of the merchant groups.[11]

Following the War of 1812 the United States faced once more the restrictive mercantilism of the British in the West Indies. Nationalist sentiment now demanded that the United States no longer subordinate pride to economic interests, and Congress responded with legislation in 1817 and 1818 restricting the importation of British West Indian products. The price of readmitting these imports, it was suggested, was the extension of reciprocity and equality in the West Indian trade. The demand was ignored; the British did not repudiate their colonial system. In Congress the nationalistic Henry Clay ruefully acknowledged the relinquishment of original American demands but prophesied that in time the nation would not settle for trade based on British terms. In the next European war, Clay predicted, the United States would come to dominate all the trade of the hemisphere.[12]

An opening in the West Indian market was eventually achieved in 1830 by President Jackson. In the grand debate on Spanish American revolutions American commentators generally saw in political independence for the mainland an unparalleled economic opportunity for the United States, with its well-developed merchant marine, to dominate hemispheric carrying trade. Here republicanism symbolized economic opportunity; one facilitated the other. In Europe's insular possessions, in Spanish Cuba and Puerto Rico or in the British West Indies, the United States sought similar economic goals, but these could be achieved within the structure of European imperialism if European colonial powers only modified their commercial policies to extend concessions to the United States.

•

Given the survival of European political and economic systems in the Caribbean—with the important exception of Haiti—it might be presumed that the United States viewed European power interests there with the same disapproval so cogently expressed in Monroe's famous message of 1823. American policy makers were alert to European machinations in the Caribbean but for special reasons—reasons that were based on what most Americans considered to be special features of Caribbean society. The larger issues with which the Monroe Doctrine has always been associated—the hemispheric balance of power, the presence of "European" political systems in the New World, and the recognition of revolutionary governments—were usually subordinated, or at least rephrased, to conform to the realities of the Caribbean world. The Haitian revolution raised a number of questions frightening in their implication—social upheaval, abolitionist bloodbaths, uncontrollable dissolution of empire, and rapacious land-grabbing by rival nations. George Canning, perhaps the most important figure in the elaboration of a British policy toward the republics of Latin America, elicited the famous Polignac Memorandum from the French, which virtually guaranteed that France would not intervene in a mainland counterrevolution. Yet Canning expressed deep-seated fears of Caribbean revolution and Polignac himself was convinced that Britain desired the return of French power to Hispaniola.[13]

To be sure, Spain, France, Great Britain, and the United States eyed one another suspiciously in the Caribbean, but all shared a respect for social tranquillity and an abiding fear of slave rebellion. Any jockeying for power or domination emanated more from a determination to preserve the status quo—as in the case of Cuba, where Spain's grip seemed to be slipping in the 1820s—rather than from a brazen effort to extend an imperial domain. A comment on the Saint Domingue revolt written in 1799 illustrated the point:

> In looking at the present State of St. Domingo, . . . the first of all Objects of Attention is the Security both of our West India Colonies, and of the Southern States of America, from the Effect which such circumstances may produce on the Slaves, who form the great Mass of Population there.[14]

The reference to "our West India Colonies" labeled the writer as British, as indeed he was, but notably he gave equal weight to the protection of slavery in British possessions *and* in the United States. With similar candor he added,

> An unrestrained Freedom of Commercial Intercourse from St. Domingo, either with our Colonies or with the United States, and still more with both, would infallibly open this Source of Ruin, the Course of which would rapidly extend from the one to the other.[15]

In Cuba too the United States and Great Britain were rivals, but their goals were similar, and both were adamant in their demands for the prevention of social-economic revolution on the island. The Cuban issue in the 1820s formed a distinct corollary to the principles of Monroe's December 1823 message. The claim of Cuba's "special relationship" to the United States—a relationship based on commerce and strategy—was a nineteenth-century concept, and the development of a Cuban policy provided an excellent illustration of American attitudes toward the Caribbean generally.[16]

United States interest in Cuba was a heritage from colonial days. The seizure of Havana in 1762 by a British naval force brought with it the confiscation of an immense amount of booty and for a few months opened the city to trade with the British Empire. During the American Revolution Spain provided aid to the thirteen colonies by opening Cuban trade to New England merchants. After 1783 the Spanish shut down the Havana market to American traders, but a generation of Americans had tasted the profits of trade with Cuba. Many were caught between the bureaucratic leniencies of wartime arrangements and the peacetime rigidities of Spanish colonialism. Oliver Pollock, appointed commercial agent to Havana, arrived at his post only to find that local officials had seized two ships Pollock had sent from New Orleans. The officials accused him of smuggling and refused to recognize his credentials. Pollock expressed the widely held belief that such arbitrary action reflected the backwardness of Spanish colonialism.

Spain feared the aggressive American merchant as instinctively as sixteenth-century officials had feared the Englishman John Hawkins. With free trade, a principle much discussed in the colonial debate of 1765–1776, the Spanish associated revolution. In the abolition of mercantilistic privileges they foresaw political upheaval. Forced to choose between Cuban trade with the United States and Spanish integrity, between pots and pans and *pundonor*, they naturally chose the latter. The irony was that they misread American motives, for every presidential administration from Washington to Monroe supported the twin concepts of free trade with Cuba and preservation of Spanish rule on the island.

As a matter of fact Cuban revolution had much less chance of success after the outbreak of revolts on the mainland in 1810. While dissidents threatened the empire from Mexico to Buenos Aires, Cuba enjoyed the sobriquet of "ever faithful isle." In the counterrevolutionary effort, Spain concentrated more men and supplies on the island, thus enhancing the bureaucratic oppressiveness of the colonial regime. Spanish armies and royalist émigrés retreated to Cuba and Puerto Rico. There was no creole counterpart to Bolívar, or San Martín, and the lower clergy, which had proved a decisive element in mainland revolutions, remained royalist in its politics. As Spanish armies retreated from the mainland they were lodged in Cuba, which became a military base by 1820.

Toward the mainland revolutionaries the Jeffersonians professed outward neutrality but privately they expressed expectations of victory for the independence movements. In Cuba, American agents warned creole leaders that an anticolonial effort would never receive American support. The Republican triumvirate of Jefferson, Madison, and Gallatin wrote long analyses of the Spanish American situation, and their attitudes toward the revolutions against Spanish authority were remarkably similar. Whatever the symbolic influence of the Declaration of Independence, revolutionary upheaval in the Caribbean was a prelude to political, economic, and social chaos. No leadership class existed to fill the political vacuum caused by the removal of Spanish power. And in the final calamitous moments of Cuban revolution, they predicted, another European power, probably Great Britain, would occupy the island under a pretext of preserving order. British domination of Cuba would guarantee the preservation of social order by preventing racial war, but it would

also mean the erection of trade barriers against American mer-
chantmen. Thus to the Jeffersonians and their political successors,
the only feasible alternative was continued support for a Spanish
Cuba.

The Florida acquisiton, which was for all purposes complete by
1819, opened the way for recognition of the mainland republics,
but its impact on United States policy toward the Caribbean, particularly Cuba, nearly brought a confrontation with Britain. In South
America the Anglo-American contest was essentially economic, a
competition for new markets, but in the Caribbean it was military
as well. In London the southward advance into Florida was looked
upon suspiciously as the first step in an American power play for
control of the Gulf-Caribbean insular domain. Cuba, and especially
Havana, were thus gateways for American expansion into the sugar
market of the Antilles; for the British, Cuba constituted the first
line of defense. Spanish colonialism in Cuba—the ability of Spain to
hold out against any Cuban uprising—thus was an important element in American and British strategy, for each feared the other
might act precipitately in the event of any disturbances on the island. Each nation had naval forces in close proximity (the United
States had begun to develop bases in Florida), and in 1822 the British began to strengthen their Caribbean squadron.

It now appeared that Spain intended to make the most of this
antagonism. From Madrid came reports of rumblings in Cuba; the
instigators of the plot, the Spanish claimed, belonged to a Free Ma-
sonic agency which had connections in Philadelphia. The American
minister John Forsyth looked upon Spanish fears as political fabri-
cations, but he nevertheless saw a possibility that the story might be
believed in London and if so would lead to British occupation of
the island. Already the British minister in Madrid was applying
pressure for a commercial treaty and Spanish recognition of British
mediation between the mother country and her former colonies. In
all of this Forsyth naturally saw a great plot.

In fact Forsyth and his Washington superiors had discerned the
general strategy of British policy in the Caribbean, but they had er-
roneously ascribed to it an aggressive behavior. Occupation of Cuba

was, in the mind of George Canning, an operation to be undertaken only in extraordinary circumstances. Forsyth's alarmism had
its counterpart in Britain, for Canning believed that American
forces might occupy Cuba as a means of eradicating pirates in the
Caribbean. Once ensconced in Havana, the Americans would
doubtless remain, and their presence would jeopardize British security in the Antilles. In Canning's view the easiest way of preventing
such eventualities was continued official support for Spain's government in Cuba.[17]

During the first year of Monroe's second administration, the cabinet had to face the threat of Cuban revolution. In this attempt—
and indeed all others in the nineteenth century—the revolutionary
junta recognized early that it could not succeed without economic
and political support in the United States. The junta broadcasted
an appeal to the American public and requested material aid from
the administration. Like the much broader issue of recognition of
the Latin American republics this problem brought out a variety of
views within the administration. In a cabinet discussion Secretary of
War Calhoun made a vigorous argument for annexation, principally on the grounds that such a course would prevent another "Haiti"
so close to the slave South, but for Adams the greater danger was
the certain war with Britain if annexation were attempted. His response was to reiterate formal backing for the monarchical government, which would improve relations with Spain, quell British
suspicions about American intentions in the Caribbean, and convince the potential revolutionaries in Cuba that they had no chance
of success. In the preservation of Spanish Cuba, Adams saw the interest that Britain and the United States shared: the prevention of
another Caribbean black republic. As for the future, Adams wrote
in 1823 to Hugh Nelson, minister to Spain, that there was no doubt
of the inevitable "gravitation" of Cuba into the American empire.

The coincidence of interests opened the way momentarily for
some kind of Anglo-American guarantee to Spanish Cuba. Scholars
of the Monroe Doctrine have shown, sometimes in great detail, the
elaborate sequence of events leading to the famous December message, especially Canning's overture to Rush for a joint statement. In
1823 Adams dispatched a special agent, Thomas Randall, to Cuba

to assess the situation. In essence Randall was to ferret out any information about a possible revolt or a transfer of the island to a third power. Randall noised it among the influential creoles that the United States would continue its recognition of Spanish Cuba and would oppose any transfer of the island to another European nation. The no-transfer doctrine, as it came to be called, had been applied by the Congress in 1811 to the Florida situation. Its application to Cuba seemed almost preordained.

Two years later Canning made his proposal for a tripartite guarantee of Spanish Cuba by Britain, France, and the United States.[18] As a political device the maneuver was designed to prevent any future unilateral American moves to annex the island and simultaneously to prevent any sudden French movements against Spanish power. Actually the offer was couched in a denunciation of French Caribbean policy, but Adams, now president, saw its real intent as a means of checking American expansion. The United States had already made its formal pledge to Madrid, and the best hope for Cuban stability lay in the termination of revolutionary activity on the mainland. Spanish authority on the mainland, except for the garrison off Veracruz, had by now virtually disappeared, and many of the retreating troops were stationed in Cuba or Puerto Rico. What the United States must prevent, Adams believed, was a revolutionary crusade from the new republics against Spanish rule on these two islands. Just as the Spanish had to accept the realities of republicanism on the mainland, the republicans of mainland Latin America must adjust to the permanence of colonialism in the Caribbean.

Canning's proposed tripartite alliance, intended to forestall American absorption of Cuba, was directed also at France. In the summer of 1825 French naval movements in the Caribbean increased considerably, and prompted a variety of rumors in three capitals— London, Washington, and Mexico City. The most prevalent theory was that French forces might be used to aid the Spanish in stifling any insurrection in Cuba. This was the information passed on to Canning in June, and he tried to use it as a lever to bring the American government around to his idea of a tripartite guarantee. The French governor of Martinique had apparently received orders for the possible use of troops in Cuba, but he had misinterpreted his instructions and instead had ordered the convoying of a Spanish contingent of troops from Martinique to Cuba. When the news was leaked in London, Canning protested the action as a violation of European "neutrality" toward the Spanish American revolutions. In Mexico City the reaction to these events was even more apprehensive. After receiving the information the Mexican foreign minister visited Joel Poinsett and Henry Ward, the American and British ministers, respectively, and presented the correspondence to them. They in turn suggested a formal statement, and on 17 August both received notes from the Mexican government protesting the French naval movements as acts inimical to the republican governments of the hemisphere. In the protest the Mexican foreign minister Lucas Alamán specifically drew attention to the principles of Monroe's December 1823 message and stated that the United States was obligated to undertake active countermeasures, if necessary. To the last point Poinsett understandably took strong exception. Actually the French "threat" was grossly exaggerated.[19]

Thus, the United States and Great Britain pursued similar goals where Cuba was concerned, but each felt compelled to convince Spain of its commitment to the preservation of Spanish Cuba. On the American side, the pledge took the form of reminders to the Spanish that their armies had been soundly defeated on the mainland and to refuse to give up the fight would be tantamount to inviting a republican attack on Cuba and Puerto Rico. Such an invasion might precipitate an internal revolt. "The United States," Clay wrote to the American minister in Madrid, "are satisfied with the present condition of the Islands [Cuba and Puerto Rico], in the hands of Spain, and with their ports open to our commerce, as they are now open." As for the future, "This Government desires no political change of that condition. The population itself...is incompetent, at present, from its composition and its amount, to maintain self government."[20]

The phrase in Clay's instruction referring to commerce held the key to much misunderstanding, for the Spanish never admitted that the twin American commitments—the pledge to a Spanish Cuba and the determination to pursue a Cuban trade—were compatible. With pressures for free trade the Spanish historically associated agitation for independence. Madrid officials remained skeptical about American pledges to Spanish rule in the island and in September 1825 refused to recognize United States commercial agents. The Spanish contended the consuls would incite insurgent elements. In October Alexander Everett, the American minister, received permission to reiterate the American pledge to recognize the continuation of a Spanish Cuba. A treaty commitment was not forthcoming, but the statement was nonetheless a strong one, and with it the American government hoped to quell any Spanish apprehensions.[21]

In the formulation of a Caribbean policy in the 1820s in both Britain and the United States two figures—Canning and Adams—stood out. Both occupied the senior posts for foreign policy in their respective countries; both subordinated any romantic or emotional illusions about Spanish America to pressing economic and political necessities; both were practitioners of realpolitik.

Canning is usually associated with the middle way between the reactionary attitudes of post-Napoleonic European diplomacy and the romantic symbol of republicanism represented in the United States. In mainland Latin America his policies were plodding and cautious but geared to the inexorable victory of the independence movements. In the Caribbean he reacted instinctively, as did a generation of Americans, to the reality of a black republic in the midst of British slave outposts. In the United States he saw a potential danger to British suzerainty in the Caribbean, both political and economic, but his prescription for dealing with the American menace was defensive in nature. He saw British occupation of Cuba as a final measure to forestall American occupation. By 1824 he believed there was no point in delaying recognition of the new republics any longer; the French threat to aid Spain had been dealt with, Spanish control on the mainland had all but disappeared, and Britain must appear at least the coequal of the United States in securing Latin American markets.[22]

In this effort the key word was *stability*, and in 1825–1826 the most disruptive agents in the New World were neither France nor Spain but the zealous governments of Mexico and Colombia where, it was rumored, plots were brewing for an invasion of Cuba and Puerto Rico. Defenders of the plan spoke of the invasion as necessary defensive action to remove the last vestiges of Spanish colonialism from the hemisphere and to prevent a counterrevolution that might utilize these islands as bases. Canning's tripartite plan for a French, American, and British guarantee of a Spanish Cuba was geared to cope with such a threat, but it was rejected by the United States. As the leading student of Canning's foreign policy notes, there is evidence that the British foreign minister applied some pressure on Mexican and Colombian officials, warning them of the consequences—possibly a slave insurrection—if the invasion were undertaken.

The tripartite scheme having failed, Canning's only recourse was reiteration of British policy at the Panama Congress, scheduled to meet in 1826. This conference had been called by Simón Bolívar, who saw in it possibilities of a strong defensive league of former Spanish colonies. Recognizing the decisive impact of British policy in Spanish America, Bolívar had extended an invitation to Canning to send an "observer" to the proceedings. In his instructions to this observer Canning was careful to distinguish between British and American policy. In the Cuban case he pointed out the possibility of American occupation if the Mexican-Colombian expedition became a reality. The right of Cuba's conquest he recognized; the expediency of a Cuban invasion he warned against. Finally, Britain would not allow the United States to annex the island.[23]

The historical rating of the Panama Congress has never been very high, principally because the participants failed to fulfill the lofty dream of a strong hemispheric alliance. At Panama a treaty was drawn up, but only Colombia ratified it. The sequel to the conference, which was scheduled for Tacubaya, Mexico, was even more disappointing. The republics fell under the sway of provincialism and self-interest. There was much emotional opposition to the idea of a hemispheric union, but certainly an important factor was the disappearance of any real threat to the integrity of the new republics from a European alliance.[24]

From the beginning the attitude of the United States toward a hemispheric union of equal and sovereign states was almost totally negative. Bolívar himself had sensed American aloofness, and he had employed a technicality—the professed neutrality of the United States in the wars of independence—to justify excluding American representatives from the Panama Congress, but the Central American states extended the United States an invitation, and the Adams administration was impelled to make some preparations. Adams and Clay believed the congress of sufficient importance to send a well-known representative, and Clay appointed Gallatin in 1825. Gallatin declined on the grounds of age and his ignorance of the Spanish language, and the appointment eventually went to Richard Anderson and John Sergeant, neither of whom measured up to Gallatin's prestige. When their nominations came before the Senate, clashing opinions over the mission were displayed in the worst circumstances. The House of Representatives, which had to fund the mission, spent four months debating the implications of the meeting, and the central issue—American participation in a hemispheric union—was overshadowed by the harangues over the appointees, the constitutionality of United States participation, the implications of Monroe's message, the survival of slavery, and the Cuban problem.[25]

Clay's sixty-four-page instruction to Anderson and Sergeant constituted a finely woven argument justifying a unilateral American policy hemispheric affairs. He ridiculed the idea of an amphictyonic union of states, restated the neutral stand of the United States, and claimed that the republics of the hemisphere were able to survive without an alliance. As the president had informed members of Congress, the representatives were to refrain from any discussions concerning the war with Spain and to avoid any "entangling alliances." They should instead promote methods to secure peace and uphold the freedom of the seas. They were encouraged to support a joint statement of hemispheric states opposing any new European colonies in the New World. Here, clearly, was the logic of Adams. Having professed its amity toward Latin America by recognizing the new governments, the United States now extended an invitation to engage in trade and commerce based on reciprocity and equality of treatment. Haitian independence posed an intellectual as well as political dilemma, but Clay avoided a long defense of Haitian policy by claiming that the black republic was still tied too closely to France economically and was thus not completely independent.

On the question of Cuba the secretary was precise: the United States steadfastly opposed the transfer of the island to another power or revolutionary movements aimed at liberating the colony. Anderson and Sergeant were instructed to learn the nature of Mexican-Colombian plans for an invasion and to make it known that a war of liberation would be transformed into a war of conquest. The invasion would be militarily hazardous, would invite foreign involvement, and would ultimately provoke American action.[26]

Clay considered the possibility of Mexican-Colombian action so dangerous that he did not hesitate to use his influence to thwart any invasion effort. In a letter to Poinsett in Mexico City he listed the eventualities resulting from any attempt to overthrow the Cuban colonial government. American political and economic interests were intimately bound to Cuba. Under Spanish rule the island's future was predictable, its harbors were open to American shippers, and European rivalries virtually guaranteed its preservation to Spain. Neither Mexico nor Colombia was capable of conquering the island if the invasion were launched or of defending the island perchance an invasion did succeed. Clay called upon the Spanish to cease any counterrevolutionary threats, and he appealed for British, French, and Russian assistance in order to apply more pressure in Madrid. In short an American secretary of state, reared on the doctrine of the two spheres and the principle of "no entangling alliances," was nevertheless soliciting European diplomatic aid to promote American policy in the Caribbean.[27]

As for the expedition, the plans were beset with frustration and delay. Before the Panama Congress, the Mexican president had informed the national assembly that the Cuban matter would be discussed fully at the conference. But during the meeting jealousies between the Mexicans and Colombians thwarted efforts to arrive at an agreement. Poinsett reported that already certain influential members of the Mexican government were expressing second thoughts on the expediency of a Cuban invasion, primarily on the grounds that it would be vigorously objected to by Britain. Others were moving to the position that the expedition should be conducted only by Mexico on the supposition that Cubans, once liberated, would welcome the opportunity to join the Mexican republic.[28]

During Adams's presidency rumors of a Cuban invasion appeared periodically. In January 1827 attention shifted from plots in Mexico to alleged Bolivarian designs to institute a dictatorship in Colombia and to attack Cuba. Bolívar accomplished the first; the second failed to materialize. In Washington, however, such talk received some credibility, and in March Clay dispatched a confidential agent to assess the Cuban situation. The purpose of the mission, the secretary wrote, was to analyze Cuba's conditions as a necessary precaution in the event of an external attack or "internal commotion." The agent was instructed to study the population, agriculture, politics, and defenses with a view to ascertaining class hostilities, sympathy for independence, or ability to resist attacks from either Mexico-Colombia or Great Britain.

Spain's rule in Cuba survived, and when the Jacksonians inherited the Cuban policy, the danger of invasion seemed remote. The perils of violent internal upheaval, so much feared by Jackson's predecessors, were now overcome by the inefficient but stable Spanish bureaucracy.[29]

Some of the more revealing documents about the Panama Congress were not made public until after Andrew Jackson's inauguration and then were circulated only because the enemies of Jackson believed that the foreign policies of Adams were being unfairly condemned. In the 1828 campaign the Jacksonians had leveled charges of ineptness at the outgoing president for his failure to procure a greater share of the West Indian market. As Jackson moved to an understanding with the British on the West Indian trade question, the "Panama policy" of Adams was brought up in the congressional debates.

Where the Caribbean was concerned, however, there was division only over the means of procuring a greater share of its trade for the United States. Few Americans argued for any change in the political relationship between Europe and the United States in the Antillean world. What Adams had written about Cuba in 1823— about the paramount need to preserve Spanish colonialism for want of anything better—applied all the more to Haiti. Britain followed the American lead and began recognizing the mainland republics; its capital and influence soon outdistanced that of the United States in virtually every one of the new republics. In Cuba the British thought they saw a menacing United States eager to attach more territory. Ironically, American diplomats in the mid-1820s interpreted British policy as an expansionist scheme. And Spain, defeated on the mainland, lodged the remnants of its western hemispheric empire in Cuba and Puerto Rico, interpreting American (and to some degree, British) pressures for trade with the islands as incitement to riot.[30]

But the Spanish government was wrong. The Caribbean was one of the few places in the Western hemisphere where the United States and Europe pursued similar long-range goals. In the late 1790s as the Haitian situation became more serious, Britain and the United States had cooperated to contain the black revolt to the island. Where the elder Adams and Jefferson might have differed greatly in their domestic and foreign policy attitudes, they shared at least one view about the future of Caribbean society. To them the Antilles constituted an unperfected society which should be left to an inefficient Spanish bureaucracy. And to them and an entire generation of American leaders, the Haitian revolution was a social and political menace that must be contained if not excised.

3 • The Balance of Power— Texas and Mexico, 1821–1848

In 1821 the western boundaries of the United States were the Sabine, Red, and Arkansas rivers in the Southwest, the forty-second parallel and the crest of the Rocky Mountains in the Far West. With Great Britain the United States possessed the right of joint occupation of the Oregon country. Twenty-five years later the boundary shifted to the Rio Grande in the Southwest and to the Pacific Ocean in the West. In the process the country signed territorial agreements with Britain and Russia, annexed the independent Texas republic, and fought a war with Mexico for the vindication of Texas annexation and the territorial prize of California.

Europe remained a formidable presence not only in the hemisphere but in North America throughout this era. The American people, who twice sent invading forces northward during the Revolution and War of 1812, had only recently in 1817 and 1818 concluded agreements with their former enemy which neutralized the Great Lakes and settled on the forty-ninth parallel as the northern boundary of the Louisiana Purchase. The rest of the line was still guarded and not accurately determined. In 1842 Daniel Webster and Lord Ashburton marked out a compromise line in the Northeast and in northeastern Minnesota; not until 1846 was the Oregon territory divided by extending the 1818 line from the Rockies to the sea. Suspicion of British diplomacy in North America remained high in Washington during these years. The American presence on the Gulf did not inhibit British agents in their efforts to influence the presumably impressionable Mexican republic and later on in their attempt to guide the international course of the independent Texas republic. When France entered upon the Texas scene with its promises of commercial exchange and possibly its military aid, it too aroused suspicions.

The Texas republic was born in 1836, at a time when Americans were fascinated by the uniqueness of their culture, by the cult of the common man and the literary romanticism that glorified it, and by their supposedly obvious differences from the Old World. When Europe displayed an unusual interest in the Texas experiment in independence, even to the point of acting as political advisor and as intermediary between the Texans and the Mexicans, the reaction of the United States was hostile. European manipulation in the affairs of the New World had been discredited officially since Monroe's pronouncement of 1823. The Anglo-French link with Texas was objectionable thus for philosophical reasons because Americans believed republicanism not monarchism was the wave of the future. It was also objectionable because it symbolized the menace of European power, the extension of an Old World balance-of-power scheme to the New World. It was no surprise then that war with Mexico was looked upon by Americans as a mission to extend the frontiers of republicanism to the Pacific and as a way of checking European influence in the continent.

The source of Anglo-American confrontation in Mexico and Central America appeared in the 1820s. In Central America especially American diplomacy operated under a number of handicaps, not the least of which was the physical difficulty of reaching a government. It suffered too from lack of information. The advantageous position of British diplomacy, by way of contrast, was not fully appreciated until the Polk administration.British influence in the area had its origin in the logwood camps along the eastern coast, and British financial preeminence had bound the monocultural economies of Central America to the pound. Political influence naturally followed. In 1825 Henry Clay observed that the geographical features of the isthmus made the region attractive for commercial and transportational ventures, yet the United States had little diplomatic contact with the United Provinces of Central America and knew little of its politics, economy, or people.[1]

American efforts in Mexico were negated for a number of reasons—the basic premises of United States policy, the shrewd calculations of British diplomats, and the behavior of the American minister, Joel R. Poinsett. In the United States Poinsett left his name to a flower; in Mexico it registered as a word, *poinsettismo*, which stood for the most execrable Yankee traits. A fervent democrat, Poinsett saw no reason why he should not become openly involved in Mexican political debates. His championing of one element in the national political arena, as well as his personal gaucheries, virtually foredoomed his mission, which was to adjust United States–Mexican relations on the basis of a trade treaty.

In other ways too the British outclassed their American counterparts in Mexico City. The United States extended diplomatic recognition to Mexico two years before London, but it was Poinsett who was received by the Mexican president the day after Henry Ward as British chargé d'affaires presented his credentials. Throughout the capital there was a suspicion of American intentions, particularly Monroe's "principles," which the Mexican chief executive referred to with cavalier disdain in a message to the national assembly. In all fairness, the failure of American policy in Mexico in the twenties cannot be ascribed to Poinsett's inabilities. He carried out a bad policy ineptly. Much of the blame ought to be laid squarely at the doorstep of John Quincy Adams, who as secretary of state and president dealt with the formulation of a unilateral Latin American policy. The Mexicans had good reason to fear a Spanish counterattack in the early days of the empire and republic—Spanish troops, after all, still occupied the fort off Veracruz— and they were sorely displeased when the United States failed to join Canning in a joint statement opposing Spanish reconquest of the mainland. When Monroe delivered his December message, Mexican disbelief of American commitments to the preservation of republicanism was already widespread. Clay's explanation, which downplayed the possibility of a French-Spanish invasion, only worsened the diplomatic situation. British policy in Mexico was equally self-serving, but Canning's frankness in calling for a pledge respecting Latin American independence and asserting that Britain did not seek the domination of Mexico was favorably received. Behind the scenes Ward spread the rumor that Poinsett had been sent to stir up trouble, to facilitate the annexation of Texas, and to promote a Mexican civil war. Poinsett's political meddling, though sincere, appeared as proof of Ward's charges. The Mexican mind, very impressionable where Yankees were concerned, remained anti-American long after Ward and Poinsett had departed.[2]

•

The Texas revolution was primarily the result of American migration into the Mexican province. The movement of Americans into Texas, at first encouraged by Mexican officials who wished to populate the sparsely settled northeastern frontier, represented the movement of the American people, the shifting of the frontier toward the Pacific Ocean. Though isolated in an alien culture, the Texans were hardly a band of valiant yeomen continually suppressed by fanatical Mexican totalitarians. Rather, despite the patience, understanding, and goodwill that existed between many Mexicans and Americans, the stronger forces of language, law, and politics provided the impetus to revolution.[3]

Those Mexicans responsible for Texas's administration sensed the tactical error of the early immigration policy which had by 1830 planted a sizable number of Anglos on Mexican soil. Midway in the twenties Poinsett, whose diplomatic improprieties eventually led to his abrupt departure from Mexcio City, observed that the Texans occupied the most fertile lands in the province. Within a short time, he predicted, they would become politically obstreperous and ungovernable. In that situation Mexico doubtless preferred to cede the province rather than deal with its reckless citizens. In August 1829 Poinsett reported that several Mexican officials were fearful of an American attack to liberate Texas with a fifteen thousand—man army assembled on the frontier. Later in the month Martin Van Buren, then secretary of state, sent Poinsett instructions discussing the possible sale of Texas. Van Buren even suggested three boundary alternatives.[4]

In Mexico the reaction was bellicose and resentful. On 8 March 1830 the secretary of foreign relations delivered a memorandum on the Texas question to the national senate. The northern province was fast slipping from federal control: Anglos outnumbered Mexicans, national laws were flouted, and Texas constituted a temptation to adventurers who infiltrated the province without regard for strict immigration laws. Immediate steps to reestablish firm federal rule, the memorandum continued, were imperative.

The new policy was promulgated in a law of 6 April that was designed to reincorporate the dissident Texans into the federal struc-

ture by a series of specific measures. The law, which emanated
from the office of Manuel Mier y Terán, recommended increased
allotments for the undermanned military garrisons at San Antonio,
Goliad, and Nacagdoches, the creation of new units at Galveston
Bay, and the shifting of troops normally stationed on the Rio
Grande to the Nueces River. This meant, in effect, a military occupation of Texas. To supplement the military measures the Mier
proposal called for countercolonization with Mexican nationals and
European (principally German and Swiss) immigrants. Finally, the
law encouraged closer Texas-Mexican economic bonds through
coastal trade. The colonists of Mexican citizenry were to be chosen
from the ranks of convict soldiers and impoverished families.[5]

The Mier prescription was a frank declaration of intent to stem
the tide. What is often forgotten is that the measures attempting to
deal with the "Texas problem" from Mexico City represented only
one facet of a political effort to strengthen the central power. The
Texas revolution was a protest against Mexican centralism and Santa Anna's revocation of the constitution in 1835, but it represented
also the failure of Mexico's immigration policy of the 1820s. The
catastrophic consequences of a tolerant immigration policy, which
the Spanish had experienced in Louisiana in the 1780s, were now
repeated. At bottom was the assumption that assimilation of Americans was the answer to the dilemma of maintaining buffer zones
against an expansionist United States. Once settled in Texas the immigrants lost none of their religious and linguistic traits, maintained their fierce hostility to centralism and their fanatical
devotion to localism, and adamantly refused spiritual incorporation
into the Mexican state. In the famous debates of the next decade,
when the slavery issue was linked to the expansionist question, abolitionists interpreted the Texas revolution as a southern-based plot
to attach another slave state to the Union. The earliest immigrants
had brought their slaves with them and the law of 1830 certainly
placed a restriction on further importation of slaves. To assert that
the revolution of 1835 was a sinister piece of slaveholding conspiracy is farfetched. If anything, slavery probably hindered immigration in the early days of Texas settlement. The sentiment of the

Texans in 1835 was proslavery, but Mexican restrictive legislation on the subject was an annoyance and not the principal reason for revolt.[6]

Politically weak, wedged between an expansionist United States and a resentful Mexico, the Texas republic offered to European diplomacy an unparalleled opportunity to preserve the balance of power on the North American continent, to check American encroachment in the Southwest, and to exploit the Texas issue as a lever to mitigate American bellicosity in the Oregon question. Economically Texas could be developed under the aegis of British finance and British-French manipulation of the republic's cotton production. Finally, the republic appeared on the international scene just as Parliament eradicated the last vestiges of slavery in the empire, and in Texas British abolitionists saw an untouched field for their proselytizing activities.

Already Mexico had become something of a testing ground for French prestige. For years French residents in Mexico had suffered from a variety of annoying measures and by 1837 the French government reached the limits of its patience in trying to satisfy the burgeoning claims of its nationals. Late in the year the French minister departed Mexico City, boarded a French vessel in the harbor of Veracruz, and presented the demands of his government. The Mexicans were granted three weeks to respond, and in righteous indignation they refused. The "Pastry War," as it came to be known, was now begun in earnest. In the summer of 1838 the French commander in the western gulf blockaded the Veracruz coast. Reinforcements in the form of another French squadron arrived in October, and the French called for negotiations to satisfy their claims and to terminate their "pacific blockade." This situation was made to order for Antonio López de Santa Anna, who called the blockade a violation of national integrity and demanded retaliation. Their overtures rejected, the French fired on the fortress of San Juan de Ulúa, compelling its surrender on 28 November, and a week later occupied the city of Veracruz.

For Santa Anna the Veracruz affair became an event of personal triumph, not only for the "grand actor" but also for his foot, shot off in the fighting. From his stretcher the general dictated what he believed was his last message, describing for the president in exaggerated fashion the exploits of the battle. Santa Anna was moved to write almost fifteen pages, terminating with comments of death and an appeal to his compatriots to look upon his foot as a symbol of courage and unity and to forget his political errors and remember him as a "good Mexican." Mourning messengers transported the foot to the president, who believed Santa Anna dead. But he was very much alive, able to watch the French take to the sea. As his countrymen mourned over his lost appendage, Santa Anna underwent amputation below the knee, without benefit of anesthetics. A few days later, he departed for his hacienda. The parish priest of Veracruz, with much solemnity, buried the foot in a shrine at Manga de Clavo.

The occupation of Mexico's most important port was only temporary, and French forces soon withdrew to their ships. There ensued a standoff between the two governments, the French unable to prosecute further military action and the Mexicans unwilling to negotiate French claims.

American newspapers covered the whole affair, but the French action failed to provoke critical editorials or inspire general condemnations. In the Congress the president was urged to transmit to that body any explanations given by France about its intentions in Mexico. The sponsor of the resolution calling for such information was Caleb Cushing, who would later negotiate the first treaty with China in 1844. Though he did not use the term "Monroe's principles," Cushing did cite the December 1823 message to Congress in his resolution.

In 1838 the United States was already at odds with the Mexican government over unsettled claims and did not have a regular diplomatic minister in residence in Mexico City. The French had launched their own blockade in anticipation that the United States would have done so out of irritation in dealing with the recalcitrant Mexicans. When Cushing proposed his resolution the Van Buren administration had already notified the French that it would be willing to assist in any mediation of the Franco-Mexican dispute. In none of its correspondence had the administration appealed to the general principles of Monroe's famous message.

In the early stages of the crisis the British cabinet had debated the French-Mexican imbroglio and arrived at the conclusion that France was intimidating the sensitive Mexican government. British naval forces off the Mexican coast were increased sizably, but when the powerful squadron arrived on the scene at Veracruz its commander found the fort already occupied by the French. The British insisted they sought only a mediatory role between the Mexicans and their European neighbor, but the French were naturally suspicious that the British display of armaments was designed to intimidate their efforts and to protect an unruly Mexican government from its deserved punishments. When the British squadron sought entrance into Veracruz harbor, the French commander demanded that the two fleets be of equal size. The British complied, and through the remainder of the crisis resigned themselves to playing the role of mediator.[7]

Americans imagined the specter of French rule in Texas as the aftermath of a revolution that would leave the Texans militarily helpless. They feared that in a critical moment unscrupulous French diplomats would try to erect a protectorate in Texas. That failing, the French would devise an elaborate marriage scheme, reminiscent of eighteenth-century European diplomacy, subordinating the republic to French manipulation. France accepted the creation of the Texas republic as the best alternative to a protectorate. Policymakers in Paris were imbued with a sense of duty to halt the march of republicanism and Protestantism. The architect of the *mission civilisatrice*, François Guizot, premier and foreign minister of Louis Philippe, was a devotee of international balances of power based on the European model. The European equilibrium, he believed, was a thing of beauty that must be transmitted to Asia and the Western hemisphere. In Asia Britain and Russia constituted countervailing forces, but what power balanced the United States in the New World? Left unchecked to predominate in the Western hemisphere, the United States in the future loomed as a threat to Europe. In erecting a barrier against further penetration by the American giant, France also stood as the champion of Latin culture. Universal democracy, as represented in the American model, was as insidious and dangerous as universal monarchy.[8]

A republic that lauded the gruff Sam Houston or the unlettered David Crockett as heroes seemed an unlikely place to find pupils for a French-instructed finishing school, but French agents in the republic were soon reporting that the Texan determination to win international diplomatic recognition provided an excellent opportunity to initiate commercial relations. In Texas the French envisaged a healthy producer of raw materials and an eager consumer of French manufactured products. On 25 September 1839 the economic link was forged in a Treaty of Amity, Navigation, and Commerce. Among other things, it provided for the sale of Texas cotton in France at a reduction in price and the importation of French manufactures into the republic at half duty.[9]

For the French the signing of the treaty was only the beginning of a grand enterprise. Their diplomats were already working on the Texas leaders, particularly Houston, on behalf of a colonization scheme whereby French settlers would be sprinkled in settlements along the Texas frontier. Sympathetic, Houston agreed to act as sponsor for the measure in the Texas legislature. By the bill's provisions the republic would grant a French corporation 3 million acres of western lands which would become by January 1849 the residence of eight thousand French immigrants. For twenty years the immigrants would be allowed to import free of duty any item, and the land itself would not be taxable until 1848. As compensation France would erect twenty forts in a line from the Red River to the Rio Grande and supply them for twenty years. In the legislature the Franco-Texienne bill precipitated an intense debate, and its sponsors, sensing the political implications of their support, soon dwindled in strength.

Following defeat of the colonization scheme, French policy in Texas became increasingly cautious and circumspect. In 1842 Guizot still believed that French efforts could play a major role in settling the Texas-Mexican impasse (Mexico claimed that Texas was a rebellious province and remained legally a part of the nation), but when the British refused to go along in an action that might mean war with Mexico, he backed down. Within two years Guizot formulated a basic policy where Texas was concerned: French policy would generally follow that of Britain. It was just as well, for French activity in Texas was based on the inaccurate belief that the republic wished to remain independent indefinitely and that the antiannexationists in the United States were much more powerful politically than the annexationists.[10]

The Francophobes in the United States doubtless studied very little the romantic notions of French visionaries such as Guizot, who saw a Frenchified Texas republic as a defensive shield for Latin culture. When in the 1840s French diplomats yielded to the primacy of British leadership in the Texas-Mexican quarrel they recognized the strength of British influence in the Gulf region.

British hostility toward American expansion in Texas clearly bore the imprint of the Latin-American policy fashioned in the age of Castlereagh and Canning. The British took a stand against the extension of the American empire into Texas because a decade earlier official policy had opposed American intrusion into the Gulf, especially Cuba. In 1825 Canning had granted his support for the continuation of Spanish Cuba (as had John Quincy Adams), but his approbation of Spanish rule had derived logically from his fear of American acquisitiveness. When Adams rejected Canning's famous appeal to Richard Rush, he kept alive the possibility of unilateral American action in Cuba and in Texas. As the British had rendered support of a Spanish Cuba in the face of an acquisitive United States, it was logical for London to champion an independent Texas, or at least to intercede on behalf of a weak Mexico. Unlike the Cuban case, which occasioned numerous memoranda detailing official policy, the Texas issue produced no counterpart to Canning's tripartite scheme of 1825, but British agents in the republic worked energetically to check American expansion there. The very fact that British agents were in Texas convinced many Americans that a conspiracy was underway in London to create a protectorate.

Lord Palmerston, the chief figure in British foreign policy in this era, saw in the building of friendly relations with the independent Texas republic a means of preserving British interests in the New World. Equally compelling was Palmerston's conviction that it was British duty to interfere in the Texas-Mexican impasse because the

creditors of Mexico resided in London and, at least, British mediation of the quarrel might prevent the renewal of hostilities. The
Texas republic made its appearance in the same year that a serious
revolt against imperial authority broke out in Upper Canada, a revolt that found widespread public support in the United States.
The Canadian upheaval and the Maine and Oregon disputes,
which hampered Anglo-American reconciliation for decades, placed
the Texas question in a continental perspective. British policy was
thus to resist American expansion into the Southwest, but not at
the expense of war.[11]

In citing the reasons for recognizing Texas independence and negotiating a treaty, British agents believed a viable Texas policy must
go beyond merely erecting a barrier against American expansion.
Diplomatic recognition led, first of all, to Anglo-Texas trade on
terms favorable to British commerce. British acceptance of Texas
independence would convince the Mexican government of the folly
of counterrevolution and the republic of its partial responsibility
for repaying the Mexican debt owed to British creditors. Finally,
recognition would lead to delimitation of a boundary, thus marking
clearly the limits of expansion by the "Anglo-American race." If
Britain refused diplomatic recognition, the "Texian Squadron"
would probably blockade the Mexican coastline at Veracruz, Tam-
pico, and Matamoras, declare common cause with the Mexican Federalists (who championed state autonomy) and try to detach the
northern tier of Mexican provinces, levy discriminatory duties
against British products, and rush headlong into the arms of another power.[12]

In slightly different form this was the argument presented to Palmerston by Texas representatives following several years of fruit-
less campaigning to obtain recognition. Despite compelling reasons
for prompt decision, the record reveals that Palmerston moved
very slowly on the Texas question because he was fearful of jeopar-
dizing British interests in Mexico. The appeal for diplomatic recognition was satisfied in 1840 (France had acted the year before), but
on the issue of a loan Palmerston was more cautious. Texas's financial desperation prompted a certain recklessness in dealing with
France and Britain. In Paris the overture took the form of the

Franco-Texienne bill, which nearly became law, but in London the Texas agents promised intimate trade relationships and preferential treatment in the obtaining of ship timber, while continually suggesting the possibility of American annexation if a loan failed to materialize immediately.[13]

Texas's European emissaries were also undermined by the military disasters that befell the republic. In the early 1840s the republic exhibited an inordinately aggressive notion of its offensive capabilities. Such exaggerated optimism led to a series of decisions aimed at preserving the independence of Texas by carrying the war against Mexico to the Gulf and to Santa Fe. The Texan navy was assigned the task of blockading the Mexican east coast in order to prevent delivery of vessels manufactured in American and British shipyards and to deprive Mexico of its foreign trade. In addition, it was announced, the Lone Star flag would be raised on the isthmus of Darién, and the republic would seek an alliance with dissident elements in Yucatán, thus flanking the Mexican enemy. When Sam Houston became president, he repudiated the Yucatán arrangement, but he failed to salvage the Santa Fe adventure, which turned into a rout. In July 1842 the Texas chargé d'affaires in Great Britain, Dr. Ashbel Smith, worked frantically to bring about a French-British-American effort to mediate the Texas-Mexican stalemate. Guizot was favorably inclined and indicated a willingness to follow London's leadership, but Lord Aberdeen, secretary for foreign affairs in the ministry of Sir Robert Peel, rejected the concept of a tripartite pact, arguing persuasively that the signatories would have to enforce the peace, which Britain was unwilling to do. Smith's labors suffered considerably as Europeans heard the news of the Santa Fe debacle. The republic's financial reputation reached its nadir, and in the United States and Europe capitalist and immigration groups favorable to Texas found it difficult to convince investors or prospective settlers that the republic's government was a sound enterprise.[14]

Within the British government the evolution of a Texas policy was hindered by the change of ministries in 1841, an alteration that brought the vacillating Aberdeen into the chair occupied previously by the more determined Palmerston. Aberdeen softened Palmerston's Mexican policy but sought a British-sponsored settlement. He had no wish to anger the Mexicans by embracing the Texas republic or to hazard war with the United States by meddling imprudently in Texas-Mexican affairs. From 1842, when Aberdeen's Texas policy crystallized, British attitudes exhibited two traits: the first was a reaffirmation of faith in Mexico's financial and political perseverance; the second, a genuine desire to convince the Texas slaveholders of the moral righteousness and international respectability that derived from an antislavery measure. How these purposes were to be achieved was never very clear, but in the case of the first, Aberdeen sought to persuade the Mexican government that Texas independence was a political and military reality and that Mexico should recognize the republic's government.

The Anglo-Texas link might have appeared improbable of success at first glance, given the obvious disparities in education and social upbringing of some of their respective leaders. Palmerston could project nationalistic fervency and cultural arrogance in his official capacity in the foreign office. About him the Germans coined a ditty: "If the devil had a son, he is surely Palmerston." Then there was Aberdeen, reared at the feet of the great William Pitt the Younger, who was so gifted that he entertained Sir Walter Scott and other literary notables at amateur theatricals. His researches into Greek culture moved Byron to endow him with the title "the Athenian Aberdeen." Yet he could charm the Texan diplomats who met him. One came away from an official encounter impressed with this "plain, matter of fact man, entirely free from ostentation, and almost free from court etiquette."

British observers and travelers saw in the republic a fruitful field for abolitionist proselytizing. If successful, British policy might bring peace to the troubled Texas-Mexican region and at the same time perform a humanitarian service by sponsoring the eradication of slavery on the doorsteps of the slave South.[15] One of Palmerston's subordinates wrote a convincing abolitionist case in 1841. "By effecting the final abolition of Slavery in Texas," he argued, "we at once extinguish that horrid traffic in a Country which, without our interference, might become one of the most extensive Slave Markets in America." A free Texas, he added, held open the prospect of a healthy republic wedged between Mexico and the United States, capable of influencing the course of slavery in the South. Treaties with Spain and Brazil would follow and put to an end the slave institution in Cuba and South America and simultaneously undermine the slave trade, in a manner more effective than any the British navy might employ.

In the United States the worst inferences were drawn from British activites, not only in Texas but in Cuba and Mexico. Over a period of half a dozen years, from about 1837 to 1843, the outlines of a British conspiracy to destroy the institution of slavery in the Texas republic and ultimately in the United States took form. Diverse information—some false, some only partly true—collected by American diplomats in Europe fed the rumor mill in the United States. Its major architect was Duff Green, influential editor, speculator, and confidant of some important people, especially John C. Calhoun. In 1841 Green obtained a post as Tyler's executive agent and was sent to London to get information about a commercial treaty. His first commitment was to slavery, so much so that John Quincy Adams referred to Green as the "roving ambassador of slavery." While in London Green saw the machinations in Parliament which brought down the Melbourne ministry and installed in its place one headed by Sir Robert Peel. Melbourne had injured his position by promoting a measure designed to increase competition between sugar produced in free-labor British West Indian colonies and the slave-labor societies of Cuba and Brazil. Peel argued that the Melbourne proposal, which would have lowered preferences to sugar produced in Jamaica, Trinidad, and British Guiana, where slavery had been abolished in 1833, would in fact indirectly support slavery and the slave trade. Peel's opposition to the proposal helped to bring him to power.

In all of this Green discerned an elaborate plot. The British economic system, now failing because of the unworkability of a free labor system in the West Indies, was striving to salvage itself by destroying the remnants of slavery everywhere, especially in the Western hemisphere. British public opinion would not tolerate the restoration of slavery in the Empire, so British politicians, urged on by fanatics and abolitionists, schemed to wreck the slave system of

the United States. A foothold would be obtained in the Texas republic by loans, then increasingly the dissemination of propaganda
designed to destroy slavery in the republic and substitute for it the
inefficient free labor system of the British West Indies. The United
States could not expand, and its slave system would be wrecked.[16]

The strong impulses in British abolitionism were not, of course,
shared by all who formulated official policy, but an intent to spread
the gospel was manifestly present among British agents throughout
the Gulf-Caribbean. Reports of abolitionist organizations in the republic greatly excited the Tyler administration. Secretary of State
Abel P. Upshur received an inaccurate report that the Aberdeen
ministry planned to guarantee a loan to Texas if the republic abolished slavery, but when Upshur made inquiries of American diplomats in Texas and Britain, he was informed that the British
government was interested solely in acquiring commercial advantages in the republic.[17]

Upshur was not satisfied with these assurances. In August and
September 1843 he sent long instructions to William Murphy,
chargé d'affaires in Texas, commenting on the British stake in the
republic's future. The British, Upshur wrote, harbored general
plans for Texas. They sought favorable commercial access to its
riches and the eradication of slavery throughout the hemisphere.
He echoed Green's theory of a plot. Removal of slavery was not
merely a moral commitment; it was a means of destroying British
competition in trade by undermining the labor system of slavery.
Financially weak and politically immature, Texas would become a
protectorate, receiving few of the blessings of empire and saddled
with all the disadvantages of a colony. The abolition of slavery, Upshur believed, constituted a first step in the subjugation of the Texas republic to the British imperial system. Because the republic was
already a customer for American products the United States could
not allow British domination there. But, more importantly, the
creation of a free republic bordering on the slave South would undermine the stability of slavery in the United States, and the federal government had an obligation to safeguard the property rights
represented in slaves.[18]

An aggressively anti-British policy in Texas, Upshur argued, benefited the North as much as the South. By supporting the perpetuation of slavery in Texas, southerners would gain only security, and in fact southern agriculture would be injured by the promotion of Texas competition. But the North would discover a new market for manufactured products, a source for cheap cotton, and a new domain for expanding its commercial and navigational interests.[19]

By tortuous logic the Tyler administration thus propounded the questionable position that a vigorous annexationist policy in Texas fostered the economic and social well-being of the entire nation, North as well as South. It is true that the election of Polk in 1844 was not really a victory of the expansionists over the antiexpansionists, for the candidates' views did not greatly differ, and Polk's triumph depended heavily on the vacillation and division within the opposition. But Tyler and Polk exploited the latent fears of European meddling in a neighboring territory, and Tyler's secretaries of state, Upshur and Calhoun, cleverly packaged the foreign threat with southern fears of an abolitionist menace. They also blended proslavery contentions with pleas for preserving democracy in Texas, without squeamishness about the obvious inconsistencies in their arguments.[20]

While Upshur and Calhoun warned of conspiracies from across the seas, New Englanders like John Quincy Adams scoffed and in turn accused southern slave interests of promoting the annexation of an additional slave state. Circumstantial evidence—the fact that Texas would be a slave state—confirmed this accusation in some minds. It was not altogether a fair charge. To accuse the South or prosouthern interests in Washington of fomenting Texas annexation in order to enlarge slave power overlooked the vital evidence that as far as Texas was concerned proslavery elements reacted defensively; they championed annexation in order to prevent the possibility of Texas's becoming a free republic. The augmented power that derived from Texas's entering the Union as a slave state was a secondary consideration compared with the paramount necessity of preventing the erection of a haven for runaways on the borders of the South. Upshur's treaty of annexation, which Calhoun inherited following his predecessor's untimely death in early 1844, was a defensive mechanism. Tyler planned to rush the treaty through the Senate before Calhoun arrived from South Carolina to assume his duties, for the president recognized that some senators would make invidious comparisons of the treaty and Calhoun's representations on behalf of slave interests. Actually Calhoun led himself neatly into the trap. In an effort to obtain ratification of the document and to divide the political opposition he decided to respond to a five-month-old letter from the British, sent from Aberdeen through Pakenham, in which the foreign minister had denied accusations that British abolitionists were striving to undermine slavery in the United States. The newly appointed secretary of state agonized a week in composing his reply, in which he elaborated an aggressive defense of slavery, employing columns of statistics to illustrate his view that southern slaves were better off than workingmen in the North or in Britain. The United States had thus negotiated the annexation treaty in order to prevent the British from wiping out what was in fact a benevolent institution. In his presentation to the Senate, Calhoun included not only the treaty but also supporting memoranda, including his famous "Pakenham letter." There the treaty was labeled, in the phrase of Thomas Hart Benton, the "Texas bombshell." It failed on 8 June by a vote of 35 to 16.[21]

The treaty's defeat, which was due as much to party factionalism as to Calhoun's theories of slavery, provided Aberdeen with the opportunity he had long awaited. While energetically denying any sinister intent in the activities of British abolitionists, Aberdeen worked hard to prevent annexation. He intended to catch the Americans off guard by concentrating on the issue of abolitionism. On 24 June, a few weeks following the shattering defeat of the Upshur-Calhoun treaty, Aberdeen approached Ashbel Smith, Texas's agent in Britain, with a proposition for a "diplomatick Act" in which Britain and France, cooperating with Mexico and Texas, and if possible the United States, would guarantee the republic's independence and ascertain its boundaries, provided Texas refused annexation to the United States.[22]

News of Aberdeen's diplomatic thrust aroused suspicions in Washington, but it also set the Texans to quarreling among themselves. In Mexico the Texas question rapidly degenerated into an issue of national honor, inciting the most rabid passions of the day against any political element that dared to negotiate away any piece of national territory. With Polk's victory in November the annexationists in Washington moved hastily to capitalize on what they felt was the "mood" of the nation and of the republic. A future member of Polk's cabinet, Robert J. Walker, had written in an article in April 1844 that the real question was not annexation but "re-annexation," a term denoting that Texas was a part of the Mississippi Valley (a debatable proposition) by an act of God. Professing neither "Southernism" nor "Northernism" in his contention, Walker declared as essential to the nation's economic health the annexation of territory containing excellent harbors that linked the Alleghenies and the Rocky Mountains. Without apparently recognizing the inherent contradictions of his plea, Walker argued that the Rio Grande was the southern boundary of Texas, that the territory between the Rio Grande and the Nueces (usually considered as Texas's natural southern boundary) was inconsequential, and that the United States should annex Texas with Mexico's approval![23]

In his December message to Congress Tyler confidently stated that Polk's November election victory sanctified the annexationist sentiment and recommended a joint resolution to effect Texas statehood. In both houses there was a withering of the ardent antiannexationist forces of the summer, and the appeal of "re-annexation" proved a successful rallying cry. On 25 January 1845 the resolution was approved in the House, and on 26 February in the Senate. It was rushed through the cabinet in early March and submitted to Texas on the day before Polk's inauguration. On 6 March the Mexican minister, following a long protest against an "illegal" and "unjust" action, demanded his passport.[24]

In Texas the British cause was by no means lost. From an observer in the republic Walker learned that the Texas cabinet, headed by Anson Jones, favored continued independence and strong commercial ties with Britain. Sam Houston's attitude, wrote the correspondent, alternated with his drinking: strongly annexationist when sober but hostile to the idea when intoxicated. (According to his enemies Houston was a "great talker" but vacillated on issues. In 1844 he advocated an alliance with Britain and France and the next year annexation to the United States.) Nonetheless, the observer noted, annexation seemed assured. Aberdeen had already set in motion his plans for a British-French declaration, and on 10 January 1845 he secured Guizot's approval. On the twenty-third, as the joint resolution was passing its hurdles in the House of Representatives, Aberdeen wrote instructions to Captain Elliot of the Royal Navy expressing his conviction that the Texas citizenry would react critically to the strident annexationists. As an independent republic, Aberdeen continued, Texas would preserve a "more permanent balance of interests in the North American continent" and "its interposition between the United States and Mexico offers the best chance of a preservation of friendly relations between those two Governments." Mexico, Aberdeen argued, was not ready to accept the fact of Texan independence. Despite House approval of the joint resolution Pakenham was confident, too, that the Texans would delay for more favorable terms, which included, in the Aberdeen plan, a British-French proposal to bring pressure on Mexico to accept Texan independence.[25]

When the joint resolution was put forward in Texas it was presented as a choice between annexation to the United States or rejection of annexation and a guarantee of recognition and independence. (In May the Mexicans had come around to the idea of recognition if Texas refuted annexation.) The public chose the former. In the final days of debate the republic's president and cabinet clung steadfastly to their antiannexation position, a view shared by those who argued that the republic had weathered its severest tests and was on its way to becoming a powerful independent republic. The formalities concluded, Texas entered the Union.[26]

European intrusion in the Mexican-Texas issue aroused the deepest suspicions within the American government because, at bottom, the British-French effort at mediation struck at a basic tenet of American foreign policy, a principle rooted in the intercolonial conflicts that opposed the existence of a balance of power on the North American continent. But the European escapade that frightened

Tyler and Polk, impelling them to leap on the expansionist band-wagon, also alienated the Mexicans.

One fundamental problem that had plagued Mexican foreign policy for generations was the legacy of Spanish relations with the United States. In 1819 John Quincy Adams and Don Luis de Onís had signed a document dealing conclusively with Florida and pre-sumably with the transcontinental boundary between American and Spanish possessions. Mexico inherited the boundary delimitation in 1821, but from the beginning political leaders refused to accept the proposition that the nation must remain a secondary power in the Gulf of Mexico or that the northern reaches of national domain must inexorably pass into the American dominion. The Poinsett mission of the 1820s, which left an emotional scar on Mexi-can–United States relations, provided circumstantial evidence to the firebrands who labored for an aggressive anti-American poli-cy.[27]

The Texan revolution inevitably worsened matters, despite the prudency of the Jackson administration in declaring a neutral stance, for Mexican reports on American reaction to the revolution emphasized the effusive support given the Texans by the press. Texas's de facto independence after 1836 was not a debatable issue in Mexican politics. Instead, until mid-1844 the Mexican position remained stringently hard line, predicated on the belief that the so-called Texas republic was an illegal usurpation of Mexican authori-ty and its architects were traitors. Following the disastrous Santa Fe expedition of 1842, in which a Texas army failed to conquer west-ern territory it claimed for the republic, the prisoners captured by Mexican forces were labeled as traitors, not prisoners of war. In April 1843, after several groups of Americans had immigrated into the republic, the Mexican minister in Washington announced that their residency was illegal, as were the consulates established in Texas by Great Britain, France, and the United States. The coun-terargument, of course, was that Mexico had lost authority in Tex-as, but its implication was an avowal that only force of arms could demonstrate the legitimacy of Mexican sovereignty in its rebellious province.[28] Admittedly, Mexican politics of the era was so chauvinis-tic as to deny the reality of Texas independence, but the American

argument—that Texas deserved recognition because of the impo-
tence of Mexican authority—gave substance to the belligerent contentions in Mexico City that punitive measures against Texas
would, if successful, receive international approbation.

Since the days of the Ward-Poinsett duel, British influence in
Mexican affairs had been paramount over that of other nations. It
was also deeply resented. The heavy involvement of British diplomacy in the Texas question stemmed directly from the sizable British investment in and trade with the Mexican republic. A war of
attrition between Mexico and its former colony was looked upon as
a strain upon the financial resources of the former, leaving it with a
depleted treasury and mounting debts. This gloomy prospect explained increasing British interest in Texas independence. If British policy were exerted in Mexico and Texas with the aim of
bringing about Mexican recognition of Texas independence, it
would constitute a master stroke. At once, British power would halt
a ruinous counterrevolution that could terminate only in a financially depressed Mexican treasury, obtain favorable commercial
concessions in return for safeguarding Texas's independence, and,
finally, block an expansionist United States. British labors in Mexico
City went beyond granting advice and attempted at times to dictate
policy only to discover that Mexico's financial situation was such
that it could not repay British bondholders and that British interference played into the hands of the jingoes who screamed for war
à outrance against the Texans. To the British and French representatives the Mexican foreign minister sent reports that the Texans
understood force and only a reconquest of the province would prevent American annexation. In 1842 Santa Anna, whose shaky government rested almost solely on military power, rejected
Pakenham's offer of mediation, for Santa Anna clearly recognized
that any administration recognizing the independence of Texas
could not survive in power.[29]

In late November 1844 a British official who interviewed Santa
Anna wrote optimistically that at last he had come around to the
idea of recognition. It was essential that Mexican "amour-propre"
be preserved, that the boundary be clarified, that Great Britain and
France guarantee the Texas-Mexico boundary and Mexico's

"northern frontier" in New Mexico, Arizona, and California. In return, Mexico would agree to suspend military operations against Texas. But it was already too late. In the American Congress, the annexationist forces were coalescing into a formidable bloc, in Britain the prospect of war with the United States if such a guarantee were consummated seemed a likely possibility, and in Mexico Santa Anna himself was rapidly losing favor. In September he had returned to his Jalapa estate following a bitter fight with the national assembly for more funds, and in the meantime his image had suffered considerably. He was now blamed, among other things, for Texas's loss. When he extended the November interview he was already desperate. In December his detractors dug up his amputated foot, which he had lost fighting in the Pastry War against the French, as a symbolic protest. A short time later he was impeached. In June 1845 Santa Anna went into exile in Havana.[30]

In the fourteen months between Polk's inauguration (March 1845) and the onset of war with Mexico (May 1846), American hostility to European intrusion in the Texas-Mexican theater was only one factor in the breakdown of relations with Mexico and the onset of war. The term *manifest destiny,* the descriptive phrase that symbolized commitment to expansionism, generated an anti-European impulse. Defenders of slavery had inveighed against the evil of British abolitionism in Texas and the erection of free territory on the borders of the slave south. Free soilers, resigned to the acceptance of Texas as a slave state, saw in the conquered Mexican territory of the Southwest the prospect of a domain free of slaves. For the free soil adherents of expansionism and war with Mexico, the slave power *and* the European monarchical structure were twin evils that had to be defeated in the West.

In the decision for war, then, European meddling in North American affairs was a secondary consideration in Polk's mind. The new president possessed an unquenchable faith in the rectitude of American mission, and he easily blended the passion for expansionism that permeated the 1840s with a precise continental strategy calling for the extension of national domain to the Pacific (in part to acquire harbor facilities along a thirteen-hundred-mile western coast) and a rectification of outstanding issues with Mexico. In order to satisfy such lofty ambitions, he was willing to risk war with Mexico by exploiting long-standing grievances—the Texas boundary dispute and the claims of American citizens against the Mexican government. The fact that he approached these issues in a truculent mood that scarcely concealed a burning ambition to lead his nation to the Pacific shore convinced many contemporaries (and several historians) that he plotted war. His manipulation of the Texas boundary imbroglio, especially his dispatching of Gen. Zachary Taylor into the disputed zone with armed forces, offered circumstantial evidence of sinister intent. But in Oregon, a lingering problem of pervasive emotional volatility, Polk was a compromiser.[31]

When the issue of European interests in North American affairs was broached, Polk was adamant in opposing any interference, armed or diplomatic, by a European power in the relations between the United States and Mexico. His interpretation of such intrusions added a corollary to Monroe's message of 1823 and was, from the view of diplomatic practice, unjustified. Great Britain and France possessed every right to render peaceful counsel to an independent Texas or Mexico. If peaceful representations led to armed intervention, thus upsetting the continental balance of power, then Polk's opposition made a more credible argument. On the eve of war with Mexico, James Buchanan, then secretary of state, predicted that Great Britain would demand explanations of American intentions in California and, if American responses proved unsatisfactory, Britain and France might join Mexico in a common war against the United States. To this prognostication Polk replied that no explanations were required; neither Britain nor France would be permitted to interfere in United States–Mexican affairs.[32]

Given the president's obstinacy, there appeared little chance of British mediation after Polk's inauguration. In late June 1845 Pakenham wrote pessimistically about United States–Mexican troubles and predicted the American intention to claim territory between the Nueces and Rio Grande would almost certainly bring war with Mexico. Its government when confronted with American territorial aims would prepare "for the worst." From London, however, the

American minister Louis McLane reported a public mood that doubted Mexico's resolution to prosecute a war against a more powerful United States. On 26 September, more certain of his impressions, McLane wrote that Mexico's chances of obtaining British credit to fight a war had dwindled considerably. Britain discouraged Mexican bellicosity on the grounds that Mexico had little chance to defeat the United States and that a war would serve only to expand American territorial interests. In addition, McLane observed, the Oregon dispute prompted a cautious British policy in the Southwest.[33]

Within the cabinet, Polk's thinking on European interference in hemispheric affairs was spelled out more precisely by Buchanan. In his instructions to John Slidell, who journeyed to Mexico in a vain attempt to settle outstanding issues by peaceful methods, Buchanan linked the dicta of Polk with the principles of Monroe's December 1823 message. Western hemispheric nations possessed distinctive histories, their governmental structures differed markedly from European monarchical institutions, and their preservation and security necessitated a "system of policy" that was "entirely distinct from that which has so long prevailed in Europe." Slidell was instructed to reject any Mexican suggestion for European mediation, for

> to tolerate any interference on the part of European sovereigns with controversies in America; to permit them to apply the worn-out dogma of the balance of power to the free States of this Continent; and above all, to suffer them to establish new colonies of their own, intermingled with our free Republics, would be to make, to the same extent, a voluntary sacrifice of our independence. . . . Separated as we are from the old world, and still further removed from it by the nature of our political institutions, the march of our free Government on this continent must not be trammeled by the intrigues and selfish interests of European powers. Liberty here must be allowed to work out its natural results; and these will, ere long, astonish the world.[34]

"Liberty," then, included the prerogative of levying war against Mexico.

Rebuffed by a chauvinistic administration in Mexico City, Slidell withdrew to Jalapa and began sending inflammatory dispatches warning of British intrigue and an Anglo-Mexican union. He misinterpreted the consultation between Mexican and British officials in the republic. The American rejection of Pakenham's offer of British "good offices" meant that there was "little prospect of my [Pakenham's] being able to lend a helping hand to Mexico."[35]

The president's war message went to the Congress on 11 May 1846. Polk's indictment of Mexico rested primarily on long-standing issues, such as the unsatisfied claims and the unprovoked Mexican "invasion" of Texas. The United States, the message continued, had exhibited unusual patience and understanding (as exhibited in the Slidell mission), but Mexican bad faith and bellicosity had brought on the hostilities.

It was a compelling portrayal of a suffering nation, but Pakenham refused to accept the president's argument. Since his inauguration, Pakenham wrote, Polk had displayed casual indifference to the likelihood of war.[36]

Following the declarations, the Paredes government requested "assistance" from London, but Aberdeen's response was unpromising and in fact critical of Mexican vacillation in the prewar years. Since 1844, Aberdeen wrote, Britain had warned that Mexico's Texas policy was dangerous, had foreseen the probability of annexation, and had strived to prevent American absorption of the republic by encouraging Mexico to recognize Texas's independence. The outbreak of war did not alter a commitment to noninterference, for interference now would certainly mean war with the United States, a nation with which Britain had no quarrel. News of the commencement of hostilities caused great excitement among the British public, McLane noted, and proved damaging to the American image, but he was convinced that the Aberdeen ministry had no intention of interfering.[37]

Inspired perhaps by the accusatory dispatches of Slidell, Polk and Buchanan next turned to the threat of monarchism in Mexico. In his annual message of 1845, Polk had revived Monroe's principles of 1823, limiting their application to North America but warning about European meddling in the affairs of the New World. Little attention was given to the activities of the Mexican monarchists, who would eventually succeed in installing Maximilian on a Mexican throne. Within the Mexican government of these troubled years were numerous monarchists, such as Lucas Alamán or even

Santa Anna, who in moments of reverie yearned for the restoration of royal rule. As their outlet the monarchist faction founded the newspaper *El Tiempo*. Though republican sentiment in Mexico was by no means moribund the appeal to monarchism with its promises of order and continuity found receptive ears among a generation of Mexicans weary of continued internal strife and the probability of conflict with another country.

In some European circles the Mexican monarchists discovered a kindred spirit and were in turn encouraged. In Spain there was talk of a Bourbon once again on the Mexican throne. All this was part conspiracy, part romanticism, but it was sufficiently circulated to cause the levelheaded British minister Charles Bankhead to ponder the question. The Spanish minister was liberally assigned funds to promote monarchism in Mexico, and in one report this zealot informed his superiors that Mexican monarchism was the only bulwark against the republicanism of the United States. Similar analyses reached the desks of French policymakers. Naturally, the Mexicans would adopt monarchism lest they be absorbed by the crass culture of Americans. In February 1846 the gist of a scheme to raise ten thousand troops for the use of the monarchical cause was brought to the attention of London.[38]

In London and Paris there was not much enthusiasm generated for the monarchists' plan. Paris had already witnessed a verbal duel between Guizot, who masterminded the anti-American Texas policy in earlier years, and his old enemy Adolphe Thiers. Thiers attacked Guizot for his Texan policies, for his failure to check American power, and for his misunderstanding of French interests. Had Texas come under British influence, Thiers charged, then London would have controlled the supply of Texas cotton, but no French commercial interests had been harmed by Texas's annexation to the United States. Guizot's grand theory of an "American balance of power" was so much nonsense; after all, the rise of republicanism in the United States confirmed the freedom of France. Guizot replied that his aim was to check American power when it reached a point of endangering French interests. Up to a point, the United States might help to check Britain and Russia, France's traditional enemies, but American ambitions in the Western hemisphere did not complement French foreign policy. As for the Texas matter, Guizot went on, the Texans had appealed to France.[39]

Without more support from European governments, of course, the Mexican monarchists could only dream of success. British and French refusal to mediate the war and their acquiescence in American territorial designs after the war began compelled the monarchists to retreat. Nicholas Trist, sent to Mexico in 1847 with Gen. Winfield Scott to negotiate with the enemy, wrote voluminously about Mexican politics. He noted the existence of a monarchical faction but ascribed little influence to it. As in Texas and in other parts of Latin America, anti-American sentiment took many forms. In Mexico the monarchists were sustained in part by genuine sympathy from European elements but also in part by some old-fashioned diplomatic maneuvering.[40]

Polk's assertive diplomacy, coupled with European reluctance to press the Mexican case, prevented an American-European showdown in the Southwest. As a matter of fact, the reputation of Mexico in London and Paris deteriorated steadily as the war progressed. British observers, characteristically pessimistic when the question of Mexico's political and economic strength was broached, believed they were witnessing the final act of some physical process, wherein Mexico would probably be swallowed up by the American giant. In France, opinion was divided; the progovernment press predicted the conflict as the initial act in a war of extermination of Latin peoples, but the opposition organs, which had consistently decried Guizot's Texan policies, were friendly to the American cause and chronicled the exploits of the American military.

What had been demonstrated in the European condemnation of American expansionism in the three years before the outbreak of war was that Britain and France cooperated little better in the New World than they did in the Old. A number of influential French politicians had made it clear that there was no entente cordiale between London and Paris, that in the Western hemisphere France still had more to fear from Britain than from the United States, and that France could hardly identify with the antislavery policies of London so long as slavery still existed in the French West Indies.[41]

Still, in European minds there remained the possibility that the American juggernaut might not stop at the Rio Grande but continue to challenge British and French interests in the Gulf and Central American regions. Though Polk's policies in Central America exhibited a decidedly anti-European bias, a more immediate possibility of territorial expansion was in Mexico. During the prosecution of the war Polk had expressed some sympathy with the "all Mexico movement," but a likelier prospect was a part of the republic, the Yucatán peninsula.

Yucatán in 1847 was openly antagonistic to control by Mexico City and looked outside the republic for sustenance. Desperate in their unsuccessful efforts to obtain protection from what were described as savage aborigines, the white Yucatecos broadcast annexationist appeals to the United States, Spain, and Great Britain. At one time the prospect of establishing a foothold in the strategically located peninsula had motivated the Texas republic to promote Yucateco separatism. In the United States the overtures of Yucatán naturally found a responsive audience among the expansionist element, which saw the area under American domination as the gateway to the Pacific, the Caribbean, and as a protective southern flank to the Gulf of Mexico. The circulation of rumors telling of American absorption of Cuba reinforced the conviction that Yucatán and Cuba in United States possession would indeed transform the Gulf into an American lake. Moses Y. Beach, John L. O'Sullivan, and Walt Whitman—two journalists and a poet—joined the chorus of voices calling for the extension of empire over the oppressed Yucatecos.

As the American military extended its control in northern Mexico in 1847 the clamor for Yucatán picked up. But compared with northern Mexico, Yucatán was not so desirable. A poor soil and erratic rainfall made the province an unlikely choice for the growing of anything except maize and limited amounts of tobacco, sugar cane, and henequen.

Americans were mostly fascinated with stories of imminent eradication of the white Yucatecos. Since Santa Anna's policies of centralism in the 1830s, there had been continual friction between Mérida and Mexico City. The white Yucatecos, who numbered about one-fourth of the peninsula's population but who considered themselves the builders of a future Yucateco society, wanted autonomy. Others looked to Mexico City for leadership. Factions developed, and both sides exploited Indians in warfare, something Europeans had done in the colonial wars but which Americans had generally avoided. The Indians committed atrocities, at first against the other faction's combatants, then indiscriminately against whites. By 1847 Americans read in the press of a war of extermination in the peninsula with the ultimate goal being eradication of the whites. In March 1848, a month after the end of the war with Mexico, the United States, Spain, and Britain received Yucatán's appeal.[42]

The offer of "dominion and sovereignty" had been made to the three governments almost simultaneously. In Washington one of the Yucatecos buttressed the argument with references to Monroe's message of 1823. Polk sent his recommendations to Congress on 19 April. Omitting a definite call for annexation, the president argued for aid to the devastated province. Once more, as he had in his December 1845 message, Polk raised the issue of European control over Western hemispheric territory and restated the American opposition to any European attempt to annex Yucatán. If the United States failed to provide aid, then Europe might, thus leading to political control.

Polk's Yucatán message lacked the forcefulness of his earlier analysis of the European menace, but it was sufficiently daring to provoke a number of congressmen, particularly Calhoun, into denunciations of the president's misinterpretation of Monroe's message. By utilizing Monroe's principles of 1823, it was argued, Polk was subtly transforming the principle of nonintervention into a policy of intervention by the United States in the affairs of another Western hemispheric state. Polk added his second corollary to the Monroe Doctrine by forbidding the transfer of sovereignty of a Western hemispheric state to a European government, but in this logic, as the most noted student of the doctrine has pointed out, he missed a vital issue. Yucatán's "sovereignty" was a debatable issue; the crux of the matter was the principle of self-determination for the Yucatecos. In the Senate, Calhoun, a critic of the "offensive war" against Mexico, now condemned the Yucateco bill as a perversion of Monroe's principles. Calhoun expanded his attack on the Yucatán message into a disquisition on the fallacies of the doctrine itself, saying that there was no comparison in the plight of Yucatán in 1848 and the political situation in the hemisphere in 1823. Britain, the opponent of Spanish reconquest in 1823, was now the bogeyman of imperialism by Polk's argument. Finally, Calhoun went on, Monroe's message of 1823 was a "declaration," not a policy.

While British residents in Belize harbored some desires for the Yucatán offer, there was little favorable inclination in London to annex the province. As for Spain, an agreement to aid the Yucatecos went out from Havana, but little more was done to bring about annexation. Another faction came to power in Mérida in April 1848; debating congressmen learned of a peace treaty between the whites and the Indians. The Yucatán project died quickly, though it had precipitated the first great public debate on the Monroe Doctrine, its meaning, and its future.[43]

4 • Central America and Cuba— Anglo-American Confrontation, 1840–1860

The Anglo-American diplomatic duel of the 1840s in Central America was not so much a clash for control of territory as a struggle for commercial dominance. In two years the United States declared war on Mexico, settled the Oregon dispute with Great Britain, and in the treaty of Guadalupe Hidalgo expanded the continental domain from sea to sea. Of the vast territory wrested from the Mexican republic, California was the most prized; its spacious harbor of San Francisco offered incalculable commercial possibilities for Pacific trade, and its gold fields beckoned a generation of American settlers. The decision for war in 1846, though based partially on alleged Mexican wrongdoing, derived logically from the movements of hundreds of families into Mexican territory, a migration the president had no power to halt.

But the crosscountry route to California was exceedingly risky, and the hazards and costs of the journey overland prompted increased attention to an alternative route via Central America or the isthmus of Panama. American diplomatic and commercial energies in this region reached back into the Monroe presidency, but the urgency to secure a foothold there was manifestly a byproduct of the expansionist forties.

In the colonial period Panama and Central America, especially the former, came to be of considerable international importance. United politically to the viceroyalty of New Granada, Panama possessed unusual strategic and commercial value, for its Caribbean shore contained an important entrepôt, Portobelo, where opulent annual fairs were held and from which the Spanish galleons laden with Peruvian silver sailed for Spain. Portobelo lay at the western terminus of the Spanish Main, which became in the sixteenth century a favored hunting area of English privateers. Peruvian silver, shipped by water from the west coast, had to be transported through the isthmian jungle by pack train, and reloaded at Portobelo. Silver often was accumulated in amounts beyond the wildest imagination. In July 1572 Sir Francis Drake struck the Panamanian isthmus, burned several Spanish vessels at Nombre de Dios, and invaded the central marketplace of the town. At the governor's house the attackers found a cache of silver. Drake planned to wait out the arrival of the Peruvian silver shipment, but a tropical storm forced the privateers to seek refuge on Slaughter Island, in the Gulf of San Blas. From this base Drake raided Cartagena, Santa Marta, and Curaçao, and in April 1573 returned to Panama to hit the treasure convoy. Fittingly, his death in 1596 was in Panama, where he planned another assault on the silver shipment, only to succumb to the most feared isthmian malady, the fever.[1]

From western Panama, the isthmus shifts northwest into Costa Rica, bulging to form Nicaragua, El Salvador, Honduras, and Guatemala. As a theater of international contact and rivalry, Central America rivaled Panama, and a cursory glance at a physical and political map reveals part of the explanation. National boundaries still do not follow natural ones, for here nature placed a formidable barrier before the Spanish. From Chiapas (on the Mexican-Guatemalan border) to Costa Rica, the isthmus is dominated by a mountain range that stretches for a thousand miles, creating climatic paradises in the highlands, but leaving between its jagged eastern periphery and the sea a vast area uninviting to human life. The Spanish settlements were erected in the high country toward the Pacific side. The oppressive climate and swampy eastern lowlands were left to the Indians and ultimately to foreign interlopers. In 1821, when Central America declared its independence, the British were already settled on the Caribbean, mostly at Belize, but their political and commercial influence with the Indians stretched as far southward as the San Juan River.[2]

In the 1820s and 1830s the states of Central America were organized in a loose federation known as the Provincias Unidas de América Central, an effort to blend the colonial Spanish administrative scheme with republican institutions. From the beginning, however, the united provinces displayed mutual jealousies and suspicions that eventually undermined the union in the late 1830s. Politically inchoate, the federation soon found its finances in a disastrous state, heavily dependent on foreign support. For the European investor, Central America—indeed, all of Latin America—offered unparalleled opportunities for investment at rewarding rates of interest.

The principal European investors in Central America were British. Although British companies competed there with other foreign concerns, their preeminence was established from the beginning. Centuries before isthmian independence, British logwood cutters and immigrants from Jamaica settled along the neglected eastern coast of the isthmus. With independence, Central American governments discovered that their rule did not prevail equally over the isthmus, that the British presence in Belize and Mosquitia constituted by 1821 an unofficial protectorate.

In addition, the federation indirectly promoted British influence in the famous 1824 loan contracted with a London firm, Barclay, Herring, Richardson, and Company. The initial sum was approximately 7 million pesos, but following deductions for commissions and discounts, the Central American federation received only one-third of a million pesos. When the lending company went bankrupt, other British investors became increasingly suspicious of the federation's solvency and viability. Had the Provincias Unidas received the full amount of the loan, and had officials spent the sum on industrial and educational enterprises instead of salaries and military expenditures, the union might have survived the vicissitudes of the next decade. Instead the member states became more provincial, instinctively distrustful of each other and of British influence, now viewed as a neocolonialism operating in the guise of trade and commerce. By the mid-1840s, the anglophobia in the region was of such proportions that American arrival was seen by many Central Americans as a means of undermining British domination.[3]

There is considerable evidence to show that the British role in Central America from the 1820s to the 1860s was misinterpreted by the federation's members and by the United States. Though aggressive in form, British diplomacy was defensive in intent, designed to maintain commercial preponderance rather than acquire territory for colonies. Where territories were seized, as in Ruatán or Tigre Island, the action was ordinarily undertaken by zealous local officials convinced that temporary possession of strategic sites enhanced British commercial security. For years historians assigned a major responsibility for defeat of the Central American federation to the machinations of British diplomacy, particularly the refusal to extend official recognition or to send a fully accredited minister to the region. But these judgments reflected no hostility to the central government; rather, the decision to operate through consuls indicated the prevalence of commercial attitudes in British thinking on Central America. The fact that the United States officially recognized the federation in 1825 and signed a trade treaty a short time later made a profound psychological impact throughout the isthmus, even though the extent of American commerce in Central America was dwarfed by that of Great Britain.[4]

Similarly, the basis of British control rested on something more than manipulation of internal politics. Domination stemmed logically from Britain's replacing of Spain as the major factor in the foreign trade of the isthmus. Without this dependence Central America would have retrogressed economically. If Britain loomed as a giant in the Central American economy, it was because Britain had attained preeminence in international trade, industrial production, and financial exchange, and constituted an ideal market for the commodities of a monocultural economy.[5]

Those who condemned British "aggression" in Central America usually centered their accusations on Belize and the Bay Islands. Belize was the evolutionary product of centuries of exploitation of the coast by British nationals who had migrated from overcrowded Jamaica and other Antillean possessions to cut logwood or engage in commerce. The political and legal status of Belize was rooted in the actuality of British settlement in the colonial period. In the case of the Bay Islands, critics were able to argue a more cogent and persuasive charge. Lying off the Honduran coast, the Bay Islands possessed fertile soils and spacious harbors that attracted mainland British residents. In 1830 Belize's superintendent ordered the occupation of Ruatán, the most important island in the group, on the grounds that Central American officials were harboring escaped slaves there. This decision was not upheld in London, but eight

years later a dissident band of ex-slaves from Cayman occupied
Ruatán and appealed to Belize for protection. On this occasion
London supported local policy, though Honduras protested em-
phatically. Actually, British forces had settled on Ruatán on several
occasions in the colonial period, and though the Anglo-Spanish
treaty of 1783 called for the renunciation of British claims, British
representatives in Central America looked upon the Bay Islands as
another Gibraltar. The occupation of 1838 was, in the strictest
sense, a reoccupation.[6]

In the shaping of British policy toward Central America, two figures—Palmerston and Frederick Chatfield—were prominent. With
Palmerston a generation of Americans associated the most blatantly
aggressive characteristics of Pax Britannica. His forte was not so
much a vigorous assertion of British superiority as a mastery of the
intricacies of foreign policy. In the assessment by his chief biographer, Sir Charles Webster, Palmerston was perhaps the last British
foreign minister who studied in detail all the issues of British foreign policy. In the case of Central America, Palmerston was dutifully respectful of national sovereignty and territorial integrity, but he
was equally determined to maintain strict observance of the rights
of British nationals located there and to preserve British commercial supremacy in the isthmian region.[7]

In Chatfield, Palmerston had a vainglorious but highly capable
representative. On Central American affairs he was largely self-edu-
cated, having undertaken a rapid study of Spanish grammar and
research into area politics before his departure from Britain. Steep-
ing himself in the sparse collection of Central Americana then exis-
tent in London archives, he became one of the best-informed men
of his generation on isthmian affairs. He developed a fondness for
the language, but Latin American politics brought out the most
cynical observations.

In carrying out his mission of preserving British interests Chatfield often appeared as the belligerent agent of imperialism, frankly
contemptuous of the sovereignty of the Central American states. In
the region's historiography, he has been caricatured as the chief vil-
lain in the splintering of the federal experiment. He angered Nicaragua by championing Costa Rica, meddled in the affairs of the

union by encouraging Guatemalan separatism, and seized Tigre Island to block an American transisthmian route through Nicaragua. But these decisions were defensive in nature, undertaken only to preserve British interests. Costa Rica was economically dependent on British commerce, and it made sense to favor San José over Managua. In fact, the Costa Ricans made the overture to Chatfield for British support in their claims against Nicaragua. Chatfield did not destroy the federation; it died for want of a common commitment by all the member states. Finally, in the Tigre affair, Chatfield went far beyond his instructions in hasty action designed to frighten American diplomats.[8]

American interest in Central America and the isthmus of Panama was, at least officially, rooted in the 1820s, when the United States recognized the Provincias Unidas and pondered the prospects of transisthmian transportation. The fact of American diplomatic approval of the federal union gave Washington a psychological advantage over London, but no administration from John Quincy Adams's to Polk's bothered to capitalize upon it. Indeed, the histories of the eleven diplomats assigned to Central America to 1849 were case studies in futility, tragedy, and comedy. Of the group, only one, John L. Stephens, a Van Buren appointee, was professionally distinguished, but Stephens was an aficionado of archeology, and his contribution lay in his descriptions of Mayan ruins, not in a zealous prosecution of American foreign policy. The others were nondescripts, political wheelhorses, and charlatans. One died before leaving for the isthmus, three succumbed en route, a fifth received his salary for a year without venturing near the Central American capital, and another wandered over much of the region in a mission to find a government. Of the four who did locate a government and were accepted, only one prolonged his stay more than a few months, and he took his life shortly after returning to the United States.[9]

It would be unfair, of course, to accuse the Department of State of gross negligence in its dealings with Central America in the two decades before the Mexican War. Continental questions with Britain and Mexico had not yet been settled. Successive administrations did show an occasional interest in the future of American policy in the isthmian area. In 1826, for instance, *Niles' Register* reported the organization of the "Central American and United States Atlantic and Pacific Canal Company." In the abstract of its contract, the company revealed that it had obtained the cooperation of the federal government of Central America, which would facilitate the construction of a transisthmian canal by obtaining legal title to lands, waters, and the right of way. In the same year the Adams administration negotiated a twelve-year commercial treaty of thirty-three articles with the Provincias Unidas.[10] As for a canal, administrations from Adams to Polk vacillated on the issue of the *means* of transisthmian communication (i.e., canal, railroad, stagecoach, etc.) as well as the location. The British headstart in Central America naturally made the isthmus of Panama more attractive for the construction of an American-dominated route. The consul in Panama summed up the case for a Panama route in 1833. For years the need of a line across the isthmus of Panama by schooner packet had been demonstrated by the growth of American commerce, particularly the whaling enterprise in the Pacific. The British, who began a regular packet between Jamaica and Chagres on the isthmus, possessed a marked commercial advantage.[11]

Any arrangement for a Panamanian route would have to be negotiated with officials in Bogotá, and in the thirties the Colombian government operated under intense pressure from European capitals, particularly London and Paris. The French almost intervened following alleged ill treatment of a consul in Cartagena. The Colombians were also fearful that an inchoate rebellion in the isolated isthmus of Panama might succeed with the connivance of a foreign power. To obtain a guarantee of territorial integrity in the isthmus, the Colombians proposed a concession to some foreign power to construct a transisthmian canal. In 1839 the Colombian representative in London sounded out Palmerston about the possibilities of a tripartite guarantee of the isthmus by Britain, France, and the United States, but Palmerston was skeptical, especially in view of the vigorous Colombian protest of British activities in Central America. In 1839–1841 a civil war intervened and a Panamanian secession crisis had to be weathered once more. With the reincorporation of the isthmus, the Colombians returned earnestly to their scheme of a national guarantee, this time appealing to Great Britain, the United States, France, Holland, and Spain, who were expected to cooperate in the construction of a canal. In January 1844 Secretary of State Upshur was informed by the Panamanian consul that two Frenchmen had arrived to study the feasibility of building either a canal or a railroad.[12]

Meanwhile, relations between Britain and Colombia steadily worsened as the British role in Mosquitia and its meddling in Costa Rica expanded and after the Colombian government learned that London financiers had underwritten three ships commanded by the ex-Ecuadorian dictator Gen. Juan José Flores, who allegedly planned to invade the isthmian region. Colombian alarm reached its peak just as Polk's expansionist views were receiving widespread attention, and in an aggressive United States the Colombians saw their protector. The president's man in Bogotá, Benjamin Bidlack, had received instructions to block any special concessions to another power in any transisthmian transaction that Colombia negotiated. Sensing the anti-British mood in the capital, Bidlack made the most of his official contacts, and his reports to Washington charged sinister designs by British and French agents. But the treaty he made was as much the product of Colombian skittishness over the Flores expedition and British-French ambitions as the contrivance of a diplomatic agent of the "Colossus of the North." Colombia wanted American protection, and in article 35 the United States guaranteed the neutrality of the isthmus and Colombian sovereignty over it in return for a concession to build a means of transit across the isthmus.[13]

Within the cabinet the stipulation of territorial integrity provoked serious debate, and Polk had to explain that article 35 was not inconsistent with the Washingtonian dictum of "no permanent entangling alliances." On 10 February 1847 he sent it to the Senate with his recommendation for approval, noting that the guarantee applied only to the isthmus of Panama, that the treaty was not a political alliance but an obligation for commercial purposes, that other European nations would sign a similar document with Colombia, and that it was necessary for the building of a canal or railroad in

Panama. Polk's successor in the White House, Zachary Taylor, tried
to secure European adherence, but neither Britain nor France
signed a similar treaty with Colombia.[14]

The Colombian venture was not a direct confrontation between
Britain and America. Rather the Colombian government had exploited fear of British manipulation in the isthmus of Panama by
employing the example of London's meddling in Central American
matters. The bogey of British imperialism in the hemisphere offered compelling reasons for a vigorous assertion of American prerogatives in Central America.

American policymakers in the forties failed to appreciate the defensive character of British policy. While a man such as Palmerston
could be verbally abusive in his representations of Pax Britannica,
he nonetheless possessed a respect for the concept of nationhood.
He did not create the anomalous "colony" of Belize nor the quasi
protectorate of Mosquitia, but he had no intention of relinquishing
political control of these regions to governments that failed to command his respect or the loyalty of the Mosquito Indians. In short,
Palmerston had no desire to enclose all of Central America within
the British Empire.[15]

British agents, especially Chatfield, were much less reserved
about the protectorate concept. In their eyes Central American politicians were hopelessly irresponsible. Left unchecked they would
promote rash measures designed to undermine Britain's historic
commercial relationship to the isthmus, to say nothing of improvident financial decisions that might wreck the reputations of a generation of British bondholders who constituted Central America's
creditors. Resident in Central America, these agents witnessed the
tragic breakup of the Provincias Unidas and the meteoric rise of
provincial caudillos. In an American victory in the Mexican war,
they saw not only the fulfilling of the continental mission but also
the prelude to a Yankee invasion of the isthmus.[16]

The British argued that Belize was at one time part of the cap-
taincy of Guatemala, which in turn belonged to the dominions of
the Spanish monarch, and thus was not a colony in the usual sense
of the word. The Central American "revolution" of 1821 was,

strictly speaking, a revolt against the king of Spain, not the Spanish nation, and the possessions of the monarch passed to the people or their chosen agency of government, the Provincias Unidas. Such a contention undermined the historical and contractual foundations of British settlement in Belize, and Chatfield rejected what he called the vague Spanish theory of empire, citing an impressive array of documents to illustrate that the Belize occupation rested on solid historical and legal precedent. Unlike Palmerston, he believed that Belize (and Britain's Central American influence) constituted a protective buffer against the land-hungry encroachments of Central America's neighbors, Mexico to the north, Colombia to the south, even the United States. Belize was not a symbol of British imperialism but a vital outlet for Central American produce to the markets of Europe.[17]

The British presence in the Mosquitia was usually singled out by Central Americans as an indication of an imperialist design for exploitation of the entire isthmian region. Historically, the Mosquitos had resisted Spanish encroachments, and in their hatred and rejection of the Spanish Empire, English, Dutch, and French buccaneers discovered a kindred spirit. Following English occupation of Jamaica, the governors viewed the Indians as a barrier to Spanish retaliation, and they covertly supplied them with weapons, encouraging the Mosquitos to raid outlying Spanish towns. In the Anglo-Spanish treaty of 1786, Madrid recognized its inability to dominate the coastal Indians and promised to leave the tribe in isolation, a pledge which, with one exception, the Spanish kept.

In 1824 the Provincias Unidas and Gran Colombia made tentative plans for a division of the coastline, but the project failed to materialize. The breakup of the union in 1839 saw no appreciable increase in Central American control over the Mosquitos, and in 1844 the British began referring to the Mosquito protectorate. Both Colombia and Central America asserted their claim to the territory, but neither possessed a strong case; the two countries that voiced strong ties with the Mosquitia—Nicaragua and Honduras—presented their arguments *after* the British announcement of the protectorate. To make matters worse, Palmerston drew de facto boundaries of the Mosquitia as the Mexican War raged; thus his actions seemed provocative, designed to advance British colonial authority and possibly violate the Monroe Doctrine while the American people focused on the conflict with Mexico. In 1847 Palmerston tried to mitigate harsh feelings by dispatching William Christie as special agent to Costa Rica and Nicaragua in a vain effort to convince their governments that Britain harbored no territorial designs in Central America.[18]

Presiding over the "kingdom" was the Mosquito "king," his power sanctified by the British Empire and his authority extending eight hundred miles along the coast, from Cape Honduras to the San Juan River. The Mosquitia, if it were a kingdom, was nonetheless a largely unoccupied one. Most of the tribe lived near Bluefields, approximately thirty miles north of the port of San Juan, which served the Mosquito king as a source of revenue, although the customs officials and residents of the town were mostly British. Nicaraguan officials, however, looked upon this arrangement with distaste and decided to end the symbolic desecration of national sovereignty by raising the flag over the port of San Juan.

On 1 January 1848 Anglo-Mosquito contingents moved into the city, renaming it Greytown as an honor to the Jamaican governor, and announced a new tariff schedule on port commerce. Ten days later Nicaragua retaliated and retook the port, imprisoning the Mosquito governor and the port captain, prompting in turn a British counterattack with two warships and two hundred fifty men. In early March Nicaraguan forces resigned themselves to defeat, and British and Nicaraguan negotiators signed a truce recognizing the Mosquito protectorate.[19]

Greytown's subjugation seemed a portent of British determination to forestall any American transactions with Nicaragua, for the city was the obvious eastern terminus for a transisthmian route. From Panama the American consul voiced fears of another invasion by British forces at Bocas del Toro on the isthmus of Panama. Colombian militia units drilled every Sunday in preparation for a British thrust. In the United States the occupation was looked upon as an unwarranted interference in Nicaraguan affairs. Britain possessed no legal claim to the Mosquitia, Secretary of State John Clayton wrote more than a year after the city fell. A Democratic periodical was horrified over the Mosquito issue:

> It seems to be no longer agitated, whether she [Great Britain] shall
> continue to protect the squalid nationality of some few hundred ille-
> gitimate savages, born of indiscriminate concubinage, and leprous
> from a commixture of every unique blood, to whom she alternately
> administers crowns, Christianity and Jamaica rum; or whether she
> shall . . . inflame international strife between Costa Rica and Nicara-
> gua. . . . What becomes of Washington's, Jefferson's, Monroe's and
> Polk's defiance to Europe, while the British flag flies over San Juan?[20]

As for Polk, his response to the Greytown occupation—in fact to
the British presence throughout the isthmus—came in the mission
of Elijah Hise in the summer of 1848. Hise was American chargé
d'affaires for Central America, and in June he received instructions
from Buchanan to support revival of the union, the dissolution of
which had allowed Britain to encroach in Honduran, Nicaraguan,
and Costa Rican affairs. Britain, Buchanan continued, wished to
dominate the eastern outlet for a transisthmian route. For the moment, Hise was obligated to confine his activities to a thorough
study of the Mosquitos and the cultivation of friendly relations with
Guatemala and El Salvador by the signing of treaties with them.
Buchanan advised against negotiation of treaties with Nicaragua,
Honduras, and Costa Rica. In any event, Hise, who was determined
to outwit his British counterpart Chatfield, encouraged a Nicaraguan diplomat's overtures, and on 21 June 1849 the two penned
their names to the Hise-Selva treaty, an unauthorized, far-reaching
document granting the United States (or its citizens) total rights in
the construction of a transisthmian route. In return the United
States agreed to defend Nicaraguan sovereignty and territorial integrity. Unlike Bidlack's treaty, which was limited in its territorial
application and which allowed for international pledges, Hise's
creation obligated the United States to a unilateral defense of Nicaragua's vague boundaries: Needless to say neither the Senate nor
the new Whig administration was very enthusiastic about ratification.[21]

Hise's successor was Ephraim George Squier, whose appointment
came at the hands of the new Taylor administration. In Squier the

president had what appeared to be an ideal candidate to weather the Central American political storm and to compete with the British diplomatic and commercial establishment. The journey to the isthmus was only the beginning of Squier's intense interest in Central Americana: he visited the area on several occasions and spent many of his remaining years exploring its terrain or studying its political and cultural system. With the possible exception of John L. Stephens, Squier was the most dedicated promoter of Central America of his generation. In his scholarly endeavors he left a dozen books on the subject. Politically, he exhibited the emotional fervor of manifest destiny and "young America" and saw in his Central American mission an unparalleled opportunity to open up new paths for American expansion.[22]

In his assignment Squier was supposed to clear the way for those private financiers who were appealing to the Nicaraguan government for transit privileges. A transisthmian route dominated by American citizens would be "indispensable" to the task of linking the Pacific coastline of the United States with the rest of the country. To the republics of Central America, especially Nicaragua, Costa Rica, and Honduras, Squier was to transmit professions of friendship and overtures for treaties. Of the three Nicaragua was the most important, and with its rulers Squier was permitted to sign a transit treaty similar to Bidlack's compact with Colombia excluding any clause guaranteeing the sovereignty of the country. Here, the secretary of state noted, the critical problem was British-controlled Mosquitia, although Nicaragua's claims appeared to be substantiated by the facts. Clayton concluded his instructions with a warning against entangling alliances, and added: "We only ask an equal right of passage for all nations on the same terms, a passage unencumbered by oppressive exactions.[23]

On the surface the Taylor administration displayed a passivity in foreign affairs that stood in marked contrast to the expansionist bellicosity of Polk, but the Central American policy of the outgoing president was continued almost without deviation. To Polk's proposal to secure an American foothold in the area Taylor and Clayton added Henry Clay's commitment to a neutral transisthmian route. A Nicaraguan canal, they believed, should be built by Americans. Toward Great Britain they displayed diplomatic cordiality, but they were unreserved about extending sympathy to those Central American states chafing under the British aegis. When Squier made his appearance in Nicaragua, he was showered with praise and heralded as the savior of the nation; in him the Nicaraguans believed they possessed a champion who would drive the British from the Mosquitia, indeed, from all Central America.[24]

Squier was a dedicated and indefatigable worker. He negotiated a transit treaty with Nicaragua (3 September 1849), providing for United States construction and protection of the route; signed a few weeks later a treaty with Honduras stipulating the cession of Tigre Island, located at the western terminus of the proposed transit route; and assiduously cultivated revival of the Central American federation.[25] The Nicaraguan agreement specifically underwrote the concession granted to Cornelius Vanderbilt's Atlantic and Pacific Ship Canal Company. (Vanderbilt's financial misfortunes and the technological hazards of constructing a Nicaraguan canal led in 1850 to the abandonment of this company. He organized a successor, the Accessory Transit Company, which transported passengers across Nicaragua at the height of the gold rush.)[26]

Squier's hastiness understandably caught Chatfield momentarily off guard, and his reaction, often cited as demonstrable proof of British high-handedness in Central America, was probably Chatfield's way of showing that he was not going to capitulate without a fight. Squier's assessment of the situation in September 1849 was that of a man of extraordinary self-confidence:

> Chatfield, the British Consul General, who has practically the whole weight of British influence in his hands, is a man of small caliber, easily excited, and more by little than great things. There is no difficulty in managing him. . . . Now, if it is desired I feel confident that I can destroy British influence in these States, and even procure their utter expulsion from this part of the Continent.[27]

For a "man of small caliber," Chatfield was surprisingly adept at anticipating his opponent's moves. His suspicion aroused by the details of Hise's treaty, Chatfield was nonetheless struck by the suddenness of Squier's diplomatic maneuvers, and he tried to follow each one with a counterplay. When the American representative attempted to revive the union, Chatfield plied the Hondurans with a proposed treaty that would have taken the state out of any federation altogether. When Squier signed the unauthorized treaty with Honduras ceding Tigre Island, Chatfield responded by ordering the seizure of the island (on 16 October), citing a "lien" that he had levied on the island in the preceding January. The occupation of Tigre by British forces was unauthorized, and when the commander of the fleet in the West Indies heard about the seizure, he ordered restoration of the island to Honduras. But the incident demonstrated that both diplomats would not hesitate to act without specific instructions if either believed he was furthering the best interests of his country.[28]

The Chatfield-Squier duel was at worst a frightening portent of an Anglo-American confrontation over Central America: their sparring, especially in the Tigre Island episode, kindled deeply rooted anglophobia in the United States. In London Squier's maneuvering was looked upon by the more bellicose as the quintessence of Yankee boisterousness and inept diplomacy. Both Squier and Chatfield overrated the importance of their roles, and both found their actions on Tigre Island repudiated by their respective superiors. Apparently Squier learned of his repudiation by drawing the worst inferences from the public press, and in mid-December 1849 he wrote angrily to Clayton that he operated under conditions of hardship, that America's vital interests were at stake in Central America, but that he would gladly submit to recall. Clayton was critical of Squier's performance, for in the same month he wrote Abbot Lawrence, minister to Great Britain, that he would probably have to explain Squier's actions to Palmerston. The United States had no territorial designs in Honduras, but Tigre Island, lying in the Gulf of Fonseca, was at the western terminus of a future canal and thus would be the site for a supply depot. Though questionable, Squier's activities paled by comparison with those of Chatfield, who was deliberately provocative by his seizure of Tigre. Britain must withdraw its forces from the island, Clayton warned, or Squier's Honduras treaty would be sent to the Senate.[29]

Had Clayton sent any one of the three treaties (Squier's treaties with Nicaragua and Honduras and Hise's treaty with Nicaragua) to the Senate for approval, the confrontation that Chatfield and Squier obviously desired would have occurred. Instead the British seized upon Clayton's intimations of peaceful settlement and dispatched Sir Henry Bulwer on a special mission to Washington to settle the entire isthmian question. Clayton alternated his rebukes of Chatfield's conduct with threats to submit Squier's diplomatic handiwork to the Senate. The essence of the problem, Bulwer noted, was the tendency of local American diplomats to support Latin American governments under pressure from British creditors. Squier's conduct naturally gave Chatfield an erroneous impression of American intentions. Britain and the United States, Bulwer concluded, must enter into a general Central American settlement.[30]

Chatfield feared that Bidlack's treaty with Colombia and Hise's and Squier's agreements with Nicaragua and Honduras were preludes to the erection of American protectorates throughout the isthmus. It was an erroneous judgment. Within the Taylor cabinet, Clayton worked laboriously to "internationalize" the Panamanian transisthmian pact by sending copies of the Bidlack treaty to Britain and France, urging the negotiation of similar treaties between these states and Colombia. He encouraged the French government to sign treaties with Colombia and Nicaragua guaranteeing isthmian neutrality. These failing, he appealed to both nations to sign canal conventions with the United States. He looked upon the Clayton-Bulwer discussions, for instance, as the best alternative to a British-Colombian treaty similar to Bidlack's pact of 1846. For these efforts he was later condemned as a vacillating secretary of state who in effect repudiated the Monroe Doctrine. Condemned because of his stand in favor of a neutral waterway, he nonetheless favored eradication of the British protectorate in the Mosquitia and even appealed for French support to pressure London into abolishing it.[31]

Clayton's efforts to negotiate an Anglo-American isthmian arrangement began in earnest in March 1849 with a proposal related to Mexico's Tehuantepec region. In his instructions to Abbot Lawrence Clayton joined the issue with the larger goals of American foreign policy in Central America:

The policy of the U.S. in regard to Tehuantepec is precisely the same as that which is to be pursued in regard to Nicaragua...We encourage and will certainly protect all routes, whether by canal or railroad, across the [Central] American isthmus, that we invite Great Britain to occupy the same ground, [and] to enjoy equal benefits with us.[32]

In relaying this information, Lawrence was to suggest treaty negotiation on the following bases: (1) guarantee by Britain and the United States of Nicaraguan, Costa Rican, and Honduran neutrality; (2) reaffirmation of British privileges derived from Anglo-Spanish treaties provided that Britain recognize the territorial integrity of Central Americans in the Mosquitia; and (3) recognition of Indian rights in the Mosquitia. Lawrence was not granted authority to negotiate a treaty.[33]

Equality of treatment, then, was not only a safeguard for American isthmian interests but a means of preventing Anglo-American conflict. Though condemned for coddling the British Clayton extended the hand of friendship by reminding London that its isthmian interests were similar to those of the United States and that neither nation needed "exclusive dominion" there. With each appeal for a general settlement he warned that unnecessary delay would compel him to send Hise's and Squier's treaties to the Senate. By November these repeated warnings had apparently convinced Palmerston that he must act quickly to negotiate a treaty, lest the isthmian question be made a partisan affair in the United States. If the public became convinced that Hise's and Squier's treaties were designed in opposition to the Mosquito protectorate, Clayton predicted, senatorial approval might be demanded amidst a great uproar over British encroachments on the isthmus.[34]

The substantive discussions were carried out in the hectic early months of the new year, just as the Congress began to deliberate the question of slavery in the Mexican cession, the admission of California into the union, and a fugitive slave law. In his task Bulwer faced a formidable obstacle. His original purpose in Washington was settlement of Anglo-American commercial entanglement, especially the procuring of British shipping privileges in American ports. Until Clayton threatened to explode the isthmian questions by sending the Nicaraguan and Honduran treaties to the Senate, Palmerston and Bulwer kept the isthmian question in the background. Clayton's maneuvering and the rising public antipathy to the Mosquito protectorate threatened another crisis as intense as the Oregon dispute. In the American press the Mosquito arrangement was viciously attacked as proof of the sinister designs of British imperialism. One editorialist averred that the British had obtained the Mosquitia "by taking up a boy chief, making him drunk, crowning him King of Mosquito, and going through the form of swearing allegiance to him."[35]

Unlike some of his predecessors Bulwer was more acutely aware of the intricate relationship between American public opinion and foreign policy. He believed in the efficacy of personal diplomacy, showing firmness in the face of bellicose criticism of British policy and moderation in debate over the construction of a transisthmian route. Recognizing the public desire for a canal, Bulwer readily accepted the Taylor-Clayton concept of a neutral waterway; yet he perceived the rising public disillusionment with expansionism that militated against a vigorous assertion of unilateral American interests in Central America. From the canal company he received assurances that its managers intended to alter their agreement with Nicaragua in order to accommodate plans for a neutral passageway.[36]

On 19 April 1850 the treaty was signed. As Clayton had predicted, the most formidable obstacle to settlement was the Mosquito question, which singularly inspired vicious anglophobia. In the negotiations Bulwer had made clear the paternal role of British policy in the Mosquitia. Validation of Central American claims to the area was, he believed, a legal and moral abandonment of the Indians to an alien rule. On this point the final draft stipulated that neither the United States nor Great Britain "will ever . . . exercise any dominion over Nicaragua, Costa Rica, the Mosquito coast, or any part of Central America" (article 1). Clayton understood this clause to mean that each signatory prohibited annexation of territory and in fact obligated both nations to settle Central American territorial questions.[37] In Britain the statement was understood to mean future acquisitions.

On the other issues—construction, control, fortification, and neutrality of a canal—the two powers were mutually considerate. They agreed to cooperate in its construction, to refrain from fortifying it, and to extend their agreement, as a general principle, to all feasible communications across the isthmus, from Panama to Tehuantepec.

The great debate on the Clayton-Bulwer treaty occurred after the document was signed. From the start, apparently, the signatories drew differing interpretations from the treaty's stipulations, particularly article 1. Most Americans believed that article 1 was in fact a prohibition of future British territorial acquisitions in Central America and a pledge to dismantle the Mosquito protectorate. Clayton yielded to British claims in Belize, but he too expected further discussion on the Mosquito question. Anticipating an American demand to get out of the Bay Islands, Palmerston drew up a strongly worded statement asserting British *de jure* claims. The variety of opinions on the British side created further confusion. Chatfield, for instance, held a much more rigid attitude toward British "rights" in Central America than Bulwer. And in the negotiations Palmerston proved to be the enigmatic figure: he sent Bulwer few instructions, yet he remained determined that nothing in the treaty would impair British claims throughout the isthmian region, including Mosquitia.[38]

Nothing was said about British *abandonment* of Mosquitia in article 1. "Central America" was never defined. Did the area encompass British Honduras? In the Senate the status of Belize was never broached during the debate. In all fairness to Clayton and Bulwer it should be noted that they negotiated the treaty in an atmosphere of political uncertainty. The Whig party had not yet faced squarely the expansionist issue, but the public demanded some kind of isthmian settlement. Ambiguity facilitated the negotiating, signing, and ratification of the document. Had both parties stated fully their views of the Mosquitia, the Bay Islands, and Belize, doubtless no treaty could have been agreed upon. On this issue the British were more tractable. In an agreement signed in 1852 between the British minister John Crampton and Daniel Webster, who had succeeded Clayton in the State Department, London stipulated that certain principles relating to the Mosquitia must be upheld. As Bulwer interpreted article 1, Britain was restricted in its operations in the Mosquitia but retained the right to protect the Mosquitos, within certain limits of action.[39]

Apparent violations of the Clayton-Bulwer treaty, or even of the Monroe Doctrine, were the de facto British establishments in Greytown and on Ruatán in the Bay Islands, but it was Greytown that proved most annoying because of local collisions between American entrepreneurs and British officials. A ramshackle village of about three hundred people, mostly Jamaicans, Greytown was nonetheless the most important trading center south of Belize. Its proximity to the eastern terminus of the trans-Nicaraguan route gave it strategic importance. In November 1851 the British levied a charge (for the cost of harbor maintenance) on one of Commodore Vanderbilt's steamers, the *Prometheus,* whose captain refused to pay on the grounds that Vanderbilt's obligations were to Nicaragua, not to the British or to the Mosquito kingdom. When local authorities tried to arrest the captain of the *Prometheus,* he ordered the ship to sea, only to be coaxed back into port by two warning shots from the British brig of war *Express.* Vanderbilt was on board the *Prometheus* and under protest paid the port charges though his complaint to Washington brought an angry response from the State Department. The navy dispatched the commander of the United States home fleet, Commo. Foxhall A. Parker, to Greytown, and in January the British government apologized.

As a matter of fact, the United States looked upon the British presence at Greytown as temporarily necessary for the safety of Americans in the town, who could expect little consideration from the Mosquito kingdom and no protection from Nicaraguan officials in Managua. Vanderbilt and his Accessory Transit Company continued their complaints of harassment from local British agents, and when the company was ordered out of the port officers of the U.S.S. *Cyane* were assigned to protect it. The *Cyane's* commander, Capt. George Hollins, viewed Greytown as a gathering place for "thieves and desperados" who intimidated Americans and destroyed their property. As complaints from Americans increased, Hollins posted notice around town that he would take more forceful measures, and in mid-July 1854 the *Cyane* trained its guns on

Greytown and commenced firing. Men from the ship set fires to complete the destruction of the town, which was accomplished in two hours. No one on either side was killed.

In the case of Ruatán the British presence dated at least to 1838 and was, according to the Monroe Doctrine's foremost student, contrary to the principles established in the December 1823 message. But the Clayton-Bulwer treaty did not deal with the status of the Bay Islands; rather the question was left to further negotiation.[40]

When Franklin Pierce became president in 1853, the new secretary of state William L. Marcy informed London that the United States expected Britain to abandon Ruatán, under the stipulations of article 1 of the treaty. Through the year and into the next the new administration kept up the pressure, and in Congress a discussion of the Bay Islands episode naturally led into a more general debate over the British position in Belize. Clayton and his treaty now came under severe attack.

In Marcy's opinion it was foolish to expect equality with Great Britain in the isthmian region if London exerted political influence "under whatever name or form, of the coast of Nicaragua on either ocean, or of insular positions capable in a military sense of commanding the waters adjacent to Nicaragua." In such circumstances the wording of a treaty meant little, and the spirit of the Clayton-Bulwer treaty could be satisfied only when "both parties stand on precisely the same footing, in regard, not only to fortifications, but to colonies, occupation, and sovereign jurisdiction, in the whole of Central America." In October 1856 the Dallas-Clarendon convention partially satisfied American demands by its provisions that Belize's boundary be defined, that the Bay Islands be made over into a free territory under Honduras, and that Mosquitia be granted autonomy and granted compensation from Nicaragua. The issue was dealt with further by negotiating in 1859 and 1860 with Honduras and Nicaragua. British Honduras was not relinquished, and Honduran jurisdiction over the Bay Islands was restated. Britain officially relinquished the Mosquito protectorate, though as late as 1894 London intervened in a dispute between Managua and the Indians. In 1860, Buchanan, now president, accepted these arrangements.[41]

•

In 1823 and 1825 John Quincy Adams and Henry Clay had fashioned a Cuban policy that adjusted American policy to the realities of the Caribbean balance of power.[42] Ensconced in Florida, the United States appeared ready in the early 1820s to threaten the precarious Spanish hold on Cuba and strangle the British-French lodging in the Lesser Antilles. Instead, Adams and Clay formally sanctioned the continuation of Spanish Cuba at the same time they were extending the hand of recognition to the mainland republics.

The commitment to perpetuation of Cuba's colonial status was unilateral. Canning's proffered tripartite pact of 1825, which obligated the United States and France to join Britain in a guarantee of Spanish Cuba, was rejected in favor of a singular American effort to thwart any invasion of the island by mainland republics, notably Mexico and Colombia. In the 1830s, the American government expected Havana authorities to respond by extending a greater portion of Cuban commerce to American shippers. Cuba had become, wrote Secretary of State John Forsyth in 1834, a natural economic outlet for the agricultural products of the United States, and the retention of rigidly exclusive commercial regulations served only to impair the island's economic growth. The economic critique—the persistent charge that Spanish mercantilism violated Cuba's "natural" economic ties with the United States—dominated the thinking of American policymakers throughout the century, and on the eve of war in 1898 the argument that only American trade and investment could prepare Cuba for the economic blessings of an industrial world offered a compelling reason for intervention.

While denying Cuban revolution, successive American governments also repudiated the idea of further European encroachments in the island's affairs. It was John Quincy Adams who argued the indirect blessings of Spanish rule in the island. He also saw clearly the dramatic impact of British (or French) interference there. In the early 1840s the nature of European meddling in Cuba was much different from that of two decades before. Canning had speculated about the idea of a temporary occupation of the island. Now American observers cited the principal danger as British abolitionism that proselytized a doctrine of slave emancipation, which if accepted by Spain meant the creation of a "free" society a hundred miles from the South. In Havana the British consul David Turnbull, a dedicated opponent of slavery, made tactless and unauthorized promises to extend the protection of the British Empire to Cuba's slaves. Though the official view in London called for negotiation of measures to check the slave trade, Turnbull's utterances did not express British policy. His statements were viewed in Washington by Tyler and Upshur as dangerously provocative, indicative of the "threat" posed by British abolitionism in the Texas republic.

Turnbull was eventually removed at the request of Spain, but the affair was sufficiently frightening in its implications that the next administration considered seriously the prospect of buying the island. A few months following Guadalupe Hidalgo and the end of the Mexican War, Stephen A. Douglas and John L. O'Sullivan, whose principal historical contribution was the creation of the phrase *Manifest Destiny,* approached Polk with a proposal to initiate negotiations for the island. In their presence the president was noncommittal, though he later left in his famous diary a notation approving the idea. In the State Department Buchanan busied himself by elaborating on the plan, writing a long instruction to Romulus Saunders in Madrid, in which the secretary argued persuasively that Spanish colonialism in Cuba was on the brink of destruction, and an injection of Anglo-Saxon political and economic institutions would salvage the island from its inevitable decay. The offering price was 100 million dollars, which represented, Buchanan wrote, twice what the colony was worth to Spain.

In his calculations Buchanan overlooked the price of national pride. Spain refused the offer, and during the next year Cuba erupted in revolt. With Taylor and Clayton came a more pronounced respect for Spanish authority, and during the next two years the administration labored feverishly to enforce the neutrality laws against Cuban filibusters operating from American waters, in a political climate that was openly and defiantly anti-Spanish. The principal figure in these expeditions, Narciso López, was ultimately captured and garroted by the Spanish in September 1851, but not until he had seduced a generation of Americans, mostly southerners and including a number of prominent politicians, into giving his voyages their money and blessings. On López's last raid he was accompanied by a contingent of Americans who were captured and spent the next year and a half in a Spanish prison.

Having stifled the rebellion, the Spanish sought to revive the old scheme of a tripartite pact. Sensing that the López expeditions were really a prelude to a drive for American annexation of Cuba, Madrid now approached the British with a simple scheme. Britain's West Indian possessions were endangered by any revolutionary movement in Cuba; if France and the United States joined London in a refurbished tripartite pact, Spanish colonialism would be guaranteed, the status quo of the Caribbean preserved, and the Yankee giant effectively checked at the shores of the Gulf of Mexico.

For British policy, however, the Caribbean situation had altered dramatically since the 1820s. In the Clayton-Bulwer treaty the United States was recognized by Britain as a Caribbean power; French interests focused more narrowly on a few islands in the Lesser Antilles and the Guianan region.

From Daniel Webster the Spanish received a firm rejection of the proposal which Britain and France had hesitantly extended. Denying the need for an international guarantee, Webster resurrected Adams's famous Cuban pronouncement of 1823: the United States recognized Spanish Cuba, harbored no designs to annex the island, but repudiated any plan to transfer it to another European power. Following Webster's death, his successor, Edward Everett, penned a more extensive analysis of the Cuban policy as it related to European involvement in the Western hemisphere. Cuba's position, Everett argued, made it a geographical extension of the North American continent. Its destiny was inevitably bound with that of the United States; its strategic importance was analogous to that of an island lying a hundred miles from Britain's coast. Both Britain and France must appreciate that Cuba played a special role in the hemispheric policy of the United States.

Everett's Cuban note is rightly regarded as the strongest American pronouncement on the relationship between the island and the United States since John Quincy Adams's instruction of 1823. It was delivered not only as a response to the tripartite pact but also as a commentary on European meddling in Cuban affairs. There is considerable evidence that both the United States and Europe—particularly Great Britain, France, and Spain—overreacted to the Cuban question in the late forties and early fifties. The widespread public sympathy for the López expeditions drew its strength not so much from expansionist forces as from the southern paranoia that Britain and France were trying to "Africanize" the island by promoting in Madrid the idea of a free labor system for Cuba, which would, it was believed, destroy slave society in the United States.

Ironically, the British and French governments had no territorial designs in Spanish Cuba but both believed that American absorption of the island was at hand, as indeed it was in 1854 when the United States attempted to intimidate Spain into selling it for 125 million dollars. For humanitarian reasons, and in order to safeguard their own labor systems in the West Indies, the British and French pressured Spain to give up the slave trade and take steps to abolish slavery on the island. Indeed, the British offered to guarantee Spanish rule in Cuba if Spain abolished slavery there. In early 1853 Palmerston informed Madrid that Spanish suppression of the notorious trafficking in Cuban slaves was the reason for continued British support of Spanish rule. Later the Spanish were told that continued tolerance of the slave trade would mean British acquiescence in American annexation.

The abrupt American rejection of the tripartite pact proposal put the British in a dilemma. As John Crampton, British minister to the United States, explained, Britain and France must inform Washington that it could not have Cuba. As the Central American question drifted without final solution, the British believed that war with the United States was possible, and that Cuba would be the place where London would have to draw the line against American expansionism. In such a conflict France could be counted on, at least up to the point of a diplomatic rupture, more so for the defense of Spanish Cuba than British interests in Central America.[43]

For a year, the Pierce administration was frantic over British and French overtures to Madrid about the fate of the island. Marcy, ordinarily levelheaded, speculated that Spain, frustrated by its inability to govern Cuba, would "render the Island worthless to any other power at the hazard of making it a source of annoyance to this

Country; and that England is disposed to concur in such a measure." He continued:

> Cuba, whatever be its political condition, whether a dependency or sovereign state, is, of necessity, our neighbor. It lies within sight of our coast. In carrying on trade between some of our principal cities our vessels must pass along its shore. . . . It must be to the United States no cause of annoyance in itself, nor must it be used by others as an instrument of annoyance.[44]

In March 1854, as the Pierce administration fashioned its Cuban purchase scheme in Washington, London, Paris, and Madrid, Buchanan wrote from the British capital that there was no Anglo-French guarantee of Spanish Cuba. Encouraged, the American government increased its pressure on Madrid to sell, but the entire affair failed when details were leaked to the American press, and antislavery newspapers publicized Pierce's Cuban policy as just another machination of wicked southern slaveocracy.[45] For two more generations, Cuba remained Spanish.

5 • The French Intervention in Mexico

Though Americans normally think of their Civil War as the most traumatic episode in the test of republican government, the internal struggles of nineteenth-century Mexico proved also to be a trying experience for the survival of liberal institutions. Americans of Lincoln's generation saw Mexico as a hapless and tragic land, victimized by incessant political bickering and financial disasters, alienated from the "civilized" European nations, compelled by force of arms to accept a humiliating territorial cession in the treaty of Guadalupe Hidalgo. Mexican leaders were looked upon as arrogant, self-serving, and capricious, ready to sell out a portion of the national domain for a price, as did Santa Anna in his last administration when he turned over the Mesilla valley in what became southern Arizona to the United States for 10 million dollars. The hero of the Pastry War, surrounded by sycophants and government orphans, assumed dictatorial powers but rejected the title of emperor and chose the more modest designation of His Most Supreme Highness.

The war with the United States, which had deprived the republic of more than one-third of its national domain, left many Mexicans disillusioned but not without a vision for the future. For one thing, the political influence of the liberals, those who believed in civilian rule with no special privileges for the military or the church, increased. Moderates were in command of the federal government from the peace of Guadalupe Hidalgo until Santa Anna's return to power in 1853. When Santa Anna's excesses brought an inevitable protest and then a revolution against his authority, the rebels built their support in the liberal-controlled states and gradually extended their control over much of northern Mexico. Munitions arrived from sympathizers in New Orleans.

It was 1855. Throughout Mexico there was confusion. Santa Anna tried to parlay more territory into liquid assets by selling more of the republic to the Americans, failed and decided to abdicate. The announcement was published in Perote in August, and the populace there celebrated the event by marching in the streets, declaring for the revolution, and burning the dictator's beautiful yellow coach. (Santa Anna left for his Venezuelan hacienda the same month. Later on, he would declare for Maximilian and arrive back at Veracruz, only to be deported by the French. After Maximilian was overthrown in 1867, Santa Anna fell in with some Americans who claimed influence with the State Department and were willing to help him return to power, but they wound up taking his savings in the venture. He was finally permitted to return to his homeland in 1872 and died an impoverished man in Mexico City four years later.)

For the next dozen years the country underwent a terrible fratricidal war and a foreign occupation of its soil.

The image of a prostrate state, unable to secure its national frontier, was reinforced by tales of filibustering expeditions. Between 1851 and 1854 there were no fewer than four major filibustering ventures from American to Mexican soil. In mid-1851 Joseph Moorehead commanded an expedition that descended on La Paz, Baja California, and Mazatlán, preparatory to an attack on Sonora. At the same time Texas border merchants conspired with dissident political factions in the state of Tamaulipas; and in 1852–1853 the French adventurer Raousset de Boulbon directed a scheme aimed at overthrowing the government of Sonora. The last was followed by the Sonora invasion of the most famous of mid-century filibusters, William Walker, whose Nicaraguan exploits fascinated a generation of Americans.[1]

Plagued by financial calamities the Mexican administrations of the fifties inevitably tried to parlay the nation's geographical advantages into liquid assets. Following the catastrophe of Guadalupe Hidalgo, successive governments dangled the prospect of a transisthmian route across the Tehuantepec isthmus before the eyes of foreign creditors. British efforts in Mexico City sought to prevent the Mexicans from delivering to the Americans liberal concessions for a Tehuantepec route. The Taylor-Fillmore, Pierce, and Buchanan administrations were alert to the possibilities of a United States–Mexican treaty. Each submitted treaty drafts to the Mexicans. Throughout the proceedings the United States insisted on exercis-

ing some kind of military safeguard for protecting the transisthmian route and inveighed against any disclosure that a European
state would be granted exclusive rights of construction. A commitment similar to article 35 in Bidlack's treaty with Colombia appeared to be in the making. In 1857 the State Department drafted
a transit treaty in which, among other things, Mexico agreed to
render "in perpetuity" to the United States the right-of-way across
the isthmus. In return American forces would protect the means of
communication.[2]

A concerted effort to secure transit rights came with the Buchanan administration and the McLane mission of 1859. Mexico was in
the throes of a terrible civil war, a struggle of city against country,
of militarists against civilians, of clerics against anticlerics. The ultimate product of Buchanan's goals can never be accurately ascertained, because the diplomatic labors of McLane were condemned
by the congressional opposition in Washington. (Two years earlier,
however, Buchanan had evidently confided to the Georgia fire-
brand Robert Toombs that his administration sought not only the
Tehuantepec concession but the purchase of Sonora. Buchanan
planned, in addition, to carry out a Cuban purchase scheme,
Toombs wrote.)[3] McLane's instructions recommended recognition
of whatever Mexican government was in fact in control of the
country and negotiation of a treaty securing the following: (1) a
right-of-way across the isthmus of Tehuantepec and across the
"northern parts" of the republic; (2) the authority to protect these
routes with troops, if necessary; and (3) if possible, a cession of Baja California. For all, McLane was authorized to offer 10 million
dollars.[4]

The government with which McLane dealt was headed by a Za-
potec Indian from Oaxaca who had risen to a number of prestigious posts in the Mexican bureaucracy, including the governorship
of Oaxaca, the supreme court, and the ministry of justice. In the
turbulent fifties Benito Juárez had identified strongly with liberalism, which in Mexico meant civilian rule, anticlericalism, and anti-
militarism. He played a significant role in the reforms of the decade
which struck out at clerical and military privileges and, in their
wake, left Mexico in a bitter civil war between the monarchists and

liberals and the clerics and the anticlerics. For three years, from 1858 until 1861, the war raged, a pitched battle that sometimes degenerated into guerrilla warfare. Juárez, named president when his predecessor vacated the office in crisis, viewed himself as the symbol of constitutionalism and reform and ruled from Veracruz. The conservative coalition against him held Mexico City. Though the opposition possessed superior military leadership, it could not move its troops into the murderous climate of Veracruz without suffering heavy losses to the fever. In the second year of the war the implacable Juárez stepped up his pressure by promulgating more ecclestiastical laws, further stripping the church of its power. It was a war which exhausted both sides, but the liberals improved, especially in military discipline, and in 1860 began winning critical battles. On 11 January 1861 Juárez entered the city of Mexico as president, without braid, generals, or armies, dressed in black and riding in a black carriage. He was the nation's first civilian president.

The Juárez government saw in McLane's mission an opportunity to check the frightening financial drain brought on by the civil war and, simultaneously, to build up a buffer against European intervention by transforming McLane's proposals into a defensive alliance. Juárez himself consented to the American occupation of San Juan de Ulúa off Veracruz to prevent its seizure by British or French forces. In June Juárez's foreign minister broached the idea of a transit concession, with the stipulation that either signatory might call upon the other to lend its military forces to maintain "order and security in the territory of the other." McLane objected to the strong wording but made it known that following the conclusion of a transit treaty, his primary goal, he would be willing to enter into another pact along the lines suggested by Juárez's foreign minister. A final document, known as the McLane-Ocampo treaty, was signed in December. The transit authorizations included not only Tehuantepec, but also a route from Matamoros, at the mouth of the Rio Grande, westward to Monterey and Mazatlán. Both nations stipulated guarantees of protection and neutrality of the routes, but failing Mexican action the United States was authorized to safeguard the communication link with the permission of the Mexican government. In the event of an immediate threat to American lives and property, however, the United States was permitted to intervene without prior Mexican approval.[5]

In defense of the McLane-Ocampo arrangement, Buchanan portrayed Mexico as a "wreck upon the ocean," defending the treaty as an act of good neighborliness. If the United States refused to undertake the task of policing Mexico, doubtless a European nation, most likely France, would intervene. The president's arguments were lost in the debate. His northern constituents condemned the document as a malicious and sinister device for promoting southern slave power. If the Senate rejected the treaty with its provisions for policing Mexican territory, Buchanan warned, the probable outcome would be European encroachment in a neighboring country and the prospect of a Franco-American conflict.[6]

For Buchanan the McLane-Ocampo treaty proved politically embarrassing but for Juárez it was a divisive issue that further alienated the opposition. The military defeats suffered by the Juarista camp, the hopeless financial posture of the government, the intense American diplomatic pressure, the lingering threat of European intervention—all had combined to shove Juárez in the direction of rapprochement with the Yankee colossus. However limited the stipulations of the treaty, the fact that it was negotiated and signed while the nation agonized under the burden of civil war was an indictment of Juarista nationalism. By now the conflict had reached the point that each side proclaimed fervent patriotic goals. The treaty acted as a political magnet, drawing the liberals into an American-dominated sphere, and compelling the conservatives to seek solace among their European friends. At bottom was the deeper issue of national independence, a question to which the conservatives responded with ringing reaffirmations of monarchy. In an act of self-preservation the clerical camp engaged in a European search for a prince to preside on a restored Mexican throne.[7]

Already, however, Mexico had run afoul of its European creditors. Its record of financial difficulties in the previous thirty years had alienated a number of powers. French forces occupied Veracruz and imposed a blockade of the Gulf coast in 1838 in retaliation for alleged mistreatment of French citizens and losses of property. Rumors of British or French reprisals on behalf of Mexico's creditors were part of national political lore two decades before the catastrophe of 1861. For successive Mexican governments the dilemma was that of an inexperienced member of the world family of nations, a country suffering from an excess of political turmoil, unable to face its international obligations squarely. Financial insolvency and international indebtedness were not Juárez's creations but products of the improvident Mexican governments which preceded his. He suffered the collective wrath of those European nations which felt victimized.[8]

One major problem Juárez inherited from his predecessor involved the so-called Jecker bonds amounting to 15 million pesos. These had been issued by Miramón in 1859 in exchange for 750 thousand pesos in cash in a desperate attempt to salvage the credit of his government. The bonds were turned over for handling to Jecker, Torre, and Company, a prestigious foreign firm in Mexico City. Miramón attached special inducements to attract purchasers. French business in Mexico alone profited in the amount of 10 million francs per year because of special considerations deriving from bond purchases. In 1861 the capability of paying off the army and a horde of bureaucrats, to say nothing of the nation's foreign creditors, was out of the question. In July Juárez decreed a two-year suspension of foreign debts. Mexico was now, in the words of Juárez's biographer, "beyond the pale of civilized nations." Enlightened European nations, which had waited patiently for years while Mexico tried to achieve political and economic progress, were aghast at what they considered a repudiation of fundamental governmental responsibility. In their view debt suspension was a heretical act committed by only the most improvident. Already the French minister was writing his government of Mexico's sordid political and economic conditions, concluding his dispatches with unsubtle pleas for intervention as the last resort.[9]

The law was directed at all foreign creditors equally, but the French looked upon it as a direct affront, and Napoleon III was now convinced that punitive action against Mexico would have to be undertaken. Britain and Spain, though suspicious of French designs, were nonetheless in agreement with the emperor that Mexico's actions warranted immediate punishment. Their representatives met in London and there signed on 31 October 1861 the Convention of London, by which the three agreed to cooperate in the seizure of Mexican ports for the purpose of adjusting the controversy over the debts. In article 2 the signatories specifically denied any intention of interfering with Mexico's internal political processes, but other clauses were sufficiently liberal to allow for varying interpretations. From the start, apparently, the French believed that the convention provided them with a legal means to prop up Juárez's conservative and clerical enemies. And in Spain the idea of reestablishing Spanish authority in Mexico— Spain returned to Santo Domingo in this year—was broached in a number of emotional pamphlets. Only Britain seemed firmly committed to refraining from interfering in Mexico's internal problems.[10]

The question of British involvement in this intervention remained the most baffling. While professing a distaste for the role of international policeman, Great Britain nonetheless had analyzed the Mexican situation before the tripartite convention was signed and concluded that the republic was in disastrous political and financial shape. As John Russell, British foreign secretary, assessed the Mexican tempest in March, the British foreign office did not prejudge the civil contest; its sole purpose was the protection of British citizens and property. Ideally, Russell wrote to the British diplomatic emissary in Mexico, the country should be free and independent, but British bond-holders had already lost "large sums of money" (660 thousand dollars) by robberies of Her Majesty's legation in the Mexican capital. For this breakdown in authority, Britain held the Mexican government morally and legally responsible. Wedded to the notion of governmental responsibility for British losses in Mexico was, however, a moralistic repudiation of the church-state strife between liberals and conservatives in Mexican society. As viewed by the British minister, Charles Wyke, the liberal assault on the churches, particularly church property, was insane. Mexico was rapidly becoming a society where institutions were in grave danger of destruction by extremist political factions. Robbers roamed the countryside at will. The country was splintering apart in much the same fashion as the Central American federation. In Wyke's opinion the abysmal conditions reflected the inability of Juárez to govern the republic, much less provide restitution to British financial losses. Intervention was the only remaining alternative.[11]

The disembarkation of troops came in December 1861 and January 1862. On 17 December sixty-five hundred Spanish troops occupied the city of Veracruz with little resistance. Remembering the wars of independence, the townspeople sought refuge in the surrounding countryside. Hatred of the Spanish was so pervasive, Wyke predicted, that the allies would require three to four times the number of soldiers allotted for the occupation. On 8 January the British and French contingents arrived and deposited approximately thrity-five hundred additional troops.[12]

Within the tripartite organization the strains among the allies had already manifested themselves. Shortly before the January landing Napoleon augmented the French contingent in order to increase French influence in the occupation. By mid-January, Russell had drawn the limits of British involvement. Britain's aims, he believed, were merely to impress upon Juárez and the Mexicans the necessity of installing a government that would deal honestly and fairly with the outside world, specifically, a government that would pay its debts. Any attempt by the tripartite forces to create a government of their choosing would only incite the population and would inevitably fall. A European-created government in Mexico lay beyond the scope and purpose of the convention of London. The skepticism that had surrounded Napoleon's intentions at the time of the convention's signing in the fall of 1861 was now transformed into genuine concern. Britain would not join in any effort to establish a monarch in Mexico; yet in 1862 London could do little to stand in Napoleon's way.[13]

Like Napoleon, the Spanish leaders were blinded by dreams of a restored monarchy. A colony of the same status as Cuba, for instance, seemed out of the question, but Spain could certainly restore "legitimate" authority in Mexico, which meant a restoration of the power of the church and the military. The Mexican expedition was viewed as a glorious opportunity to recover lost prestige.

Juárez had insulted all Castilians by his expulsion of the Spanish minister. The Indian background of Juárez made comparisons of him and Montezuma all the more compelling; from the vantage of Veracruz the lure of the heathen's capital in the interior was irresistible.[14]

One in the Spanish command who did resist the Cortesian legend was Don Juan Prim. His deepening pessimism about the fruitlessness of the occupation marked the gradual separation of the tripartite powers, once ensconced on Mexican soil. His letters from Mexico were bitter reflections on the senselessness of installing a European-protected government in the country. Spanish and French soldiers fought bravely, he wrote to Napoleon, but so did the Mexican resisters. It was folly to consider a restoration of monarchy in a society that vehemently opposed it.[15]

In April 1862 the allies dissolved their partnership. The French were primarily responsible for the splitting up, because shortly after Veracruz was occupied the French commander Saligny stipulated an immediate Mexican payment of 12 million pesos. It was a ruse to bring Juárez onto the battlefield against the tripartite forces. Instead Juárez's secretary of foreign relations Manuel Doblado sought out Prim and extracted from the Spanish commander a pledge not to interfere in Mexico's internal problems. When the French repeated their outrageous claims and brought in fresh troops, the British and Spanish decided to end the alliance. The final conference was held on 9 April in Orizaba, the French determined to push the issue, the British and Spanish committed to withdrawal. In a heated exchange Saligny boasted that France would never negotiate with Juárez and accused Prim of undermining the French effort in order to install himself on the Mexican throne. He again demanded the 12 million pesos, knowing Juárez could not pay. The French closed the proceeding with a declaration of renewed hostilities against the Juárez government.[16]

Confronted with the possible dissolution of Mexico at the hands of European powers, William H. Seward followed the crisis of 1861–1862 with uneasy detachment. From the first, the United States refused to join the tripartite convention. Instead, Seward prudently extracted a pledge from the British disavowing any in-

tentions of annexing Mexican territory or interfering in the republic's internal quarrels. The American representative in Mexico,
Thomas Corwin, was from the beginning of the occupation greatly
excited over the prospect that he was witnessing the final dissolution of the nation, and he urged Seward to sustain Juárez in his
hour of need. The secretary's response came in September 1861.
Corwin was permitted to sign a treaty providing for a loan to satisfy the interest on Mexico's foreign indebtedness (3 percent on 62
million dollars) for five years, provided the Senate approved. In return, Juárez's government would extend a lien on the public lands
and mineral rights in Lower California, Chihuahua, Sinaloa, and
Sonora.[17] This seemed the most practical way to preserve Mexican
integrity, but the treaty encountered opposition in the Senate, for
its implications of territorial aggrandizement were embarrassingly
similar to the rejected McLane-Ocampo document.

But neither Lincoln nor Seward relinquished the opportunity to
render a stinging indictment of the occupation, once Napoleon
made it clear that a French army would remain in Mexico. In
March 1862, as the tripartite arrangement approached the final
stages of dissolution, Seward sent a frank memorandum on the intervention to William Dayton in Paris and Charles Francis Adams
in London. The president, he wrote, had accepted in good faith
the contentions of the allies when the occupation began. It now appeared that one aim of the intervention was re-creation of a Mexican monarchy. Such a course, Seward warned, was manifestly
foolish, because "no monarchical government which could be
founded in Mexico, in the presence of foreign navies and armies in
the waters and upon the soil of Mexico, would have any prospect
of security or permanence." Neither would the United States "look
with indifference upon an armed European intervention for political ends in a country situated so near, and connected with us so
closely as Mexico."

Seward's principal goal in Mexico in 1861 was combatting Confederate propaganda and overtures to the Juárez government.
Given the precariousness of their position, the Mexicans might naturally turn to the Confederacy, establish diplomatic relations, sign
commercial conventions, or even extend territorial concessions.

From the beginning, then, Corwin's role was made difficult by at least three considerations: (1) the American Civil War, which meant that Washington could view Mexico only as a secondary problem and make pronouncements against the threat of monarchy in the hemisphere but could take no military countermeasures to stop it; (2) the European pressure against Mexico, now limited but likely to expand; and (3) the Confederate appeal to Juárez, who might very well turn to the South in Mexico's hour of peril. To his Mexican counterparts, Corwin could do little more than reiterate the secretary of state's well-publicized disquisitions about the triumph of republicanism, and the inevitable failure of monarchy in the Western hemisphere. And he could not thwart the European determination to gain at least a financial satisfaction from the impoverished Juárez government, though he did cultivate a friendship with Sir Charles Wyke, the British minister, whom Corwin met en route from Veracruz to the capital. Their relationship remained cordial during Wyke's tenure in Mexico City.

Confederate pressure was another matter, but here too Corwin succeeded in frightening Juárez with predictions of an expansionist Confederacy, using as an example, ironically, the past expansionist tendencies of the United States. Tall, awkward, the physical specimen of the ungainly American in a society universally suspicious of Yankees, Corwin charmed his way into the inner social circles of the city. He sympathized with the plight of Mexico, with Mexican history and its thirty-six governments and seventy-three presidents in the previous forty years, with its internal monarchical conspiracies, with its endemic militarism and clericalism, with its civil strife. Corwin's diplomacy and Matías Romero's warnings from Washington about the aggressive designs of southern leaders were sufficient to turn the Juaristas against cultivating a close relationship with the Confederacy. John T. Pickett, the Confederate agent to Mexico, whose manner was alternately warm and threatening, arrived in Veracruz boasting of a Mexican-Confederate understanding. By the time he reached Mexico City, he demanded diplomatic recognition for the Confederacy. When Juárez granted the Union the right to march troops from Guaymas to Arizona, Pickett was furious, and in response offered to send a proposal whereby Mexico's losses in the Mexican war would be returned. But this overture proved almost useless in impugning Corwin's diplomacy, and by September 1861 Juárez and his ministers looked upon the Confederacy with a mixture of contempt and suspicion. Mexico needed money, and the Confederacy was not the place to borrow it.[18]

For Napoleon III the year 1861, of such momentous import for Lincoln and Juárez, was to be the year of advancing the French empire deep into the heart of Mexico. His intellectual training had always been geared to lofty pursuits. In 1836, following a calamitous effort to restore Bonapartism in France, he had been put to sea and, after four months, was allowed to disembark in New York, where he spent another three months observing the economy, society, and politics of Jacksonian America. Returning to France, he once more tried to inspire the army to rebel, failed, and spent the next five years in a tower in a fifteenth-century French prison where Joan of Arc had been incarcerated. In prison he read broadly and emerged with a grasp of world politics, including plans for a transisthmian canal across Nicaragua. In 1846 The English reading public discovered the product of his studies in a slim pamphlet entitled *Canal of Nicaragua* by "N.L.B." But he had grander work in the Western hemisphere, and the coup which brought him to power in 1851 signaled only the beginning of a new French empire.

Napoleon's Mexican design was fundamentally an expression of his imperial view. French power lay at the center of a world scheme, with lines of influence radiating outward from the seat of empire on the Seine. The emperor possessed, in the words of one historian of the intervention, a "global spirit," a burning patriotism, and, frankly, some fuzzy notions of the interdependence of all nations and the well-being of all men. Despite inclination to engage in fanciful preoccupations, he developed a catholicity of interest, which naturally included the Latin peoples of the Western hemisphere. He wanted the restoration of French prestige in the New World. In prison he had dreamed even of a French-ruled "India" in Central America.[19]

In the hemispheric context, then, the Mexican intervention was of a critical importance. In a letter to the commander of the French expeditionary forces Napoleon candidly detailed his purposes in Mexico. He relegated the outstanding claims and abuses of French nationals to a secondary category; the primary mission of the French military in Mexico was to contain the United States in the Gulf. The intervention was a barrier to American encroachment and, at the same time, an effort to bind the Latin "race" with ties of Catholicism, monarchy, and French trade.[20] Torn by a civil war, the United States could do little militarily to halt the French march. In fact, Napoleon believed, the American people had demonstrated their unwillingness to incorporate Mexico in 1848 and therefore would have no objection if France provided that country with stable rule. The Monroe Doctrine? Its proscriptions were not violated, for the United States had recognized the empire of Brazil, and "responsible" elements in Mexico desired the re-creation of monarchical tutelage.[21]

Thus was born one of France's most bizarre ventures. The intervention held out the prospect of resurrecting the moribund Spanish imperial glory, sustained by French bayonets, and of whetting the financial appetites of France's Mexican bondholders.

A variety of pressures—Mexican monarchists and clerics, ambitious soldiers and adventurers, and optimistic financiers and entrepreneurs—coalesced in Paris to make the dream a reality. At the center was Napoleon and the Empress Eugénie, who harbored a deep affection for the Mexican clerics dispossessed of their churches by Juárez. Paris was a seedbed of émigré activity. For years the monarchists and clerics had been migrating into Europe's capitals, bringing with them their accumulated fortunes and tales of a nation desecrated by irresponsible *Liberales*. One of them, the pamphleteer José Gutiérrez de Estrada, had lived in Europe for two decades, ever since the publication of an 1840 booklet extolling the virtues of monarchical rule. Gutiérrez was the "Tom Paine" of the Mexican émigrés. With unflagging zeal he peddled the plan of a restored Mexican monarchy headed by a European prince who would finally put an end to the dangerous civilian politics of the nation. Rebuffed for ten years in Madrid, London, and Paris, Gutiérrez finally converted José Manuel Hidalgo, equally influential, with the argument that a restored sovereign was compatible with the famous 1821 *Plan de Iguala,* the proclamation of Mexico's separation from the Spanish Empire.[22]

The course of the intervention made such ideas more palatable. In May 1862 a makeshift Mexican army won an incredible victory over the enemy at Puebla, compelling the French to fall back to their bases at Orizaba and on the coast. Puebla cost the French a thousand men, but the military triumph of Juárez's forces spelled political disaster for Mexico, for news of the defeat angered French public opinion. The Parisian press demanded satisfaction of the nation's honor, and momentarily the incipient opposition to the Mexican expedition was quieted by cries for vindication. The next year the French with thirty thousand reinforcements took Puebla and drove on to the capital, forcing Juárez to flee northward with his government. By mid-1864 his armies controlled only the northern reaches of the country, and a foreign monarch resided in the ancient citadel of the Aztecs.

Within the military command in Paris the expedition was a popular enterprise because it offered the essential grooming and experience for the rising officer caste. Napoleon had launched his coup of 1851 with a promise to restore much of the martial glory of his illustrious predecessor, but hidden in the background were the voices of dissent, some of which were becoming increasingly strident in their criticism of the expedition. As Prof. Lynn Case has demonstrated in his collection of documents on French opinion of the expedition, the opposition to the intervention was present from the first, deriving its strength from the public apathy with the glories of French armies in Mexico and the legislative outcries that the costs of the enterprise far outweighed the most optimistic returns.[23]

As the French army moved deeper into Mexican territory, the United States reiterated its hopes that the emperor had no desire to manipulate Mexico's internal affairs and that the country was only being chastised for its refusal to honor its international obligations. In early April 1863, shortly after the capture of Puebla, William Dayton, the minister in Paris, sent Seward the report of his conversations with Napoleon's foreign minister, Drouyn de Lhuys. The city was taken "to give some sort of order to the condition of things there, [to] repay themselves for debts, expenses, etc." Following satisfaction of these legitimate grievances, Drouyn de Lhuys continued, the French intended to quit Mexico. The Union government should "rest assured that [the French] were not going to charge themselves with the Government of Mexico." When Dayton interjected the observation that Mexico could not possibly pay its obligations plus the expenses of the French expedition out of an exhausted national treasury, he was informed that France hoped to realize repayment from the mining wealth of the interior. On this point Dayton rightly indicated that that might necessitate an occupation of several years.[24]

Seward, however, was a long way from open condemnation of Napoleon's Mexican foray. In June 1862, for instance, he had written to Dayton the following instruction: "France has a right to make war against Mexico and to determine for herself the cause. We have a right and interest to insist that France shall not improve the war she makes to raise up in Mexico anti-republican or anti-American governments." Now, in mid-1863, the military situation was totally different: the French had retaken Puebla and Mexico City lay before their army. Still Seward refused to commit Union forces and in fact told Dayton that the Lincoln government would not interfere in the French-Mexican conflict. In September 1863 he sent Dayton a longer analysis of the intervention, arguing that the United States had safeguarded Mexico from foreign intervention before 1860 but was now unable to intervene. But, he warned, the American people recognized that Mexico preferred a republican government, and any French effort to launch a monarchical institution in Mexico might lead to a Franco-American collision.[25]

The French army ensconced in the land of Cortéz and the clericals and monarchists operating in the courts of Madrid, Paris maneuvered quickly to find its emperor. Their ultimate choice, Maximilian, was hardly the iron-fisted ruler who could bring law and order to a ravaged land. He was a Hapsburg, thus satisfying the monarchists' dream of imperial succession from the days of Spanish authority, a continuity interrupted only by a terrible republican interregnum. His justification for accepting the crown of Mexico, and thus for plunging into a nightmarish political conflict with the unyielding Juárez, was based on two motives: the attractiveness of an imperial crown, a yearning for power sustained largely by his wife, the empress Carlota; and a naive but sincere determination to lift the Mexicans from their "wretched, backward ways" by carrying out the credos of enlightened despotism. On the latter point, the émigrés around him at Miramar continually bombarded his ears with reports of a popular outpouring of enthusiasm when his candidacy was announced. The Mexican people, he was led to believe, awaited their savior. Skeptical at first about the Mexican venture, Maximilian was brought around by the importunings of his wife, the conservatives, and, at the last moment, an arranged plebiscite (which Maximilian had insisted should be held) by the French emperor. Juárez was driven further from Mexico City, and the French commandeered more monarchical votes in the cities.[26]

The man who was to restore Hapsburg order to Mexico arrived in Veracruz believing himself to be the Moses of the Mexican people. No arrangements for a celebration had been made, and so he and Carlota dined alone aboard ship. The railroad ran inland only a few miles from the coast, and the new emperor was conveyed to his capital in a coach pulled by mules. Things were in such disorder that his first night in Mexico City was spent trying to sleep on a billiard table.

The clerics and conservatives who had found their man in Europe soon discovered more about Maximilian's character, to their regret. Far from purging the capital of its liberals, repudiating the reform laws and restoring church property, Maximilian decided to work with the moderates. The clerics were soon dispatching protests to the pope, who sent emissaries to convince the emperor to restore clerical properties, only to have them return with stories of Maximilian's capacity for argument. Some of the conservatives, frustrated, concluded that the emperor was worse than Juárez!

Nor was the emperor content to stave off the incessant importunings of the old guard. Maximilian began spending money on beautifying the city and rebuilding Chapultepec palace and its floating gardens. In the first six months of his rule, he dazzled his guests with a dozen receptions, seventy luncheons, sixteen balls, and twenty banquets. The first year's wine bill alone totaled one hundred thousand pesos. He promulgated laws, encouraged the building of schools, abolished peonage, drafted a naval code, studied botany, and endlessly dreamed of absorbing Central America and Panama into his empire. He loved Mexico and its people, to the point of studying Spanish and walking around Mexico City in common garb. In 1864 the grand task of restoring Mexico to riches and order seemed within his grasp.

The role of Eugénie in Maximilian's venture is more difficult to assess. As partial atonement for his succession of mistresses, Napoleon allowed her to dabble in politics. She was from the beginning in the forefront of the movement to pressure Maximilian into accepting the Mexican crown. For years she had listened approvingly as the Mexican émigrés recounted the disasters of the republic. She had a missionary commitment to save societies eroded by republicanism. Mexico particularly fell into the category of corrupted states and long before the intervention she had pondered the prospect of redeeming the stricken land. Several historians have contended that she sought to push Maximilian into the emperorship as a means of pursuing power and helping France, but she was only tangentially involved in the final negotiations between Maximilian and the Mexican émigrés. And, finally, she was uncompromising in her attitude that French troops must depart from Mexico on schedule.[27]

Maximilian's acceptance of the throne precipitated wild rumors in Paris about an imminent Franco-American clash. Dayton predicted Confederate recognition of Maximilian's government and, in a dispatch sent on the last day of 1863, passed along the rumor—later proved false—to Seward that Jefferson Davis's government might possibly transfer Texas to Mexico in exchange for recognition. As a matter of fact Confederate agents in Paris were alarmed over talk about reviving Mexico's pre-1836 boundaries by absorbing Texas into Maximilian's empire. Briefly, the French had aroused the Confederacy by offhand questions about the viability of a Confederate Texas, inquiries from which the worst inferences were drawn in Richmond. Less trusting southerners contended that Napoleon III was first the friend of Maximilian, to the possible detriment of the Confederacy. As for Maximilian, he was affable, even gracious, in the midst of visiting Confederates, such as Matthew Fontaine Maury, the oceanographer, who was so impressed by the emperor in 1863 that he offered to command a Mexican ironclad navy. Once Confederate envoys arrived in Mexico City, however, the prospects of an understanding with Richmond diminished, and Confederate relations with the empire became less cordial. John Slidell, Confederate diplomat seized in the famous *Trent* episode of 1861, tried unsuccessfully to gain an audience with Maximilian. Slidell blamed the deterioration in Mexican-Confederate relations on Napoleon III and France's shift in policy after the battle of Gettysburg.

Washington rumors of a Richmond—Mexico City understanding coincided with Union troop movements into Brownsville, on the Texas-Mexican border at the mouth of the Rio Grande. Maximilian's empire awakened dormant anti-French sentiment in the Congress, which considered resolutions condemning the affair as a violation of the Monroe Doctrine. In his instructions to Dayton, however, Seward was much more cautious than congressional firebrands. He pledged to Napoleon that the Union government had no desire to meddle in Mexico's internal affairs but added the warning that the American public was deeply disturbed about the introduction, with French military support, of a monarchy into a neighboring country. When the press became too vociferous in its condemnation of French policy, Seward delivered strongly worded statements in order to satisfy the alarmists, but in his official messages to Paris he generally employed milder language. The United States, he wrote for Parisian consumption, was more anglophobe than Francophobe; American dissatisfaction with British Canada was a greater danger than French involvement in Mexico. Seward believed Napoleon wanted to be rid of the Mexican enterprise as quickly as possible. If the Union refused Maximilian recognition and maintained an official aloofness, the French would eventually retire, leaving Maximilian militarily helpless to fight off the persistent Juarista foe.[28]

Debate in Congress represented, in part, the growing executive-legislative contest for control of Union policy, a struggle tragically manifested in the debate over reconstruction of the South. But in part congressional dissatisfaction with Seward's refusal to invoke the Monroe Doctrine was the product of the labors of a determined Juarista official in Washington, Matías Romero. Envoy extraordinary and minister plenipotentiary since 1863, Romero was a lobbyist for the Juarista cause, arguing that French intervention was a gross violation of Monroe's message of December 1823. If the Union could do little in terms of military assistance to the beleaguered republic, at least the Lincoln government could respond with vigorous reassertions of the Monroe Doctrine instead of Seward's reprehensible policy of "cautious moderation." In January 1863 a California Democrat, James A. McDougall, introduced resolutions in the Senate condemning French activity in the republic and calling upon the Union to grant aid "to the Republic of Mexico, as is or may be required to prevent the forcible interposition of any of the States of Europe in the political affairs of the Republic." In an emotional speech, McDougall told his colleagues that a Franco-American war would unite the spirit of all Unionists. The resolutions were tabled following an effective counterargument by Charles Sumner, who contended that the Union must avoid a collision with France. But when news arrived that Maximilian would take the Mexican throne McDougall introduced even harsher resolutions demanding war with France if French troops were not withdrawn from Mexico. Once more Sumner performed yeoman service for Seward's policy by killing the resolutions in committee.

In these months Romero was in the midst of the debate. He backed the candidacy of George McClellan against Lincoln in 1864 because, he argued, the Democrats were traditionally aggressive in foreign policy. And apparently Romero was instrumental in fomenting the executive-legislative debate over control of foreign policy. He convinced Rep. Henry Davis, for example, of the inadequacy of Seward's mild policy in Mexico, and in mid-December 1864 Davis sponsored a resolution declaring that foreign policy must represent the people's will. Implicitly, then, the Union's Mexican policy must be one of condemnation of French intervention and a strong support for the Monroe Doctrine. Once more loyal Republicans prevented a showdown, but these events demonstrated that pressure for a strong anti-French policy, which Seward began to adopt after Appomattox, had been present in Congress throughout the war.

To his contemporaries and to some of his later interpreters Seward's actions were baffling. More direct condemnation of French involvement as a violation of the Monroe Doctrine or more pronounced support for the warring Juárez might very well have quieted congressional criticism of his policy and certainly would have earned him wider public support. Yet, though his statements and actions seemed contradictory to his critics and exasperating to the Juaristas, the secretary of state maintained a surprising consistency, inspired in part by necessity, in part by stubbornness. The Civil War must be the first priority, Seward told Romero, and he never wavered from that priority. The United States recognized Juárez as the rightful leader of Mexico, he explained, yet the Mexican people must choose their own form of government, whether monarchical or republican. By inference, of course, Napoleon III might conclude from Seward's expressions some hope for continuing the Mexican intervention, without fear of American retaliation. Yet as the war drew to a close Seward's position hardened, and to him belongs no small amount of the credit for pressuring the French to withdraw.[29]

Actually Napoleon III was made very much aware of the precariousness of the Mexican situation months before Lee's surrender to Grant. As the prospects for Confederate survival were dashed by the southward march of Union armies, he consoled Maximilian with the idea that the war would last a long time, that even a victorious North would be too exhausted to launch a punitive expedition into Mexico, and that the United States dared not to confront Britain and France. In contemplation, however, he sensed the implications of the inexorable Union triumph for his Mexican policy: the possibility of an angry northern public demanding a vindication of the Monroe Doctrine, the revelations of financial and military recklessness sustained by the French to maintain Maximilian's tottering empire, and the political threat posed by rising public opposition to the expedition.[30]

Through the last months of the war John Bigelow, who succeeded Dayton at Paris, maintained the spirit and temper of Seward's cautious policy. In mid-February he assured the French minister of finance that the American people had no desire to fight a war in Mexico, the Union armies would be quickly demobilized, and the United States would "conquer" Mexico by emigration, not war. In the same conversation Bigelow informed the minister that he "took no responsibility in saying that Mexico will not become a primary cause of war between France and the United States."[31] Nonetheless stories of Union vindictiveness for the "rape" of the Monroe Doctrine were disquieting, and by May they had apparently reached such proportions that Bigelow was moved to reiterate his conciliatory statements. A policy of forbearance, he wrote to Seward, would pay dividends; the French would vacate Mexico if Napoleon confronted a steady, firm diplomatic pressure, but bellicose newspaper editorials from the United States might affect French public opinion, now opposed to the support of Maximilian.[32]

It is difficult if not impossible to fix the precise date for Napoleon's decision to withdraw from the Mexican adventure. The utterances of a few Union generals on the Mexican situation in the aftermath of the war reflected the bitterness felt over Seward's policies. Their position weak in northern Mexico, the French believed that Union armies might now be sent on a sweep through the provinces. One Union general who strongly supported a more forceful policy against the French intervention in Mexico was U. S. Grant, who informed Pres. Andrew Johnson that the Rio Grande area was pro-Confederate and that the French presence in Mexico was a challenge to republican institutions. As the war at home drew to a close Grant dispatched Gen. Phil Sheridan with fifty thousand troops to southern Texas, with orders to harass the French. Supplies were piled at the border and disappeared into the Juarista camps. Through intermediaries but in a manner known to the French, Sheridan communicated with Juárez himself, and rumors of an invasion spread throughout northern Mexico. In Washington the French protested, and Seward ordered strict neutrality, but it was obvious to the French that in the country there was a resolve even more determined than Seward's to remove French influence from Mexico.

The secretary's policy was clear and unmistakable: aside from some arms-smuggling to the Juaristas, the course he followed was calculated to frighten the French but to avoid an armed clash. Seward gambled that in a war of will Napoleon would back down. Thus it was a coincidence of factors that the French emperor was compelled to weigh in the summer of 1865. The French army had been dispatched to Mexico when the Confederacy was at high tide, when it was estimated that Juárez could be crushed within a few years. Now in 1865 the Confederacy was defeated and Juárez was stronger than ever. Maximilian was no longer a protégé but a liability, and the French public was becoming increasingly apprehensive about American intentions and angry about the costs of the expedition. As long as the American Civil War lasted there was hope of salvaging Maximilian, but with the Confederate defeat and continued pressure from Washington a campaign to save Maximilian was no longer worth the effort.[33]

Unlike his critics Seward viewed the Mexican problem in historical perspective. He opposed the establishment of a Mexican monarchy because it violated his determination to promote republicanism in the hemisphere. He believed the United States had a primary role in Latin America and that Mexico would eventually be absorbed by a gradual expansionism of the American people. At the same time he sought to preserve cordial relations between the United States and France. Thus he refrained from using the term *Monroe Doctrine* in his statements on the French intervention because, he argued, that policy had only alienated Europe. If exploited, it might damage his plan of gradual pressure against the intervention. Convinced that the course of history was on the side of republicanism, Seward saw no reason to antagonize Napoleon with bellicose utterances predicated on Monroe's dictum. In the meantime he rejected all diplomatic gestures from Maximilian, made more nervous by the Confederacy's defeat, and when a special agent of the emperor appealed for an audience with Seward in June 1865 the secretary refused.[34]

What then prompted Seward in 1866 to adopt a harder line by demanding a specific timetable for the withdrawal of French forces? In part, it seems, this attitude represented the natural inclination to push the French along at a faster pace once Napoleon had steered French policy in the direction of a withdrawal. And it revealed Seward's willingness to bend a little to congressional and popular dissatisfaction with his wartime policies. Matías Romero had not been idle in the months following the surrender of Confederate forces. He sought to maintain public interest in the Mexican situation by encouraging a congressional inquiry into Maximilian's government, especially the Hapsburg's infamous "black decrees" of October 1865 reintroducing slavery into Mexico. In December Romero's wishes were fulfilled. One congressman called for an investigation of the "black decrees," and two others, Benjamin Wade and Robert Schenck, introduced resolutions in the Senate and House condemning the government of Maximilian as a violation of republican institutions upheld by European military force and requesting the president "to take such steps concerning this grave matter as will vindicate the recognized policy and protect the honor and interests of our government." Seward's instructions to Bigelow became more forceful, and on 12 February 1866 he demanded a time limit for the French military presence.[35]

Seward's conversion of 1866 was incidental to the alterations in attitudes within France. In the spring of 1865 proponents of the intervention found themselves increasingly on the defensive. Bigelow's copy of the French senatorial debates of March showed a number of diehards predicting prolongation of the American Civil War. One senator exclaimed his wish for a war that would exhaust North and South and was hooted down. Another questioned the will or ability of the United States to enforce the Monroe Doctrine in Mexico, which would require, he reckoned, an armed force of six hundred thousand. More exasperating for Napoleon's ministers were the sessions of the Corps Legislatif, where the political opposition exploited the intervention as a gross miscalculation and introduced measures calling for the immediate withdrawal of French troops.[36]

Failure to crush Juárez prompted a reassessment of a man who would otherwise have remained an obscure public figure to the French people. Throughout the intervention the Indian played the role of a determined, unbending, necessarily ruthless leader striving to overcome monarchy and foreign influence. Unwittingly French propagandists elevated Juárez in the eyes of world observers and the Mexican people. In 1861 the émigrés in European courts had painted the portrait of an uncivilized figure presiding over the wreck of Mexican society, but by 1865 Juárez had been shoved by events into a position of respect, even awe, and the French army was on trial.

The excited public that had demanded revenge for the repulse at Puebla in 1862 had lost its enthusiasm for military glory. France was generally prosperous but the glories of empire brought with them the burdens of empire. The army fought not only in Mexico but also sent detachments to Egypt, Algiers, and the Far East. Compared with the Juarista irregulars, French soldiers were disciplined and well equipped, but their numbers were too small for a campaign such as Juárez waged. Finally, Napoleon and the military had not counted on fighting an implacable enemy dedicated to the nationalist goal of destroying Maximilian and driving the foreigner from Mexican soil.[37]

On the occasion of the opening of the legislative session in January 1866 Napoleon announced that Maximilian had dispersed the Juaristas and had consolidated his rule. The date for recalling French troops had been agreed upon with Maximilian. It was a statement of pride rather than fact. An observation closer to truth appeared in an August edition of Le Temps: "The Mexican question is dead, and its friends in France are mourning for it."[38]

In the last year of his life Maximilian was compelled to suffer a series of successive blows, from Juárez and from his French ally. More and more the question of abdication was broached. In June the minister of foreign affairs informed Bigelow that under no circumstances would France invest more funds in Maximilian's government. The burden of previous financial commitments, thought French treasury officials, and the prospect of economic austerity at home made impractical further subsidization of Maximilian's empire. For a time Maximilian considered Napoleon's warnings of retrenchment only considerations for the moment, delivered mainly for political consumption and subject to future modification. But when Carlota left for Europe to procure funds for the empire's benefit, she was greeted with general indifference on the part of Napoleon and his ministers. She arrived just as attention focused on the war between Prussia and Austria, a conflict which was in fact a portent of the military humiliation of France five years later. Rebuffed in Paris she journeyed to Miramar and even to the Vatican to seek the solace of the pope. By this time she was alternately lucid and enraged, writing Maximilian long accounts of the debasement of Napoleon's regime and whispering to confidants her fears of Napoleon's spies dispatched to poison her. In these last weeks of her sojourn irrationality dominated completely: she would eat nothing unless it was prepared before her eyes. The pope's physician declared her insane. Though contrary to custom, she was permitted an overnight stay in the Vatican itself, and in the morning the attendants found Carlota sitting rigid in a chair, trying to sleep.[39]

Napoleon made complete his repudiation of Maximilian in the first months of the new year. On 5 February 1867 Maximilian watched thoughtfully as the last French soldiers shuffled out of the capital, turned to his secretary, and declared that at last he was a free man. "The idea which had presided over the expedition to Mexico," Napoleon informed the national assembly, "was a grand one; to regenerate a people; to implant amongst them ideas of order and of progress." But change and circumstance, he continued, had dictated a withdrawal; the support of a faraway empire was no longer in the national interest. The deputies and senators approved with thunderous applause.[40]

Thus eleven hundred officers and almost twenty-eight thousand Frenchmen, Belgians, and Austrians departed the country which they had tried vainly to pacify for the cause of benevolent despotism. Even in the military there was little confidence the battle could be won against the Juaristas. Gen. Achille Francois Bazaine, the fourth commander of French forces in Mexico, sailed for Europe, praising his men for their glorious struggle and privately confessing that Maximilian must resign because the Mexicans never wanted an emperor anyway. Though more succinctly stated, it was the identical logic Seward had expressed to the French in 1862.[41]

Maximilian displayed in these last few months of his reign and his life the outward appearance of man relieved to be on his own. Juárez's forces moved systematically from the north, preparing to cut off the routes to the sea and lay siege to the capital. The emperor was now almost totally dominated by the conservatives within the government, but he now decided boldly to take to the field, to intercept Juárez to the north at Querétaro. He knew such a move would be folly, that he could never hold out against the encircling foe. Yet his final act of power was more than a death wish; it was a defiant gesture to the Indian who had claimed to the world that the source of strength of the transplanted empire was the French army and that Maximilian was in fact the pawn of others. In defeat he could triumph.

In a country scarred by years of war, the one-hundred-day siege of Querétaro seemed almost anticlimactic. The town itself was divided in sentiment. Maximilian was on the verge of abdication when one of his lieutenants, Gen. Leonardo Márquez, concocted a wild scheme which called for a detachment of troops to burst through the Juarista lines in a dash for the capital and reinforcements. Maximilian sent with him an act of abdication but Márquez failed to announce it and did not return to the beleaguered city. The emperor made a few efforts to break through but was turned back. He was deprived of a military confrontation when a traitor opened the gates in the middle of the night to the enemy.

Maximilian was tried by a military court but refused to appear, insisting instead that he must confer personally with Juárez. Confronted by the enemy whom he had fought for years, Juárez would nonetheless have sensed the humility and decency of his captive, Maximilian believed, and in a gesture of clemency pardon the emperor for his follies and send him back to Miramar. But this was the one consideration that Juárez could not afford, despite the pleas of mercy from European and American governments. The claimants to power in Mexico would learn a more profound lesson in politics by Maximilian's death; the clerics who abominated republicanism would at last be taught a truth they had not learned during the wars of the reform. Ruthless in battle, Juárez remained unmoved by pleas for compassion in the moment of his triumph.

Maximilian was executed with two of his generals on 19 June

1867, at a place called the Hill of the Bells near Querétaro. With him died the hopes of the Mexican monarchists, who since the wars of independence had dreamed and plotted the restoration of a Hapsburg and who saw in republican Mexico political drift and social degeneracy. The emperor they chose was a man of culture and humility who facing death spoke comfortingly to his executioners and even relinquished the center spot to one of his two generals condemned with him. Juárez, whose firmness, steadfastness, and ruthlessness had done so much to preserve the republican cause, lived until 1872. In his wake Mexico underwent other political calamities until 1876, when a former Juarista officer named Porfirio Díaz began a thirty-five-year rule that opened up Mexico to foreign influence of a different kind but gained for the country a respect from Europe and the United States unmatched by any "backward" society.

Napoleon III and France suffered in the aftermath of the intervention. In 1866 a Prussian army defeated Austria at Sadowa. Napoleon's health and prestige deteriorated, and when France went to war against Prussia in 1870 Napoleon's imperial dreams were already shattered by the costs in men and materiel and the crisis in public confidence. In the Western hemisphere the republicanism of Mexico whose victory Seward had predicted in 1862 had triumphed.

6 • The New Empire

For four long years the European powers watched the struggle over slavery and union in the United States, yet the victory of Grant's army did not produce a major reassessment of Caribbean policy in London, Paris, or Madrid. The one exception was of course the Mexican situation, but there the factors explaining French withdrawal were more complex than the fear of a liberating republican force from the north. France pulled back to its Antillean possessions of Guadeloupe and Martinique and in 1879 plunged into the labor of canal construction on the Panamanian isthmus. In 1878, in an apparent violation of the Monroe Doctrine, the French acquired tiny Saint Bartholomew's island from Sweden, which ironically the Swedes had offered to sell to the United States in 1818−1819, 1825, and again when Seward was secretary. But his attempts to acquire the Danish West Indies in 1867 negated any need for Saint Bartholomew's and in any event there was no protest over the French acquisition. Technically the transfer was a retrocession for at one time the island had been French.

Though the years of Spanish reoccupation of Santo Domingo coincided with those of the American Civil War, the decision to withdraw in 1865 was more closely linked to Madrid's pessimistic assessment of the internal political and financial crisis on the island than to American pronouncements on the destiny of republicanism in the Western hemisphere. Spain clung fiercely to its prerogatives of rule in Cuba and Puerto Rico. Britain held her insular possessions in the Caribbean world and exercised political and financial influence in Mexico and Central America.

Yet the three decades between the war and the crusade against Spanish colonialism in Cuba witnessed subtle but significant alterations in American policy toward the Caribbean world. One was frankly military in character and had as its most obvious goal the strengthening of American naval power. In Washington this was looked upon by some to be almost exclusively at the expense of the taxpayer, but in the Gulf and Caribbean it was to the detriment of the European powers as well. A more formidable American naval presence made their possessions more vulnerable. Another change was, for want of a better description, an intellectual one that by 1898 arrogantly presumed only the United States could provide the "backward" Caribbean societies with the moral and political precepts they required to advance. Its arguments derived in part from American social scientists who looked upon European colonialism in the Western hemisphere and especially Spanish rule in the Caribbean as poor preparation for the twentieth century. The last and perhaps the most significant impact on policy came in the economic sphere. In the years following Appomattox, Americans came to accept neomercantilistic doctrines that urged an "outward look" in order to satisfy the demand for outlets for American foodstuffs and industrial products. There was nothing Marxian nor conspiratorial in the efforts of secretaries of state, navy, agriculture, and presidents in advancing global economic interests. The country had always been an exporter of raw materials, but the difference was the urgency with which the nation sought new markets after the war. Farm journals continually exhorted Washington to find new buyers for agricultural surpluses. Businessmen discovered that their industrial machine could produce more than the domestic consumer used and thus they naturally looked to the outside world. Some observers argued the best way to avoid depression—these years saw two of the worst in American history—and resulting political and social strife was to promote vigorously an expansionist trade policy.[1]

William Henry Seward went far in promoting this "new empire." He foresaw increasing American domination in adjacent lands and waters and the gradual disappearance of European colonies and institutions in the New World. The West Indies would evolve into a friendly black confederacy; strategic island outposts and the isthmian region would come under American ownership or at least American hegemony. He rejected the idea of South American colonies but eagerly accepted the concept of a chain of island bases in the Caribbean in order to safeguard the region from European encroachment and promote American military and commercial interests. His ill-fated venture into negotiations with Denmark for the cession of the Virgin Islands reflected these attitudes.[2]

Seward may have been more outspoken than his successors, but they were no less interested in the drafting of a grand design for the Caribbean. In 1870 when the Grant administration was requested by the Senate to examine the state of United States–Latin American trade, Secretary of State Hamilton Fish responded by vigorously reasserting the Monroe Doctrine and the no-transfer principle. Taking his cue from the Senate statement urging a greater share of the Latin American trade, Fish boasted that the inevitable course of American foreign policy in this region was the emancipation of Latin America from European dependence.[3]

The foreign policies of Garfield and Arthur continued to promote the idea of American commercial and military domination in the Caribbean and Latin America and, as a matter of fact, anticipated the goals of McKinley and Roosevelt. Secretary of State James G. Blaine's advocacy of a Pan American conference in 1881 reflected his concern about United States–Latin American trade. Blaine's Pan American invitations were canceled by his successor Frederick T. Frelinghuysen, but Frelinghuysen sought similar ends by exploiting different means. He signed a canal treaty with Nicaragua and, equally as important to American commercial expansion in the Caribbean, negotiated a series of bilateral reciprocity treaties with Mexico, Colombia, the British West Indies, El Salvador, the Dominican Republic, and Spanish Cuba and Puerto Rico. Viewed together, these treaties opened up a vast market in the Caribbean region to American industrial products by providing for lower tariffs on manufactured products in return for reductions on imports from these countries. Frelinghuysen's dream extended beyond the commercial realm: the treaties would promote American political, as well as economic, influence in the Caribbean region. And each country (or colony, in the case of Cuba, Puerto Rico, and the British West Indies) lay near the sea approaches to the isthmian canal region. In short, as a British diplomat observed, the treaties provided for all the benefits of colonial rule without any of the disadvantages of outright ownership.[4]

The belief that America must reach beyond its borders for an industrial outlet paralleled the fundamental reassessment of naval strategy. For such farsighted naval theorists as Alfred Thayer Mahan the postwar naval policy was a disaster. Mahan watched help-lessly as the advancements in technology and strategy achieved during the war years were quietly forgotten in the peacetime pro-gram of retrenchment. The nation had survived the domestic threat to disunion, it possessed no overseas territories that required a large naval defense, and public opinion was frankly antagonistic toward spending to build a modern navy. The deterioration in the merchant marine mirrored a dismal naval outlook. In naval tech-nology the United States fell rapidly behind other nations, some of them much smaller in population and industrial potential, in the ten years after Appomattox. In naval strategy the governing mood remained roughly what it had been fifty years before: the wartime function of the navy was coastal defense and commercial raiding. This attitude prevailed into the 1880s.[5]

By all accounts the ideologue of the late nineteenth-century cru-sade for a modern navy was Mahan. He was a navy man and a na-val strategist; he became very influential in the 1890's, especially among a group of vigorous, expansionist young Republicans. He not only championed a large navy but he also promoted the con-cept of sea power, and the impact of his thinking abroad was equal to the impression he made on a growing band of followers in the United States. Naval journals in Britain quoted his works, and in 1894 on a visit Mahan was feted by the queen and prime minister, given honorary degrees at Oxford and Cambridge, and received as a guest of honor at the Royal Navy Club.[6] In his naval studies Brit-ain and British power had served as historical illustrations of the influence of sea power in the evolution of national power and prestige.

The future of American sea power was equally compelling. If Britain commanded paramountcy among the great powers because its navy ruled the Atlantic, then the United States must look natu-rally to the Caribbean and Pacific. Mahan believed, for instance, that in the twentieth century America and Europe would face a formidable enemy in the form of Asian civilization. European ar-mies would guard Eurasia in this confrontation, but American sea power would safeguard the Pacific.[7] To achieve naval supremacy in the Pacific the United States must possess naval superiority in the

Caribbean, which would become, with completion of an isthmian canal, the Mediterranean of the Western hemisphere. Consider his comments on the crucial role of an isthmian passageway:

> If . . . [a canal] be made, and fulfill the hopes of its builders, the Caribbean will be changed from a terminus, and place of local traffic, or at best a broken and imperfect line of travel . . . into one of the great highways of the world. Along this path a great commerce will travel, bringing the interests of other great nations, the European nations, close along our shores, as they have never been before. . . . The position of the United States with reference to this route will resemble that of England to the Channel, and of the Mediterranean countries to the Suez route.[8]

Here Mahan's predictions raised questions about the role of European powers in the Caribbean. In the wake of the Spanish-American War the United States became increasingly intolerant of European influence in the Caribbean and in fact justified its interventionist policy there partly on the grounds that American intervention prevented a much more dangerous and unsettling European intervention.

Like many other Americans Mahan was no easy convert to expansionist philosophies. He shared with many of his countrymen in the 1870s and 1880s a pessimistic view toward territorial possessions, which required heavy administrative and financial burdens, an inordinately large defense force, and a cumbersome bureaucracy. And, frankly, he feared the destruction of free government by imperial rule. But the example of Britain with its large navy, small standing army, and commitment to republican institutions may have removed the last of his inhibitions to accepting expansionism. By 1890 it is clear that his conversion was complete, for in that year he produced the famous article calling for an America "looking outward" to its global mission. Moreover, the industrial revolution had made superfluous many of the eighteenth-century mercantilistic necessities—colonies and merchant marines—which Mahan considered inimical to democratic processes. To the old mercantilistic school the role of the colony was to serve as a producer of raw material, a purchaser of manufactured products, and a dumping ground for population. Increasingly Mahan deemphasized the role of the merchant marine—because with technological and industrial ingenuity it no longer played such a crucial part in the search for markets—and wrote of the colonial possession as a waystation for naval bases and a link between the American metropole and a vast market in Latin America and Asia.

Mahan's views were shared by others, notably Commo. Stephen Luce, founder of the Naval War College at Newport, Rhode Island, in 1884, and Benjamin Tracy, secretary of the navy in the expansionist Harrison administration. Like Mahan, Luce believed that there was more to naval strategy than experience at sea, a concept assailed by the old navy men. Though at first condemned by the old guard the War College continued and helped to produce a new breed of naval officer, one versed in tactics, strategy, history, and politics.

Tracy was a political appointee, but he had less suspicion of military men than many of his contemporaries and vigorously advocated a modernized naval force. In 1889 when Tracy took over in the navy department, the thinking was still oriented toward the idea of a peacetime navy only reluctantly giving up sail in favor of steam. Modern weaponry now appeared on naval vessels, but the concept of the navy as essentially a defensive force remained. Tracy sought to unite the principle of modernization with the "outward thrust" views of Mahan. He succeeded in an administrative overhauling within the department, and a number of crises—the Chilean war scare of 1891, the Samoan squabble, and an energetic search for Caribbean bases—provided the opportunity for using the navy department as an advocate for an expansionist, assertive foreign policy. When Tracy left office in 1893, his successors, appointed by the opposition party, did not revert to pre-1889 thinking but continued his program.[9]

Inevitably the revolution in naval thinking and the more aggressive foreign policy that accompanied it altered the relationship between the United States and Europe in the Caribbean world. More and more, Americans came to look upon the remnants of European, particularly Spanish, colonialism as outdated, even archaic, a hindrance to social and political modernization. Going further, the American people in the last thirty years of the nineteenth century came to look upon themselves as the final arbiters of international conflict in the Caribbean. They became more critical of European interference there until finally they allocated unto themselves the sole right of intervention in the Caribbean.

In Hispaniola, Cuba, Central America, and Venezuela, American power displayed increased antagonism toward European meddling after the Civil War.

The Dominican issue had been festering for years. In the 1850s, politics there was dominated by two unscrupulous men, Pedro Santana and Buenaventura Báez, who sought to outdo one another by promoting economic alliances with foreign powers. Britain, France, Spain, and the United States possessed designs on the republic; each sought to check the influence of the other in the fledgling Dominican government. France, eager to serve as matchmaker between the Dominicans and Haitians, promoted the candidacy of Báez over Santana as a means of achieving this goal. Britain naturally wished to check any rising French interference in the Caribbean but was reluctant to annex additional territory. The Spanish, though hesitant to attach another colony in the West Indies, nonetheless agreed to do so in order to forestall American annexation of Dominican territory. Indeed, the question of American action in the republic was unclear: Daniel Webster had declared that the United States must preserve the integrity of the republic by protecting it from European-directed intrigues in Haiti, but Webster's plan of action was not reaffirmed by his successors.[10]

Reelected in February 1853, Santana looked to Washington and the expansionist Pierce administration for guidance. European dabbling in the politics of Haiti and the Dominican Republic in previous years now awakened new fears of possible violation of the Monroe Doctrine. Determined to check the political erosion of Dominican independence, the Pierce administration dispatched to the scene a special agent, "General" William L. Cazneau, an avid promoter of American economic and political power in the Caribbean. Cazneau was supposed to collect information on the republic, noting especially its ability to maintain independence in the face of European and Haitian encroachments. He returned with a glowing report of political and economic conditions, and the administration promptly sent him back with instructions to negotiate a treaty, which he did. Article 28 in this treaty provided for the cession of a naval and coaling station at Samaná Bay.

Though involved in the Crimean War, the British and French were sufficiently aroused by Cazneau's treaty, especially the Samaná Bay proviso, that their diplomatic representatives in the republic joined forces to defeat it. Santana was informed that article 28 must be dropped from the document. A new treaty, concluded by Santana's vice-president on 5 October, omitted the clause, but the local British and French representatives continued their opposition and called upon several warships to make an appearance in Dominican waters. Santana feared he might be overthrown. On 23 November Cazneau withdrew the treaty.[11]

The Spanish reoccupation of the Dominican Republic in 1861 served as a momentary deterrent to American intentions. Professing a program of great works for the economically depressed republic, the Spanish soon made a mockery of colonial administration. They promised in 1861 to fortify the ports, introduce postal houses in every commune, begin steam transit between the republic and other Antillean ports, and build roads between the main towns. Instead the colonial establishment became a dumping ground for jobseekers from Spain, Puerto Rico, and Cuba.

Lincoln and Seward saw in the reoccupation a threat to American interests, perhaps part of a larger scheme aimed at the suffocation of republican governments throughout the hemisphere. In a note to the Spanish minister in Washington Seward warned that further extensions of monarchical rule into the republican states of the continent would be met with "effective resistance." He sent a copy of the note to Mexico, Guatemala, El Salvador, Nicaragua, Costa Rica, Honduras, and Colombia. In 1865 the Spanish departed, partly because of the growing animosity of the United States, but mostly because of widespread hostility to the regime among the Dominicans themselves.[12]

Rather than annex the republic outright Seward sought instead a means whereby the United States might obtain only cession of Samaná Bay and the surrounding area. The plan was put into operation following Lee's surrender and the Spanish departure from the island. For the mission to Santo Domingo, the secretary selected his son Frederick, then assistant secretary of state, who was instructed to arrange a convention with Dominican authorities for ceding or leasing the bay. Article 4 of the proposal made clear that Seward was interested in transforming the backward and undeveloped Samaná into a military outpost, for it provided for American fortifications and garrisons safeguarded by United States land and naval forces. If the Dominican government decided to cede rather than lease the bay and its environs, Frederick Seward was instructed to offer 2 million dollars for a cession of thirty years. Half the sum would be paid in cash, half in arms and munitions.[13]

Seward's plans for American posts in Hispaniola and the Virgin Islands failed to materialize while he served as secretary of state. Nevertheless, others hoped to succeed. The Alaskan venture, with its windfall of favors to a select few, only whetted the appetites of a band of promoter-adventurers who saw infinite possibilities in the annexation of the Dominican Republic to the United States. With Grant in the White House, Hamilton Fish laboring energetically on the pressing issues of Anglo-American relations, and the pliable Báez back in power in Santo Domingo, the opportunity beckoned to resurrect the annexation scheme. Cazneau, a principal in the abortive negotiations of the fifties, once more assumed a primary role in working out the specifics with the Dominican leader, who proved only too willing to auction off his country to the American purchaser. The plan was sold to Grant as a business venture that would, among other things, draw American money and settlers into the remote regions near the Haitian border. Actually Cazneau and his associates spent only a few thousand promoting what they claimed to be a million dollar deal. In the republic his maneuvering and concession-hunting were ridiculed, but in Washington the scheme was given the utmost consideration.[14]

The treaty failed in June 1870. In part failure was because of Charles Sumner's strong moral objections to what many considered an indefensible affair, and in part to Grant's inability to win over the strong bloc of Cuban sympathizers, who were strongly for intervention in the Ten Years' War in Cuba, but strongly against annexation of the Dominican Republic. At first courteous in his questioning of the merits of the Dominican scheme, Sumner became increasingly strident in his condemnations of Grant's diplomacy and at one point, according to observers, even hysterical. The debate on annexation continued off and on through the remainder of 1870, and on 21 December Sumner delivered a devastating attack on the treaty. His opposition to the Dominican affair now extended to a general assault on Grant's policies of expansionism; the Dominican Republic could never be American because by "higher law," Sumner said, it was destined for the "colored race," who had poured into its soil their blood and sweat.

Many who were angry over Fish's hardnosed diplomacy in the Cuban issue could not be brought around to the Dominican proposal, which smacked of backstairs intrigue and reckless adventuring. In the *New York Sun*, Charles Henry Dana condemned the annexation as a foolish enterprise that would draw the American people into a grisly counterinsurgency in the republic, the kind of operation that had cost Spain twenty thousand men and 30 million dollars. In a message recommending favorable action on the treaty Grant attempted to tie the Dominican plan to larger and nobler purposes—reaffirmation of the Monroe Doctrine, promotion of American commerce, and, finally, undermining of slavery in Cuba, Puerto Rico, and even in Brazil—but his congressional readers remained unconvinced. Some, such as Carl Schurz, whose anti-imperialism grew with the years, opposed it simply because he believed the incorporation of tropical and "backward" societies would wreck American political and social institutions.[15]

Though perhaps exaggerated by Seward, fear of European designs also played a role in the abortive effort to purchase the Danish West Indies. With the Spanish in the Dominican Republic and the French in Mexico, it appeared to some Americans that the Caribbean balance of power was shifting back in favor of the old order. At any other time the Prussian-Danish troubles of 1864 would have occurred virtually unnoticed in the United States, but the prospect that an aggressive Prussian state might force the Danes to cede their West Indian possessions loomed as a frightening specter on the horizon. Seward did not need the Prussian-Danish imbroglio to convince him of the necessity of purchasing the islands, for he was already committed to the philosophy of American military and economic expansion southward. Narrowing his choices to the islands of Saint Thomas and Saint John, the secretary pushed the issue with all deliberate speed. On 2 July 1867 he obtained the blessing of the cabinet, despite some dissension and doubt, and was able to settle on an offer of 7.5 million dollars.[16]

Like its Dominican counterpart, the Danish West Indies annexation scheme ran afoul of congressional sentiment. The treaty was completed on 24 October, but its provisions had already incurred a great deal of criticism in the Danish government. Its fate in the Congress of the United States was disastrous. In the House, Rep. C. C. Washburn of Wisconsin introduced a resolution condemning additional purchases of territory as unnecessary and calling upon his colleagues to refuse to appropriate funds to pay for the two islands. The historian of this abortive purchase plan, Charles Callan Tansill, has observed that the "real reason for the rejection of the Danish treaty was the evident disinclination of the American public to follow Seward in his schemes for colonial dominion." Too few Americans were prepared in the seventies and eighties to emulate Britain and France in imperialistic ventures.[17]

There can be little doubt that the climate for expansion was much more favorable in the nineties than at any other time between the Civil War and the Spanish-American conflict. But rejection of the proposed Dominican and Danish West Indian annexations did not necessarily represent a rejection of Seward's thinking. He was far ahead of his generation in his concepts of American economic and military involvement in the Caribbean. He saw more clearly than his contemporaries the inevitable deterioration of European influence in the region and sought to fill the vacuum with American power. Policymakers and public opinion were moving slowly but perceptibly in this direction. Finally, the rejection of Seward's annexation treaty may have been due, at least in part, to the determination of Congress to restore the legislative-executive balance of power. Refusing to finance the Danish West Indian arrangement was one way of achieving this goal.

•

The post–Civil War years demonstrated also that Spanish Cuba was rapidly slipping from European orbit and, as John Quincy Adams had predicted one-half century before, was gravitating toward the United States. In 1868 the island erupted into a prolonged, brutal revolt, the Ten Years' War. Like previous Cuban rebellions in the nineteenth century, the rebellion aroused the American conscience and very nearly dragged the country into a conflict with Spain. Public and congressional sympathy lay almost exclusively with the Cuban insurgents, whose political activities in the United States were geared to disseminating atrocity stories designed to bring about American intervention. Cuban rebels looked naturally to the restored American union as a source of compassion and material aid; a few foolishly believed that the Grant administration would place at their disposal a vast quantity of arms and munitions left over from the Civil War.[18]

Cuban rebels had not counted on the skepticism of Hamilton Fish, Grant's secretary of state. In his superb biography of Fish, Allan Nevins noted that the Ten Years' War was one of the secretary's most trying and demanding experiences. While he felt deep emotional attachment to the Cuban struggle for independence from a backward and decrepit colonialism, he pondered the legal consequences of American recognition of the Cuban insurgency and the political implications of American intervention. It was not only a matter of the rebels' failure to produce a government worthy of recognition; it was also a question of the Cubans' ability to govern themselves. Evolutionary change from Madrid might be preferable. Thus in 1869 Fish put into operation a masterly design to resolve the Cuban dilemma by approaching Spain with a plan to grant Cuban independence under certain conditions, one of which was a 1-million-dollar payment to Spain guaranteed by the United States.[19] In this way Cubans would achieve independent status under the shadow of American power.

Too few had counted on the elusive factor of Spanish pride, and Fish's arrangement was curtly rejected in Madrid. He spent the next years writing instructions condemnatory of Spain and beating off the congressional hawks in the rear who were clamoring for American recognition, which Grant was inclined to render.

In the course of things his own thinking about Cuba underwent a transformation that McKinley and the generation of 1898 took for granted. On at least two previous occasions, in 1823–1825 and 1849–1851, American administrations had had to contend with Cuban unrest, Spanish vacillation, and the possibility of European intervention. In 1825 and 1852 the United States had granted a feeble reaffirmation of Spanish colonialism but rejected a British proposal for a tripartite pact—among Britain, France, and the United States—which would have guaranteed Spanish rule over the island. Fish's attitude on Cuba mirrored a crucial alteration of views: Spanish rule was now on trial, Cuba had a right to revolution, European powers had no right to intervene in that revolution, and the United States might have to intervene if another Ten Years' War erupted in the future. Shortly after the *Virginius* incident of November 1873, when fifty-three Cuban gunrunners (a few of them American citizens) died before a firing squad in Santiago, Fish wrote: "I have long been of the opinion that Spain must soon admit the fact that the Island has fallen from her control."[20] The nation expected Spain to reform Cuba or leave the island.

Britain and France opposed American diplomatic involvement in any settlement of the Ten Years' War. Their sympathy went out to Madrid in 1869, and again in 1898, and Fish may have been less eager to push Madrid to the wall because he knew such a policy would be opposed in both Paris and London. But neither was there British insistence on another tripartite arrangement and, in fact, London came part way toward recognizing the American case where Cuba was concerned. At last the British were prepared to admit the tenuous Spanish hold on Cuba, but, unlike 1825 and 1852, Britain now sought a practical solution to the Cuban problem as a means of preserving its commercial interests in the West Indies. Cuba's balance-of-power role was of less consequence than it had been in Canning's or Palmerston's day.[21]

It seemed inevitable, too, that Europe must relinquish its grip on Central America, but the 1880s brought a new threat in the form of the de Lesseps-French enterprise in the jungle of Panama. The United States was hardly a newcomer to the isthmus when Ferdinand de Lesseps, fresh from his Suez triumph, announced the Panama venture. Rather, American efforts had not gone much beyond the accomplishments of the 1850s, when the transisthmian railroad in Panama and a transit route through Nicaragua were completed. As far as canal sites were concerned, Nicaragua remained the favored choice in Washington for technical reasons, though Bidlack's treaty with Colombia provided a stronger legal foundation for an American-dominated isthmian route in Panama. In 1867 the Andrew Johnson administration made a feeble attempt to pursue the Nicaraguan scheme in the Dickinson-Ayón treaty, which called for an American guarantee of a Nicaraguan canal but carefully avoided any violation of British prerogatives under the Clayton-Bulwer treaty. The United States did not insist on exclusive domination of the canal. There followed surveys of potential sites, and in 1872 Grant appointed an Interoceanic Canal Commission, headed by Rear Adm. Daniel Ammen. Four years later the commission gave its blessings to the Nicaraguan canal route. Fish promptly drew up a proposed treaty with Nicaragua, which refused to accept the terms, and the plans were shelved. De Lesseps's Panamanian foray jarred American planners from their complacency once more, and in 1879 with Grant's aid Ammen and his associates created the Maritime Canal Company of Nicaragua. The founders proposed a fifty-mile canal across the republic, using the San Juan River, Lake Nicaragua, and some twelve locks to complete the transit.[22]

The Hayes administration saw in de Lesseps's endeavors the specter of European domination of the isthmus. Indeed the French effort to cut a waterway through the Panamanian jungle, in retrospect, did not speed up American attempts to build a canal; instead de Lesseps's work served to remind Americans of the political implications of the enterprise. Within the Congress and the cabinet the long-range impact of the French project was debated, to the hazard of the Clayton-Bulwer treaty and the concept of an international waterway. In March 1880 Hayes boldly informed the Congress that an interoceanic channel represented "virtually a part of the coast line of the United States." Next year Secretary of State William Evarts tried unsuccessfully to pressure the Colombians into reinterpreting the 1846 treaty so that the United States might exer-

cise much greater control over a Panamanian canal. In the hue and
cry the Clayton-Bulwer document, which symbolized the highwater
mark of Anglo-American understanding on the subject, was fair
game for political and editorial assaults, and the Monroe Doctrine
was continually invoked as de Lesseps lost his way in the Panamanian quagmire.[23]

Evarts's successor at the State Department, James G. Blaine,
plunged headlong into the debate over American rights under the
1846 treaty. Blaine's contention was essentially that the United
States now possessed a long Pacific coastline, that most of the traffic
through the Panamanian route would be engaged in east
coast—west coast shipping, and that the nation must enjoy supervi-
sory powers over the interoceanic canal for security reasons. European investment in a hemispheric canal was tolerable, but any
political or military control over the Panamanian route by a European power was contrary to American policy. The secretary wrote a
summation of his argument and sent it to all American legations in
Europe. By implication Blaine employed the Monroe Doctrine
through his assertion that only the United States and Colombia had
any right to guarantee the neutrality of the canal. Even the Colombians were taken aback by the brashness of Blaine's maneuver, but
following an explanation by the American minister, they were sufficiently soothed. In Europe, especially in Britain, Blaine's interpretations of the 1846 treaty were looked upon as the product of
typical American impetuosity. To the British Blaine had stretched
Bidlack's treaty to the breaking point: by its provisions the United
States guaranteed the neutrality of the transit route, not the security of the province of Panama. Besides, Blaine had cavalierly ignored the Clayton-Bulwer treaty, and this omission alone was
enough to raise a storm in London. For the next two years, the foreign office dredged up every scrap of diplomatic memorabilia in order to assail Blaine's contentions. Far from being an outmoded
arrangement, the British argued, the Clayton-Bulwer treaty remained a vital part of Anglo-American isthmian understanding,
and twice, in 1860 and 1869, the United States had alluded to it in
a spirit of reaffirmation.[24]

Thus the British won the battle to preserve the 1850 canal treaty, though it was obvious the pact was doomed and that the United States would demand a much greater role in any interoceanic canal than Clayton and Bulwer had anticipated. Twenty years hence the British would give up the diplomatic struggle to preserve the 1850 agreement, but they would win greater compensation for their loss.

Blaine's sparring with the British over the meaning of the Clayton-Bulwer treaty raised questions that went far beyond the neutrality of an isthmian canal. The debate struck deeply at the British presence in Central America. Belize was no longer a major issue in Anglo-American relations, for the decline of the mahogany trade and the altered routing of commerce in the Gulf-Caribbean had transformed the outpost into a sleepy port town. British rule at least protected it from the political turmoil of its Central American neighbors.[25] The Nicaraguan Mosquitia, which lingered as a symbol of British influence into the 1890s, was a more volatile issue. Americans were no longer committed to the idea of an internationally controlled isthmian canal. The Nicaraguan government saw the American interest in a Nicaraguan canal as an opportunity to remove the last vestiges of British imperialism from their eastern shores. Repeatedly London intervened in the Mosquito-Nicaragua dispute, arguing that Managua possessed little concern for the welfare of the Indians. The Nicaraguans claimed that the Mosquito protectorate was merely a guise to prevent the incorporation of the people into the Nicaraguan state and, more importantly, to impede American-Nicaraguan canal negotiations. When Nicaragua asserted its military authority over the proposed eastern terminus of the projected canal, the British raised objections. Concerning the squabble, Thomas F. Bayard, then secretary of state, observed that the Cleveland administration looked upon British paternalism in the Mosquitia as a de facto protectorate, which denied Nicaragua her full sovereignty in the area. "The United States," Bayard wrote, "can never see with indifference the re-establishment of such a protectorate." Such a move would violate the often expressed opposition of the United States to the enlargement of European influence on the continent and also violate the Clayton-Bulwer treaty.[26]

Admittedly such language was not much stronger than that employed four decades previously, but in the forties the Central American states still struggled to surmount the political agonies following the dissolution of the federation. At that time the United States constituted a political force that could be exploited to retard British influence. The Clayton-Bulwer treaty was signed, Britain accepted the American entrée into the isthmus, and the question of the Mosquitia was left unsettled. The nineties brought a more nationalistic government into power in Nicaragua, a government whose leadership resolved to settle once and for all the "symbolic imperialism" and residue of British rule. The Mosquitia became Managua's "Eastern Question."

In April 1895 Nicaraguan authorities ran a British consular official out of the port of Corinto. Affronted, London demanded a 75-thousand-pound indemnity and dispatched a warship to the scene. An ultimatum was delivered, and when Nicaragua refused to reply, the city was occupied, but only for a week. With assistance from El Salvador, Nicaragua was able to pool the funds to pay the British demand, and the troops departed. Though trivial the incident provoked passionate editorials in the United States, and the Cleveland administration was accused of knuckling under to a "patent violation" of the Monroe Doctrine.[27]

When questioned about the implications of the Corinto affair, Secretary of State Walter Q. Gresham, in a note to Nicaragua, refuted the notion that the Monroe Doctrine was violated. The occupation, he wrote, was not permanent in character because Britain had no intention of remaining in Corinto. American good offices were employed in the dispute to give the Nicaraguans an opportunity to amass the necessary funds to pay the indemnity and to bring about a peaceful settlement of the entire affair. More importantly, many Americans condemned what they considered arbitrary British methods in dealing with Managua, and the Cleveland administration was taken to task for its presumed complacency.

In the same year London gave up all pretensions of a Mosquito protectorate. Nicaragua proclaimed its sovereignty over the Indians, despite the special concessions of the 1860 treaty, and in diplomatic rejoinders the United States adhered to the Nicaraguan position. By the end of 1895 Managua had fully asserted its authority in the Mosquitia, and Britain acquiesced by accepting the Nicaraguan position.[28]

The most serious American-European confrontation in the Gulf-Caribbean excepting only the Spanish-American War was the Venezuelan crisis of 1895. It was made more serious by the abysmal ignorance of Washington and London about each other's foreign policy goals and political leadership. Bayard, who became the first American to hold ambassadorial rank at the Court of Saint James's, came to know the British mind as well as any diplomat, yet he lost influence with his own government during the crisis. There was Lord Salisbury, whose character made him a man of influence in British foreign policy but whose diplomatic orientation was toward Europe, not the United States. He looked upon America as a blustering would-be power, a parvenu in a world still dominated by the European giants. He did not have much regard for those Americans who like Secretary of State Richard Olney exploited the language of threat. His somber ways were incomprehensible to Cleveland and Olney; they were a mystery to his countrymen who did not know him well. Some said his life was "consecrated" and indeed he began every working day with chapel prayer.

Though his American counterpart probably cared as little for public opinion his social and political grooming was hardly as exquisitely tailored as Salisbury's. Where Salisbury was polished and to his friends charming, Cleveland was blunt, determined, and usually absolute. He had learned most about life as sheriff and mayor among the rowdy elements of the Democratic party in Buffalo, New York. His moral code however was of a loftier variety, and his honesty derived naturally from his moral disgust of unsavory politics and not from prayer. He took the details of every job, even the presidency, as serious business. Once as sheriff he had even undertaken the task of personally pulling the lever to hang two men rather than assign an underling to the job.

Thus it was not surprising that Cleveland found emotional and professional compatibility in the man who moved from the Justice Department to become secretary of state following Gresham's death in 1895. Like Cleveland, Richard Olney was straightforward and businesslike publicly but could reveal acceptable traces of humor privately. Their relationship was one of the more interesting in the history of presidential–secretary-of-state collaborations. In the manner that Col. E. M. House understood Woodrow Wilson or Harry Hopkins knew the mind of Franklin Roosevelt, Olney could read Cleveland's thoughts. They admired each other. But their personal codes were unusually severe. Cleveland would have understood and respected Olney's decision to banish his daughter from the house when after marriage she chose to live with her husband in Berlin rather than in Olney's house.

Before the crisis was passed the Americans nearly pushed the British into a war neither really wanted, and Olney and Cleveland formally invoked the Monroe Doctrine for the first time by transforming it from a policy statement into a doctrine of hemispheric public law.

The Venezuelan question involved a boundary controversy between Britain and Venezuela over territory between the Essequibo and Orinoco rivers. In the early stages of the dispute each nation sought to secure the territory because it commanded the interior trade routes, and its mineral resources (including a newly discovered gold field) made the region an even more desirable prize. In the late 1840s a British surveyor, Sir Robert Schomburgh, had surveyed a boundary line along a course lying near the Orinoco. Venezuela insisted that the true border lay on the Essequibo, farther to the east. Each party encroached upon the other's claims.

Until the mid-1870s Venezuela tried to settle the issue without appeals to other countries, although there had been desultory warnings in the United States Congress about possible violations of the Monroe Doctrine as far back as 1848, when a Connecticut senator had raised the issue. When the United States did become heavily involved, it matter-of-factly accepted the legality of the Venezuelan position. In the 1880s relations between Britain and Venezuela rapidly deteriorated. An arbitration treaty was drawn up in the last days of the Gladstone administration, but his successor refused to go ahead, and London fell back on Schomburgh's line. Already Venezuela had become increasingly anti-British, and British subjects under her jurisdiction were ill treated. One incident brought compensation only after London issued an ultimatum. Diplomatic relations were suspended in 1887.[29]

The Venezuelans had long since begun their importunings to Washington. An appeal of 1876 invoked the Monroe Doctrine, arguing that a European power was in the process of violating the principles of 1823 by territorial expansion in Guiana. Secretary of State William Evarts apparently refused to accept the British action as a direct affront to the doctrine, but expressed the opinion that the United States could not look with indifference on the "forcible acquisition" of South American lands by a European power. Though he did not force the issue, Evarts reiterated his fears on the occasion of a telegraph installation in the Orinoco region in 1881. One of his successors in the State Department, Frederick Frelinghuysen, professed ignorance of the legal questions involved but agreed to suggest third-party arbitration if Venezuela desired. The matter was further complicated by the ancillary question of Venezuelan indebtedness to creditors in France, the Netherlands, the United States, Spain, Britain, and Germany.[30]

The Cleveland administration adhered almost fanatically to the arbitral solution. Gresham could not understand why Britain would "maintain that the validity of their claim to territory long in dispute between the countries shall be conceded as a condition precedent to the arbitration of the question."[31] Indeed, there existed pervasive ignorance of opposing positions in each of the capitals—London, Washington, and Caracas. British delay in the crisis revealed an incredible misreading of the seriousness with which the dispute was argued in Washington. Cleveland, suspicious of backstage maneuvering in the Hawaiian episode, was blind to the fact that Venezuela exploited the crisis as a cover for serious internal economic difficulties. So grave was the financial situation in Caracas that the government retailed its postage at a discount, and the only blessing on the horizon was the boundary claim. If Venezuela could salvage the disputed territory, the land and the gold would put matters aright. Though there was a great deal to be said for arbitration, London had a point in its argument that such a settlement might be a bad precedent.[32]

At stake, of course, was more than the acreage and the mineral resources. The traditional nineteenth-century manner of dealing with smaller states, a practice developed into a fine art by Palmerston, was, so far as Cleveland and Olney were concerned, outmoded and unacceptable. In the debates on Monroe's message since 1823, politicians had concentrated on outright European seizure of territory as the primary menace, and indirect European influence—such as the British role in Central America in the 1840s—as an ancillary evil. Policymakers had not forbidden forceful action aimed at redressing legitimate grievances, as long as it did not lead to permanent occupation or control. Seward, for example, carefully distinguished between the tripartite powers' *right* to obtain redress in Mexico and the French *intention* to install a monarchy in that country. The Venezuelan crisis, however, brought such punitive measures within the purview of forbidden items in Monroe's dicta. Gresham himself gave an intimation of the altered thinking shortly before his death:

> Her Majesty's government is aware of the interest which the government and people of the United States feel in matters affecting the peace and welfare of the independent states of this hemisphere. While we do not assume to dictate to these states, or to exercise an undue influence over them, as to what their relations with other powers of the world shall be, yet their fortunes have always been objects of our solicitude, and we cannot view without anxiety the continuance of disputes in which their peace and happiness are deeply involved.

Cleveland's commitment to arbitration, Gresham added, was sustained by a joint resolution of Congress on 20 February 1895.[33]

Compared with his successor's analysis Gresham's note decidedly understated the American position. Olney was a fin de siècle policymaker who adopted Mahan's plea for an "outward-looking" foreign policy. He did not precipitate the Venezuelan question, yet he succeeded in transforming it from one of those routine nineteenth-century boundary disputes into an international cause célèbre. The controversy was one of the first things he began working on when he inherited Gresham's office, and by early July he was able to place in Cleveland's hands a position paper. Cleveland suggested some changes in the phraseology, but his overall reaction was that Olney's handiwork was an excellent piece of work which succeeded, among other things, in vigorously reaffirming the Monroe Doctrine. On 20 July Olney sent the message to Bayard in London.[34]

In time the note would earn the well-deserved sobriquet of "bombshell." In print its length came to about twenty pages of legal contentions interspersed with pontifical political observations. Tracing the historical record Olney came down hard on the British case, stating that London had encroached on Venezuela's claims successively in 1886, 1890, and as late as 1893 and that the republic was expected to accept the British claim as a precondition of arbitration. Throughout the controversy, Britain remained the obstinate party: Venezuela had sought arbitration for twenty-five years, a suggestion later seconded by Washington, but British rigidity had prevented any action. Basic to his argument was his contention of the applicability of the Monroe Doctrine to the situation and the absolute necessity of accepting the American proposal. "Today the United States is practically sovereign on this continent," Olney declared, "and its fiat is law upon the subjects to which it confines its interposition." By virtue of its preeminence in the hemisphere, the United States had every right to see to it that Venezuelan territory was not appropriated by a European power, and Britain had no right to exploit her might in dealing with a weak Latin American state. After all, Olney wrote soothingly, the British were noted for their "love of justice and fair play." The honor of the United States depended on British consent to accept arbitration; if not the president would have to present the matter to Congress.[35]

Bayard read Olney's note to Lord Salisbury, who "expressed regret, and surprise that it had been considered necessary to present so far reaching and important a principle and such wide and profound policies of international action in relation to a subject so comparatively small." Indeed, as the months passed and Salisbury delayed a reply, British tardiness appeared more and more as a refusal to take the whole matter seriously. Olney's instruction of 8 October revealed a growing irritation at the way London was handling the problem, implying that Salisbury and his colleagues were adopting a casual attitude toward the entire affair. There prevailed in some circles the belief that Venezuela was striving to stampede Britain into a war. The *London Morning Post*, for example, editorialized: "Unfortunately there is too much reason to believe that Venezuela is seeking to show that we are not so much concerned with the question of boundary as with that of extending our territorial possessions in South America."[36] Going further, the *Post* noted that such a move by the British government would be interpreted in Washington as a violation of the Monroe Doctrine. Venezuela had arrived at a similar conclusion. But war between the British and American peoples would be unthinkable, for it would be "civil war, and neither branch of the Anglo-Saxon race is going to shed brothers' blood for a mile or two of barren mountains in Guiana."[37]

Olney kept up the pressure throughout October and November, but it was soon clear that Salisbury was not going to be rushed into submitting his reply. From Bayard's reports Olney learned that the foreign office gave greater consideration to the Eastern Question, and on 20 November he demanded to know Salisbury's reasons for delaying to respond to his 20 July note. As a matter of fact, Salisbury did plan on having the draft ready in time to send before Congress met. Unfortunately Salisbury got the date confused. (Here, apparently, Bayard was not much help.) Since Salisbury's response was dispatched on 26 November by steamer instead of by cable, it did not reach Washington before Cleveland delivered his State of the Union address. This message contained a hint of the truculent mood that now dominated Cleveland's and Olney's thinking on the Venezuelan question and noted the imminent arrival of Salisbury's statement. A few days later the message came in, and Lord Pauncefote, the British ambassador, read it to Olney at the secretary's home.[38]

Actually, Salisbury sent two notes, the first refuting Olney's characterizations of the Monroe Doctrine; the second noting the British position on the boundary dispute. His analysis of Olney's 20 July assertions remains something of a literary masterpiece. Arguing that the United States had never formally advanced a statement known as the Monroe Doctrine in any written form to another government, Salisbury noted that it was an utterance whose validity was more or less taken for granted by American politicians and writers. In any event Olney's description of the doctrine's meaning went far beyond what Monroe had intended, for the circumstances of the Anglo-Venezuelan boundary imbroglio ill fitted the state of affairs in the hemisphere in 1823. The controversy was a quarrel between two sovereign states, Great Britain and Venezuela, not an issue involving European colonization of the Western world. "No statesmen, however eminent, and no nation, however powerful, are competent to insert into the code of international law a novel principle which was never recognized before."

The second note merely refuted Venezuela's interpretation of the facts; Schomburgh's line, Salisbury explained, actually did not encompass additional territories which Britain might claim as a right but did not out of consideration for a less powerful state. As British settlers penetrated ever further into the disputed territory, London made other overtures for a peaceful settlement to Caracas; these were rebuffed, and Britain therefore decided to hold steadfast to Schomburgh's line. While Britain did not reject the idea of arbitration, it would not entertain arbitration by a third party whose evidence included "extravagant pretensions" of eighteenth-century Spanish officials, nor would it accept settlement which would mean relinquishing mineral resources of "untold value" and British subjects in Guiana to the jurisdiction of a society of different language and unstable politics.

Under such circumstances London would continue to reject the idea of arbitration. The wording was clear but noticeably polite, especially when contrasted with Olney's abrasive tone. Salisbury provided Cleveland and Olney a way out, but his experience taught him that they might press their cause further. In any event he was certain that his colleagues and the empire would stand up to a belligerent United States. Here he miscalculated: Cleveland did take the issue before the Congress, and Salisbury's associates refused to confront the American challenge.[39]

Salisbury's rejection of Olney's logic infuriated Cleveland, who sent a special message on the subject to Congress on the seventeenth of December. In it he requested a special appropriation to establish an investigating commission and in succeeding passages implied that the commission would doubtless find in Venezuela's favor. If Britain remained adamant, then war was the only alternative. The public response to Cleveland's outburst was mixed but generally favorable, and in a few instances wildly enthusiastic. The *New York World* and *Baltimore Sun*, both Democratic periodicals, called the message "A Jingo Bugaboo" and "Stretching the Monroe Doctrine without Sufficient Reason." But such condemnations were overshadowed by editorial praise for what the *Washington Star* labeled "Neither Jingoistic nor Supine, but Dignified and Firm."[40]

In London the American position was now taken in utmost seriousness, "casting all other questions," Bayard wrote, "into comparative unimportance." Earlier Bayard was seriously faulted for having made too minor a thing of Olney's and Cleveland's feelings about the boundary dispute. This failure was tangential when compared to the attitudes of Salisbury, Joseph Chamberlain, and a host of others in Britain who had consistently refused to accept American power as anything but a negligible factor in the balance of power. Cleveland's determined stand threw the foreign office into a momentary panic: the South American situation suddenly mushroomed in importance, and the press screamed headlines about saving honor but avoiding war. The pressure for arbitration was now exerted. Eight hundred English workers urged an arbitral solution, vowing that an Anglo-American conflict would constitute "a crime against the laws of God and Man."[41]

Actually there is little in the record to demonstrate that the foreign office wanted anything but a peaceful settlement of the boundary dispute. Venezuela's position had always been so extreme, it was claimed, that to submit to arbitration would have meant approbation of patently ridiculous claims. It had been a point of pride in London; now the matter was a point of pride in Washington.

The Admiralty took no extraordinary measures to deal with the Caribbean situation. Had the British government decided to stand up to Cleveland's challenge, wrote one historian, it would have proved exceedingly difficult to reinforce Caribbean naval contingents, given the European situation.

The United States boasted of three first-class capital ships, hardly a match for British naval strength, but the Admiralty could spare no more ships for service in the Caribbean without undermining naval power elsewhere. In the Caribbean the days of British naval preponderance were gone. Though German and British interests in the area were often compatible and though Salisbury might have rejected the Monroe Doctrine in favor of an understanding with

Germany over Latin America, he did not. In the future British policy might have to rely on a friendly United States. Finally, as a British scholar of Salisbury's foreign policy has pointed out, the prime minister was not a bluffing man. Foreign policy must be supported by adequate military strength, otherwise it could lead to disastrous consequences. In the Venezuelan issue he perhaps possessed more faith in Britain's ability to stand firm than did some in the Admiralty, and within the cabinet he clung to the concept of a firm stand until the last. When the cabinet met again on 11 January 1896, most were ready to give up the fight. The prime minister had toyed with the idea of calling a high-level international conference in which the United States would defend the Monroe Doctrine and other states might grant it legal recognition, but by the time of the January meeting his colleagues were no longer interested in pursuing such a course. The blunders in South Africa, the attitude of Germany, the Turkish situation—all of these dictated a policy of conciliation toward the United States.[42]

The boundary settlement was not achieved until 1899, and the months following Cleveland's demand and Salisbury's capitulation seemed anticlimactic. Having accepted, in fact if not in theory, American participation in adjudicating the controversy, the British set themselves to retain control of at least the settled portions of the disputed territory. From the beginning of the Anglo-Venezuelan debate the fate of loyal settlers in the disputed region prompted the British to reject the idea of unconditional arbitration. In 1896 London fought to preserve all settled areas from the arbitral judgment, but Olney refused to accept such a principle, and the two nations finally agreed on a fifty-year rule, which stood as the guideline for determining legal possession. For a few months in 1896 Salisbury and Chamberlain believed they might obtain more favorable terms from Cleveland's successor, but Henry White, a career diplomat, and John Hay, a future secretary of state, both Republicans, apparently convinced the British of the flaws in such thinking. Chamberlain visited the United States in September, and although too much has been made of the significance of his sojourn, his meetings with Olney helped to break the tension of the previous winter. In November the fifty-year rule was agreed upon, and a five-member commission—two British, two American, and a neutral party—was named. The commission announced its judgment in October 1899. Though losing the mouth of the Orinoco, British Guiana survived the adjudication with a sizable territorial victory.[43]

Years later the perceptive French student of nineteenth-century British history Élie Halévy wrote that the first Venezuelan crisis compelled two nations to recognize their common interests by bringing them so close to war. Intellectual, religious, and political leaders in both countries, particularly in Britain, condemned the idea of fratricidal conflict. A rapprochement with the United States—these years witnessed the beginning of what Bradford Perkins has called "The Great Rapprochement"—offered a better alternative than open hostility, for in early 1896 Britain incurred the anger of not only the Americans but the French, Turks, Germans, and Russians. Finally, Britain was already coming around to the intellectual justification of American suzerainty in Latin America. The United States was the Anglo-Saxon scion in the New World, and Britain must now defer to its protégé in the Western hemisphere.[44]

Olney's strong statement of 20 July 1895 not only invigorated the Monroe Doctrine but also laid the foundation for the interventionist policies of the twentieth century. By interfering in the Anglo-Venezuelan dispute the United States assumed responsibility for its settlement. The implication of American involvement was unmistakable: if the American government asserted its right to interfere in Latin American—European quarrels, then it simultaneously assumed some responsibility for preventing such quarrels. Just how this could be accomplished was not clear, certainly not in 1895, but in 1898 diplomatic representatives argued their case against the perpetuation of Spanish Cuba and the right and duty of the United States to terminate a war. Thus by processes of escalation, the principle of intervention as a means of preventing European intervention was derived in part from what Olney said. The secretary himself was more modest about his actions. In January 1897 he declined to write an article about the Monroe Doctrine for the *Forum*, an important outlet for the views of political leaders, contending that he had in fact reduced the scope of the doctrine.[45]

Cleveland's and Olney's reaction to the Venezuelan imbroglio was symptomatic of the jingoism of the times, but it is difficult to say what influences the belligerency of both the public and press had upon their policies. Certainly Cleveland, who withstood severe buffeting from the expansionists in the Hawaiian and Cuban crises, was not a man to buckle under to popular excitement. In some respects the bellicose attitude of the administration followed logically as the culmination of ideas and processes that stretched back to the immediate post–Civil War period. A central question which Olney and Cleveland confronted was the economic and political necessity of establishing American hegemony in the Caribbean periphery in order to ease the impact of the depression at home and secure permanent outlets for American industrial products. Foreign policy and economic considerations were intricately bound together.

No single explanation of past events can be completely satisfactory, and the interpretations given here, advanced by two leading scholars of the 1890s, do not explain to everyone's satisfaction why this decade was dominated by expansionism.[46] Cleveland was not the kind of president to be rushed into a war with Britain through popular agitation. He saw that vital American economic interests were at stake in the Venezuelan confrontation. On the other hand Richard Olney calculated in 1895 that Americans owned 50 million dollars in property interests in Cuba, but the administration resolutely refused to go to war to rid the island of its Spanish grip, an act which, when carried out by Cleveland's successor, opened the doors to unrestricted American capital investment.

Perhaps historians of this crucial decade concentrate so much on the decision-making processes in London, Paris, Madrid, and Washington that they overlook the vitally important factor of Caribbean nationalism. In the early nineteenth century the Haitian Revolution, with all its political and social implications, set the tone for the evolution of a Cuban policy. In the same manner, nationalistic movements in the Gulf-Caribbean in the late nineteenth and early twentieth centuries—in Nicaragua, Cuba, Venezuela, and Panama—precipitated a series of crises. In these four countries, it can be argued, nationalistic and revolutionary movements served as catalytic agents that brought a confrontation among major powers. In each case these countries (or colonies) gambled on the expediency of encouraging American aid in their struggle—the Cuban rebels against Spain; the Venezuelans and Nicaraguans against Britain; and, later on the Panamanian revolutionists against Colombia. Initially their strategy was successful, but ultimately American power replaced that of Britain, Spain, and Colombia.

7 • The Spanish-American War and After

In 1898 the United States waged war against Spain and ultimately inherited the Spanish Empire in Puerto Rico and the Philippines. The war itself was the consequence of multiple forces, and the results of the conflict, so far as Spain's Caribbean empire was concerned, stemmed logically from certain assumptions in the nineteenth-century Caribbean policy of the United States. In Cuba, for instance, the American people looked upon themselves as the responsible arbiter for the termination of the rebellion against Spain. By advocating the application of American military power to end a civil war the United States assumed a principal role in determining the destiny of the Cuban republic.

In arrogating unto itself the right to end Spanish rule in Cuba the United States rejected any European participation in the crusade. This represented no abrupt reversal of policy, for in 1825 and 1852 the American government specifically repudiated an overture to join with Britain and France in guaranteeing Spanish Cuba. Neither was there an official commitment to Cuban rebellion in Washington until 1898, though in 1875 a secretary of state boldly declared that Spanish colonialism in the Western hemisphere was inevitably doomed. The decision to intervene was founded on a long-standing historical case against Spain, and a strenuous diplomatic effort was made in European courts to justify the intervention. With Spain's defeat and removal from the hemisphere, the traditional European role in the Caribbean was diminished but not terminated.

For most Americans the intervention in Cuba was a necessary, even humanitarian, measure aimed at terminating what was to them a horrible war. Much of the political leadership, however, saw clearly the impact of the war on American policy throughout the Caribbean and in the Pacific. Historians have long debated the question of America's imperial course: on the one side arguing that the conflict with Spain produced an "aberration" in policy that unwisely led an essentially anti-imperialistic people to emulate the colonial policies of European nations and on the other contending that the jingoistic and imperial notions of the 1890s had been in the making since 1865.

Clearly the Spanish-American conflict gave the late nineteenth century imperialists a stature and influence few of them had attained before. The experience in Cuba and to a lesser degree in Puerto Rico made more convincing the argument that America had a special responsibility in the Caribbean world. It was one thing to render a negative assessment of the self-governing capabilities of Caribbean societies, as John Quincy Adams had in the 1820s, but it was quite another matter to hold such a view yet demand the withdrawal of the European governing presence there. In other words, having condemned the Spanish for four hundred years of misrule in the West Indies, it seemed objectionable and even inhumane to presume the Cubans and Puerto Ricans could survive without some tutelage.

From this point it was an easy and logical step to the belief that Europe and particularly Britain must not exploit its financial and political influence in the Gulf-Caribbean world to the detriment of American strategic, political, and economic needs. Nothing in Monroe's message said anything about curtailing trade and investments from Europe to Latin America. But within five years of the defeat of Spain the United States compelled a thoroughgoing revision of the old 1850 canal treaty with Britain, demanded that the European creditors of an indebted Latin American state accept the mediation of Washington, and laid the foundation for an economic protectorate in the Dominican Republic.

The American indictment of Spanish rule in Cuba was a blend of idealism, politics, and economics.[1] When Cuban exiles in the United States and revolutionaries on the island renewed their efforts in the insurrection of 1895, they directed an emotional appeal to the American public, a repetition of their propaganda campaigns of the Ten Years' War. Official participation in that holocaust had been prevented by the untiring Fish, and in 1895 the Cubans encountered an equally obdurate force in the Cleveland administration. Harassed by a jingoistic Congress, Cleveland and Olney consistently refused to extend diplomatic recognition to the Cuban rebels, but they took a pessimistic view of the permanency of Spanish authority over the island. Fish's predictions of 1875 were now repeated by Olney. The Spanish gave assurances of their ability to quell the strife within a reasonable time. In September 1895 the ex-mayor of Havana predicted the crushing of the rebellion following the rainy season, which always hampered military operations. Olney was skeptical. If anything, he wrote, the rebellion was rapidly spreading; the prospect was for more disaffection with Spanish colonialism, particularly among propertied elements, and a worsening of the situation on the battlefield.

Such sentiments did not place Cleveland and Olney in the vanguard of the interventionists. Their assessment of the Cuban drama was much the same as Fish's: a steady deterioration of public confidence in Cuba would inevitably result in a Spanish withdrawal. They resisted repeated congressional attempts to compel the administration to do something on behalf of the insurrectionists. In April 1896 Congress approved a concurrent resolution recognizing the belligerent status of the revolutionaries, but the president refused to yield. Apparently both Cleveland and Olney believed that if the war worsened Spain would recognize her inability to gain Cuban confidence and simply leave the island. They failed to give sufficient weight to Spanish obstinacy and pride. Instead, they wrote long analyses of the breakdown of order on the island, the prevailing anarchy of the countryside, the growing effectiveness of the insurgents, and, finally, the steady decline of Cuba's economic productivity.

Interventionists found no commitment to their cause in Cleveland's annual message of December 1896. He concluded that Spain and the insurrectionists were now engaged in a brutal war of attrition with neither able to establish control. The anarchical state of the island and the consequent losses for American commerce and capital were deplorable, but the nation must adhere to a policy of neutrality. Congress angrily passed another resolution which in effect extended legislative recognition of Cuban independence, but Cleveland and Olney resisted with a sharp statement reaffirming executive control of foreign policy. Had the administration accepted the proffered resolution, Olney observed, it would have had to be willing to declare war against Spain.

Historians have often compared an unbending Cleveland to a pliable William McKinley—usually to the detriment of McKinley—because the latter supposedly blindly followed a jingoistic public into an unnecessary conflict with a nation that would have accepted peace. He was his own secretary of state. Recent investigators of McKinley's foreign policies have shown that McKinley generally accepted Cleveland's judgments on the Cuban problem, with one crucial exception. While his predecessor refused to yield on the question of war with Spain, McKinley accepted the possibility of a conflict, failing a solution of the Cuban problem by peaceful means. McKinley built his Cuban case on the grounds that the United States wanted to preserve peace with Spain, but not at the expense of another Ten Years' War. That earlier upheaval was, like the revolt of 1895, a brutal, internecine war. The present disaster was in reality a struggle for self-determination which would forever alter Spain's relationship to the island. The insurrection impaired American economic interests in Cuba and more importantly it inflicted intolerable damage to the productive capacity of the island, which McKinley and the generation of 1898 looked upon as a "humanitarian" concern.

Those who subsequently argued that Spain yielded substantially to American demands based their contention on the late 1897 grant of autonomy; the removal of the hated Gen. Valeriano Weyler, whose record as captain-general of Cuba had earned him the American epithet "Butcher"; and Madrid's response to McKinley's March 1898 demands.

The February 1898 crises of Dupuy de Lôme's letter and the *Maine* explosion were not in themselves sufficient provocations for war, nor did McKinley exploit the issues for the purpose of waging war. The letter, written by the Spanish minister to the United States to a private correspondent, had been purloined from the Havana mails by a rebel sympathizer in December 1897. It was not delivered to the press until the Spanish-American relationship had been severely shaken by the public commotion in Havana in January. In the letter de Lôme described McKinley as a politician catering to bellicose elements in the country, a comment often accepted by later historians as an apt description of McKinley's character.

More important than the letter's phrases was what could be read between the lines, namely, that Spain had professed for several months through official negotiations with Washington to be settling the Cuban problem, but in fact de Lôme's unflattering assessment reflected Spanish contempt for American efforts to terminate the war. The final months of peace witnessed a frantic Spanish attempt to stifle the rebellion and search for European allies.

The *Maine* had sailed to Havana for possible duty in rescuing American citizens there whose safety might be endangered. The two incidents were heaped upon the growing pile of grievances against Madrid—longstanding grievances which had now culminated in revolt. The grant of autonomy had not resulted in a material improvement of the situation, in part because the revolutionary leaders killed all chances of success by threatening anyone who agreed to accept autonomous status for the island, and in part because the Spanish did not appear to be seriously committed to reform. De Lôme's letter, for instance, implied that the concessions from Madrid were designed for American consumption. The famous March demands were (1) revocation of the *reconcentrado* system, a counterguerrilla measure that called for the herding of the population into garrison towns; (2) granting of self-government to Cuba; and (3) mediation of the war by the president of the United States.

The Spanish reply to McKinley's note has been the subject of heated historiographical debate. Spain did agree to relinquish the *reconcentrado*, but she responded to the plea for self-government and American mediation by restating the conditions for autonomy and by appealing to the insurgents to lay down their arms. Thus in Madrid men still looked upon the Cuban problem as essentially a matter of internal concern, not to be subjected to the prescription of the president of the United States. But McKinley and the American public believed they did have a right, even duty, to settle the Cuban question, that their case had a moral legitimacy which transcended the legal definitions of Spanish authority in Cuba, and that the United States was obligated to interfere because Spanish colonialism and counterrevolution had failed.

•

Spain on the eve of the war is often protrayed as the proud nation refusing to be humiliated by the moral piety of a McKinley or the jingoistic cockiness of a Theodore Roosevelt. When the revolt of 1895 erupted, Spain's military capability in Cuba was, in the opinion of one Spanish historian, "deplorable." Fourteen thousand troops guarded the interior, and four ramshackle ships patrolled the island's coastline. The hurried dispatching of six thousand additional men, the substitution in the captaincy-generalship, and, much to the outrage of the American observers, the introduction of the *reconcentrado* system were designed to accomplish what McKinley ultimately demanded—a speedy conclusion of the war. As the rebellion progressed, however, the Spanish manner of conducting the counterrevolution became an explosive issue, and most Americans were convinced that Spain could not win according to "humane" rules of war.

With McKinley's timetable hanging over their heads the Spanish ministers at first took the route of least resistance. Autonomy was extended to Cuba and Puerto Rico, and the hated Weyler was replaced. At the same time, however, the Madrid cabinet made known its collective judgment that the Cuban rebellion would have been stifled had it not been for the moral and material support the United States extended to rebel leaders.[2] When the grant of autonomy failed to satisfy the insurrectionists, Spain no longer felt compelled to extend concessions. In itself, autonomy constituted a radical departure from established policy in Madrid. (Military authority in Cuba rested on a royal decree of 1825 granting extensive power to the captain-general.) McKinley's March demands went further than his previous instructions because Spain was now expected to halt the fighting unilaterally and accept American mediation. In the Madrid cabinet the dominant mood was one of cynicism about the prospects for peace coupled with resentment over the unceasing American bullying. The government feared the possibility of insurrection at home if it yielded anything more to Washington. "Believe that this is the hour of life or death for a nation," a Spanish congressman told his colleagues, "cast your gaze on the pennant of the country, and let us not make, for God's sake, a peace without honor."[3]

Adm. Pascual Cervera's naval squadron, or at least the mention of it, struck a momentary fear among Americans along the Atlantic seaboard in the beginning of the war. Had the public known Cervera's innermost thoughts two months before, it might not have been so skittish. Cervera noted the sad state of Spanish naval forces. The eight vessels stationed at Havana, he wrote, "have no military value whatever, and, besides, are badly wornout." Spain's remaining seaborne force, compared with that of the United States, was about one to three, making any effective blockade of any American port "a dream, almost a feverish fancy." A military undertaking against the United States, he concluded, would have to be either "a defensive or a disastrous one, *unless we have some alliances*, in which case the tables may be turned."[4]

And the prospects for an alliance were not good. From the start McKinley had made clear his opposition to any European interference in the Spanish—United States discussions, an attitude which his special emissary Stewart Woodford relayed to Madrid in October 1897. The major European powers were of course desirous of keeping the peace, but how to reconcile two views of Cuba, one a product of centuries of imperial consciousness, the other a manifestation of international political morality? Either Spain must yield to McKinley's prescription or the United States must reconsider its demands.

Spain did relinquish a great deal in the final six months of peace, but never to American satisfaction, for Washington valued Spanish conciliation according to the results it produced in Cuba. Following the grant of autonomy things seemed to get worse. As for American reevaluation of its demands of Madrid, there was little chance for European diplomatic overtures short of a threat to come to Spain's aid in the event of hostilities. In a last-minute effort, in fact, the Spanish appealed for help to sustain a sister imperial state, but the response was, considering the desperation of the plea, disappointing. In the first place, a European alliance to prop up Spanish Cuba was not at all practicable. In the second, an alliance with Spain would mean a confrontation with a presumed newcomer to the imperial club, a nation that seemed determined to carve out an empire in the Caribbean.[5]

In April the powers made two diplomatic overtures on Spain's behalf. The first was an appeal from Britain, Germany, France, Austria-Hungary, Russia, and Italy for continued negotiations between Spain and the United States. McKinley's reply, dated five days before his 11 April war message, was a succinct presentation of the Cuban case which he was preparing to lay before Congress. The United States, he informed the diplomatic representatives of the powers, labored to bring a peaceful settlement to the Cuban horror "by affording the necessary guarantees for the re-establishment of order in the island." The war unfolded at the doorstep of America and shocked "its sentiment of humanity."

The second attempt was made on 14 April at the suggestion of the Austrian minister, who asked that each of his European colleagues recommend to his superiors the dispatch of an identic note to the State Department. The participants met later at the British embassy, where Sir Julian Pauncefote drew up a proposed statement that presumably was not offensive to the American position. But others apparently objected to its mildness, and the French and German ambassadors reworked it to the point of transformation from an amicable plea to a rejection of the validity of the American defense. Unfortunately the harsher note escaped Pauncefote's attention, and it was sent to Europe for approval. Salisbury and Kaiser Wilhelm II objected to the moral rigidity of the statement.[6]

Sympathy for Spain probably was strongest in France. The Paris government was apparently not at all moved by Woodford's stirring accounts of Cuban suffering to the French ambassador in Madrid, though strategists might have appreciated the American's analogue of a "Cuba" lying a hundred miles from the Brittany coastline. In the legislative assembly in early March the prospects of American intervention in Cuba were referred to as acts of piracy. While McKinley confidently asserted that Spanish colonialism was on trial, the *Journal des Debats* indicted American expansionism, hypocrisy, and selfishness for forcing Spain against a wall. The crucial test was Spain's "capitulation" to the March demands of McKinley. By demanding more the president merely revealed his ulterior motive of replacing Spanish with American domination over Cuba. McKinley's April message, the *Journal* went on, was in reality a mandate for economic imperialism, reminiscent of the machinations of the Holy Alliance, clothed in the rhetoric of Christian piety. The war, a French historian later wrote, merely unleashed the colonial ambitions of the United States.[7]

German policy was more difficult to assess. Both Germany and the United States exemplified the unifying force of nationalism; both were relative newcomers to the imperial family. But the Monroe Doctrine remained a distasteful document in Germany. By implication it proscribed German expansion into the Western hemisphere. Pan-Americanism militated against the identification of German settlers in Latin America—for instance, in Brazil—with Wilhelm's *Reich*. The Kaiser was enthusiastic at first about Spain's request for diplomatic support following the *Maine* disaster: he saw in Madrid's plea a means of reaffirming the monarchical tradition and of warning the British and Americans. His eagerness to get involved soon dissipated. Although Germany supported the collective note to Washington, the Kaiser no longer wanted to assume a principal role in reprimanding the United States.[8]

Thus in the few weeks before the outbreak of war, Germany settled on the collective diplomatic appeal as the best chance for preserving peace. Such a gesture disguised the fears of Wilhelm about the impact of a Spanish-American war on monarchism and, more importantly, on the European balance of power and colonial enterprise. It was commonly assumed that the United States was preparing to embark on colonial pursuits, which ran contrary to German interests, but the German foreign office balanced this assumption against the expected American reaction if Germany followed an aggressive anti-American course in 1898.[9]

As was the case with France, the Spanish reply to McKinley's demands elicited favorable responses in Berlin, and the American ambassador Andrew White was instructed to explain American refusal to accept the Spanish gesture. Madrid's "offer of an armistice," Secretary of State John Sherman wrote White, was in reality "an appeal by the autonomy government of Cuba urging the insurgents to lay down [their] arms . . . , an invitation to the insurgents to submit." Thereafter it would be the autonomists, not the rebels, who would decide just how much home rule Cuba needed.[10]

Though the German press, with the exception of two or three

papers, maintained consistent hostility toward America, the German foreign office softened its earlier criticism of American policy. The Department of State paid much less attention to German editorial posture than to official statements emanating from the German embassy and the informal expressions of "influential" men. In his autobiography White recounted the war months in Germany, noting the pervasive anti-Americanism in the press and among the public. The foreign office was a different matter, and on one occasion it informed White of a Spanish ship, presumably stacked with arms for use in Cuba, preparing to sail from Hamburg. White intervened, and the vessel was inspected.[11]

Clearly in Berlin the Spanish-American War was generally interpreted within the context of imperial power politics, and America's prosecution of war was looked upon as pursuit of empire. Europe could not be convinced that the American hegemony in the Caribbean was as much a result of the war with Spain as a primary cause of conflict. The Kaiser's imagination flirted with rumors of a British-American-German "triple alliance"—the press associated the idea with Joseph Chamberlain—and Wilhelm wrote his mother that if such a thought were seriously under consideration in London then the British foreign office might very well pursue the prospect through official channels![12]

The American war against decrepit Spain made a decidedly different impression in Britain, which ultimately reflected a curious duality: on the one side deep disgust of the Yankee diplomatic boorishness that sought to humiliate an aging monarchy, but on the other a resignation to the American contention that Spanish rule in Cuba was a failure. Britain was the sole European power with historical Caribbean interests that extended any serious consideration of the concept of an American-policed Caribbean.

A few months after eruption of the 1895 revolt, the *Times* editorialized on the Cuban dilemma confronted by Spain. The paper opposed loss of the island by the Spanish, annexation to the United States, and erection of another banana republic. The alternatives were few: Spain could prosecute a grueling counterrevolutionary offensive or impose an occupational force of fifty thousand soldiers and prepare for another Ten Years' War. Much more sensible would be an extension of autonomy, which might satisfy the insurgents and quell any movement for American annexation. For the next two years autonomy was looked upon as the key to preserving peace, and in June 1897 the State Department requested John Hay in London to assess "the drift to influential British sentiment . . . as respects the practical bases upon which the autonomy or even the complete self-government of Cuba may rest."[13]

Autonomy failed to bring peace. Insurgent obstinacy, Spanish dalliance, and American dissatisfaction all made it inadequate as a solution. When McKinley's demands were delivered in Madrid in March 1898 and war, failing a complete Spanish acquiescence, seemed all but inevitable, there could be no falling back on the 1895 contentions of the *Times's* editorial. While press opinion naturally sympathized with the plight of Madrid, it expressed little affection for the forgotton glories of Spain's empire of the Western hemisphere, but instead invoked the legacy of Anglo-Saxon fraternity:

> Whatever may have been our differences with the United States [wrote the London *Daily Chronicle*] the heart of our people will go out to the great attempt to be made to liberate an American colony from a cruel yoke. . . . Spain will have no allies. She will fight alone.[14]

The sanguinary bond was, of course, more meaningful than the imperial association:

> We may yet be saved from the sad spectacle of a contest between two friendly nations both bound to us by the bonds of old friendship, though, should the worst come to the worst, we shall not of course forget, whilst maintaining the duties of neutrality towards both, that one of them is knitted to us yet more closely by the ties of blood.[15]

On the eve of war Hay wrote confidently that British financial leaders looked to the United States to resolve the Cuban imbroglio.[16]

Lord Salisbury was not the kind of man to go rushing into the arms of McKinley. In the Venezuelan crisis he had consistently argued for a tougher line against American policy. He viewed the Spanish-American duel as an unfortunate affair between a humiliated European nation and a jingoistic parvenu, but he felt that any British advice to Spain would almost certainly be rejected. Unlike Arthur Balfour and Joseph Chamberlain he did not share the growing enthusiasm for a rejection of "splendid isolation" and the pursuit of a rapprochement with the United States.

In April 1898 during Salisbury's illness Balfour wrangled with the Spanish-American question, and he saw the future somewhat differently. Among other things he sought an understanding with Berlin and German-British-American cooperation in the Far East.[17] Balfour was an intellectual devotee of the idea of Anglo-Saxon mission, and saw American policy in Cuba as a fulfillment of British traditions of paternalism in backward lands. Of course the monarchy could not serve as a common bond, but other institutions, such as law, literature, and language, symbolized the "fundamental harmony" of Britain and America. Americans were, after all, ready to take up the "white man's burden" in Havana. The Victorian press exhausted the theme of divine mission in endless articles and editorials. If Pax Britannica rested solidly on a moral foundation, then so must Pax Americana, which yearned only to clean up the Cuban pesthole. The caricature of the cruel, despotic Spaniard may not have been believable in Madrid, Paris, or Vienna, but it was in Washington and London. The American indictment of Spanish oppression and cruelty was reaffirmed in Britain.[18]

The victory over Spain was a fitting example of the naval revolution that Mahan had championed. By grossly overestimating the military capability of Admiral Cervera's ships, American planners inadvertently insured victory in that July battle off Santiago. McKinley's peace terms, enunciated in June, indicated that the United States now wanted more than the Spanish evacuation of Cuba. The proposed cession of Puerto Rico, in lieu of a financial indemnity, and discussion of a harbor for a coaling station in the Philippines ominously forecasted a readjustment of the naval balance of power.[19]

The implications of American naval strength in the Caribbean had tremendous impact in Britain. American acquisition of Puerto Rico and the erection of a military protectorate in Cuba were viewed, correctly, as necessary steps for control of a future isthmian waterway. Britain's legal safeguard was the Clayton-Bulwer treaty, maligned by secretaries of state and congressmen since the Hayes administration and now almost certainly doomed. In December 1898 a British military intelligence official produced a memorandum on the treaty, aruging that American control of a future canal would result in tremendous military advantages for the United States in the event of an Anglo-American conflict. But, the memorandum continued, Britain might recognize some practical benefits by conceding to the termination of the contract.[20]

Just what practical benefits could result was not entirely clear. Certainly the Admiralty was not yet disposed toward total acquiescence in an American-dominated canal, nor did the foreign office seem inclined to go further than the provisions of the so-called first Hay-Pauncefote treaty (5 February 1900), which amended the 1850 canal treaty. In large part it was the product of John Hay's anglophilia; it provided for American construction and management of the new canal, stipulated that the waterway would be neutral, and invited other nations to guarantee the treaty. Its inadequacies were readily apparent. The document did not completely supplant the odious Clayton-Bulwer pact, it laid the legal basis for neutralization, and its provisions precluded American military fortifications. A few military officials pointed out that canal defense would rely mostly on control-of-sea approaches rather than land defenses, but the psychological impact of a waterway without fortifications was a crucial factor in the criticism. Theodore Roosevelt, then governor of New York, prudently observed that Hay's handiwork was militarily defective because it allowed enemy shipping to exploit the canal. Roosevelt viewed the appeal to other nations to adhere to the document as an implicit violation of the Monroe Doctrine.[21]

In early January the Admiralty summarized naval thinking on the new treaty and dourly concluded that any transisthmian canal would "greatly" enhance American military power, to the hazard of British interests in the event of war. The Admiralty's consensus was that the foreign office should oppose its construction. Such an assessment was of little value to Lord Lansdowne, who had inherited the foreign office from Salisbury in October. Lansdowne gauged accurately the tone of senatorial debate over the first Hay-Pauncefote treaty. The Americans were going to build a canal and insist on fortifying it. If the major consideration of defense was not fortifications but naval domination of the sea, then the Senate's squabbling about land defenses created only an incidental concern. If Britain wished to maintain her naval position in the Caribbean, Lansdowne concluded, she would have to relinquish her grip in other areas of equal importance. For the moment he rejected the Senate's amendments to the first treaty, but he prepared to acquiesce in Washington's insistence on full control of the canal's land appurtenances.[22]

By April Hay had written a new canal convention, and this time he circulated the draft to the most outspoken senators. Lansdowne's curt rejection of the amended earlier treaty had been unsettling, but further correspondence revealed London's willingness to accept an alteration. Actually Lansdowne was bluffing: he had refused to accept the amended first treaty because the Senate's amendments excluded international participation. The draft that Hay now produced was, at least, less offensive in tone. The 1850 treaty was abrogated and the United States was given unilateral authority to construct a canal. Nothing was said about fortifications, thus by implication allowing the Americans to provide for land defenses in the canal area. Finally, the United States agreed to keep the canal "free and open to the vessels of commerce and of war of all nations" on a basis of equal treatment. (Years later this clause was interpreted as a commitment to Britain only, but at the time it seemed to buttress the concept of an international waterway.)[23]

London's acceptance of the second Hay-Pauncefote instrument was of profound strategic importance for the future of British military strength in the Caribbean. For centuries the Caribbean arena was one of several crucial areas of British naval strength. The signing of the treaty was one of the climactic moments of an era reaching into the eighteenth-century world of Caribbean combat. No longer was there any question of holding the line against American power, as Bulwer had done in 1850. The United States insisted not only on its right to build, maintain, and fortify the transisthmian waterway but also on the necessity of holding military supremacy in the Caribbean region.[24]

•

Would Britain—or any European power, for that matter—accept the American guidance in the New World's Mediterranean? If Europe deferred to American authority in the Caribbean, there would have to be a drastic change in the diplomatic and financial relations between European powers and the republics of the area.

Of all the republics, Venezuela seemed the least reliable in its dealings with foreign creditors and thus was the most vulnerable to some kind of retaliation. At the turn of the century the Venezuelan government found itself in a typical nineteenth-century Latin American condition. Plagued by civil disorders and commotions, successive administrations had permitted the outstanding foreign indebtedness to soar. In 1881 the republic's obligations to creditors in Spain, the United States, Holland, France, Great Britain, Germany, and Denmark amounted to 24 million francs. The two countries eventually taking punitive action, Germany and Great Britain, were at this time far down on the list, and the most impatient government of these years was the French, which severed diplomatic relations in 1895, following Venezuela's refusal to arbitrate.[25]

In 1899 a revolution brought to power Don Cipriano Castro. Vain, ambitious, and a libertine, Castro came to power just in time to witness a catastrophic plunge in government income from 40 million bolivars in 1898–1899 to 27 million in 1899–1900, his first year of power. Castro's habits only worsened the situation. He personified the Latin American wastrel that a generation of progressive Americans held in contempt. Violent, romantic, egotistical, Castro was a fin de siècle caudillo whose financial policies were no longer tolerable.[26]

European representatives focused their attention on violations emanating from the disorders of 1899 which brought Castro to power. There were 725 new claims, ranging all the way from property destruction and forced loans to false arrest of foreigners and seizure of foreign-owned cattle. In foreign capitals the consensus was that Castro was a bandit whose mockery of international law and deportment would have to be punished. Germany felt particularly aggravated because Castro was seven years behind in interest payments on 5-percent Venezuelan bonds, failed to pay the guaranteed dividend on a railroad built by a German corporation, and refused to answer for property losses and damages to German residents in the revolt of 1899. The firm that had been hard hit by Venezuela's inattentiveness was the Diskonto Gesellschaft, which had helped to finance the Great Venezuelan Railroad Company. The line was completed in 1894, the dividend on the investment guaranteed by Venezuela. Two years later, in order to satisfy the claimants, the republic agreed to the company's assumption of 5-percent Venezuelan bonds to cover the guarantees. Venezuela defaulted again, owing its German creditors almost 13 million dollars. The Diskonto Gesellschaft became so irritated with Venezuelan dalliance that it tried in 1899 to influence the foreign office to intervene in the republic, with possible cooperation from Britain and the United States. On this occasion, however, the foreign office declined to pursue the idea, arguing that such a course might impair the unsteady German-American relationship.[27]

Anglo-German cooperation in dealing with Venezuela was prompted, at least in part, by London's decision to improve relations with Berlin. In 1901 Lord Lansdowne became foreign minister, and the "splendid isolation" of Salisbury was soon superseded by a determined effort to achieve a broad diplomatic understanding with Germany. Salisbury, lingering in the background, had little sympathy for an alliance, but in mid-1902 he retired, and the opportunity to create some kind of bond with Germany against a common irritant (Castro) could not be bypassed.[28]

The German foreign office had already explored the possibility of action against Venezuela, with particular care given to possible reaction of the United States. In December 1901 legal officials had drawn up a list of grievances against the republic, and German ambassador Theodor von Holleben later presented the summary to Hay. Though Germany wanted to avoid any clash with the United States, the ambassador reported, the claims were of such magnitude that their collection could no longer be delayed. If Castro refused to pay, the German government would be compelled to blockade crucial Venezuelan ports to forestall collection of tariffs. That failing, actual occupation of the ports might follow. On 12 December von Holleben met with Roosevelt and Hay, informing them of Germany's intentions. Apparently, Roosevelt stressed only the possibility of continuous occupation of Venezuelan territory—a violation of the Monroe Doctrine—and implied that Germany had the right to undertake limited punitive measures against Castro's government.[29]

With such implicit understanding of their dilemma in Washington, the two governments moved ahead to deal with the Latin American menace. The year 1902 was marked with a series of civil disturbances in the republic, to say nothing of Colombian-Venezuelan difficulties, in which foreign residents suffered more property losses and infringements of liberty. By mid-July Italy, also a Venezuelan creditor, had joined the ranks of European powers beseeching Caracas with a barrage of complaints.

It was matter-of-factly assumed that the Americans would be satisfied if they were informed of Anglo-German action in due time. On 13 August 1902 the British ambassador in Washington, Sir Michael Herbert, reported a conversation on the subject with Hay, who expressed regret that the powers must resort to force but could not object to the proposed measures, "provided no acquisition of territory was contemplated." Thus, as the leading student of the Monroe Doctrine later noted, the United States did little to discourage Anglo-German plans and in fact gave implied encouragement of the operation.[30]

Castro received the ultimatums on 7 December and made no response. The next day the German and British ministers departed the capital. Naval action on the ninth brought capture of several Venezuelan gunboats, two of which the Germans sank. During the next ten days Venezuela's ports were systematically harassed: a British detachment disembarked at La Guayra to evacuate some British subjects; on the thirteenth two cruisers, one British and one German, approached Puerto Cabello, whose officials had imprisoned the crew of a British steamer, issued ultimatums, shelled the fort, and dispatched a force ashore to complete its destruction; on the twentieth, the two powers proclaimed the blockade of the republic.[31]

Venezuela's plight, however, was of great concern. Castro had already set into motion a plea to Herbert Bowen, the American minister, to act as Venezuela's arbitrator in solving her difficulties with

London and Berlin. Hay was agreeable, provided that Venezuela propose the arbitral settlement and that Germany and Britain accept. All parties settled on Roosevelt himself as the arbitrator, but he was apparently dissuaded from accepting by Hay, who argued that the United States held claims against Venezuela and that the matter should rightly be submitted to the Hague Court. The blockade continued. Among the American public it rapidly became the subject of much debate, eliciting concern for Venezuela's predicament and prompting speculation about ulterior motives behind Germany's participation. The documents, as Dexter Perkins has observed, simply do not support a conclusion of German designs on territory in the Western hemisphere; Berlin followed London in teaching Castro a lesson. But in the United States the German "menace" was widely discussed, and in Britain the public wondered if the nation had made a bad bargain by cooperating with Germany in interfering in New World affairs, at the possible expense of Anglo-American friendship.[32]

During World War I when Roosevelt's anti-German feelings were at their peak, the former president gave the impression that he had employed force to frighten the Germans into backing down during the second Venezuelan crisis. If certain allowances are made for Roosevelt's Germanophobia during the war years and if one takes into account the human tendency to exaggerate things in recounting an incident, Roosevelt's assessment was not altogether a fabrication. The sudden anger of the public at the height of the crisis constituted an important factor in Britain's decision to accept the Venezuelan protocol and call off the blockade. Moreover, the extreme caution with which Britain and Germany proceeded in 1901–1902 was not so much in deference to the Monroe Doctrine as a prudent acknowledgment of the Caribbean military situation.

In the McKinley years the General Board had arrived at a basic plan of Caribbean naval operations in wartime and had strongly urged the acquisition of certain locations and bases in Cuba and near Puerto Rico for peacetime safeguards. While Germany and Britain made their preparations for dealing with Castro, the navy was coincidentally just getting into shape its base at Culebra, near eastern Puerto Rico. During the initial phases of the Venezuelan affair, operations were not far along, but the General Board drew defense plans for the Venezuelan coastline and sent them to the Caribbean commander, who was ordered to study the terrain to ascertain possible German landing sites. Following issuance of the December demand to Castro, a fleet officer was named military attaché to the Caracas legation and ordered to study Venezuelan defense capabilities.[33]

By early January Bowen was obviously playing a primary role as interlocutor between the blockading powers and Castro's government. His task was not made easier by either Venezuela or Germany. Early in the month the German foreign office tried to smooth matters over by replacing von Holleben with Baron Speck von Sternburg, who had developed a friendship with Roosevelt. The American image of Germany was not improved by news of more action on the Venezuelan coast. On the seventeenth the guns of Fort Carlos at Maracaibo fired on a German vessel, and four days later several German ships returned to shell the fort. One of the attacking vessels was the *Panther*, which had already sunk two Venezuelan ships. American public criticism of the German misdeed was widespread. Venezuela was in the mood for some kind of settlement, but the blockading powers—Britain, Germany, and Italy— asserted that their claims should be granted preferential treatment. They had, after all, gone to the trouble of compelling Castro to come to terms. Roosevelt was approached with the proposition that he decide the issue of preferential treatment, but once again he deferred to the Hague tribunal.[34]

No one outside Venezuela paid serious attention anymore to Castro's grand assertions about compelling the European powers to accept a settlement within the framework of Venezuelan law. But similarly the blockading powers recognized their predicament and yielded to American manipulation of the affair. The protocol was signed on 13 February. By its provisions the Venezuelans agreed to rank the claims according to first, second, and third categories. The seriousness with which the British and Germans looked at the first-line claims was in part responsible for the maintenance of the blockade, for to satisfy these claims Castro had to promise to make a cash and short-term securities settlement. The second and third categories of claims referred to abuses to individuals and foreign-owned companies in the republic. On the fourteenth the British lifted their blockade of Venezuela's eastern ports, and German ships terminated their blockade of the western ports the following day.

The matter of a German-American confrontation, in which a determined American president challenged the power of a reckless German leader, later became a subject of popular and scholarly controversy. Roosevelt himself precipitated the debate years later in 1916 when he responded to William Roscoe Thayer's request for more information about the Venezuelan controversy. Roosevelt's reply, in martial tones, revealed a markedly anti-German slant that many observers in 1902–1903 had failed to notice in his dealings with Berlin. Thayer published the letter as an appendix to the latest edition of his biography of John Hay. In recounting the Venezuelan affair Roosevelt now claimed that he had actually threatened Germany with war. Since then several scholars have been inclined to discount Roosevelt's 1916 version on the plausible grounds that it was written over a decade after the facts and during an era in which anti-German hysteria in the United States, for which Roosevelt bore some responsibility, reached its peak.

Moreover Roosevelt's well-publicized comments about the fiscal irresponsibility of Latin American governments, particularly their inattention to foreign creditors, and his marked sympathy to the European claims against the improvident Venezuelans would seem to indicate that pushing Germany into conflict was the farthest thing from his mind. Roosevelt's comments came after the incident when Germany and Britain had agreed to accept American demands for arbitration. During the most crucial weeks of the crisis, that is, in December-January 1902–1903, Roosevelt did apply considerable pressure, including maneuvering the fleet, to bring Germany around. Documenting the story is made difficult, however, by the fact that it rests on bits and pieces of evidence—American expressions of concern over German naval activity in the Caribbean since 1900, private warnings relayed to Berlin through third parties, and other official comments from Hay to London and Berlin, written politely but revealing an American firmness.

Circumstantial evidence bore out Roosevelt's version of the episode though no record of any ultimatum has ever been found. Moreover, after the incident Roosevelt was publicly gracious in his references to Germany, leaving in the minds of later observers doubts concerning his 1916 account to Thayer. Roosevelt did have greater respect for Europeans than for Latin Americans, but he also respected the Monroe Doctrine. While he was very much attuned to the concept that "backward" societies must be taught a lesson by "advanced" ones, he was equally aware that British and German activity against Venezuela possibly violated the strictures of Monroe's famous message and jeopardized American political and military interests in the Caribbean. Once Germany had backed down, Roosevelt accorded it the deference normally given by one power to another. Roosevelt's handling of the crisis exhibited prudence and caution in comparison with the Cleveland-Olney rigidity of 1895, though of course the victory over Spain and subsequent expansion into the Caribbean reinforced American determination in dealing with Europe in the Western hemisphere.[35]

In some respects the second Venezuelan crisis was not so serious a confrontation as the first of 1895. In the affair of 1895 the British proved exasperatingly misinformed about American intentions and attitudes. A close scrutiny of the two crises might very well indicate that Cleveland and Olney were unnecessarily provocative. The same thing could not easily be said of Roosevelt, despite his later account of the episode. The settling of the boundary dispute was in accordance with American ground rules, but the British foreign office did not admit the applicability of the principles laid down in Olney's note of 20 July. The volatility of the American reaction to British policy in the first Venezuelan episode convinced London that it must thereafter proceed with caution in dealing with a Latin American state, but it did not necessarily produce a corresponding acquiescence to the idea of American hegemony in the Caribbean.

Britain's deference to the American argument against Spain played an important role in acceptance of the belief that the United States must pick up the burden of imperialism in the Caribbean. To this philosophy Roosevelt himself was a convert. In the 1890s he had exhibited, along with Henry Cabot Lodge, the anglophobia that was still a part of American political rhetoric, but his anti-British feeling of those days was much more of a pose than a conviction. In 1901, while serving as vice-president, he told Cecil Spring Rice that the new century would be the era of English-speaking peoples. The Anglo-Saxon cultural heritage naturally made American world goals coincidental with those of Britain, but he demanded that British power defer to America in certain areas. The Spanish-American conflict proved the viability of American domination in the Caribbean, and thus Britain, Roosevelt believed, must accept gracefully American primacy there.

In the midst of the second Venezuelan crisis London paid careful attention to American sensitivities, accepted an American diplomat as a negotiator for Venezuela, promised not to confront the Venezuelans on their own soil, and by implication repudiated the sterner German demands. In part, it is true, this was due to the surfacing of anti-German feelings in Britain in 1902–1903, but it also reflected a sincere willingness to accept the American preeminence in the Caribbean. It was of no small importance that the principal adversary to emerge in the public commotion over the crisis was not John Bull but the Hun.[36]

From the position taken in the Venezuelan affair, it was inevitable that the United States would undertake more drastic steps in its dealings with Caribbean governments. When the Hague tribunal in February 1904 announced that the blockading powers—Germany, Britain, and Italy—were deserving of preferential treatment in the Venezuelan claims settlement, the decision troubled Roosevelt. Though convinced that he had compelled Europe to recognize the Monroe Doctrine, Roosevelt was now faced with another predicament: a similar situation might develop in any of the Caribbean republics, for most were heavily indebted to European creditors. The next crisis might not be so easy to resolve.

One Latin American nation in financial straits was the Dominican Republic, whose political troubles since 1899 read like a catalog of horrors. In 1882 control of the republic was in the grasp of Úlises Heaureaux, whose rule was dictatorial but provided sufficient stability to attract both trade and foreign investment. North American and Italian investors pumped some 6 million dollars into the sugar industry alone, and the San Domingo Improvement Company, a New York corporation, laid rail lines. Little in material benefits filtered down to the Dominican people, for Heaureaux like Castro showed slight inclination to spend funds wisely. One financial arrangement—the Hartmont loan—was originally held by British bankers, with financial reinforcement from Dutch moneylenders in 1888. To obtain additional funds in 1888 Heaureaux agreed to allow European bankers to send representatives to collect Dominican customs. When the republic tried to float a loan in 1890 and failed, the Dutch bankers considered selling their holdings to French and German bankers, but instead the bonds were purchased by the San Domingo Improvement Company, which became in 1893 the republic's banker.

For the next half dozen years the company floated other loans for Heaureaux, managing to keep his government alive, despite reckless spending and widespread rake-offs, by selling bonds to European investors. No effective controls were established to police the customs receipts, however, and in 1899, when Heaureaux was killed by political opponents, the financial situation of the republic was chaotic.

The American government did not rush to the aid of the Improvement Company when Heaureaux's successor dismissed its representatives from the customhouses. The republic began paying off some of its European creditors, but ill feeling in the country against the Improvement Company prevented any imminent resolution of its demands. In 1902 negotiations between the government and the company broke down. At this point the American government began urging both parties to arbitrate, and after considerable haggling an agreement was signed in July 1903. The American minister in Santo Domingo, William F. Powell, was inept in his efforts to settle other claims. He argued with the republic's president, the third since Heaureaux's assassination, over the right of Dominicans to transform Samaná and Manzanillo into free ports. Powell suspected German designs to build a coaling station in the republic.

In this complex affair the United States was initially concerned with a fair settlement for American investors. By 1903 Roosevelt was worried that the plight of Venezuela might resurface in the Dominican Republic. During the 1903 political succession European governments had dispatched war vessels to Dominican waters to protect their citizens. Germany, Spain, and Italy were especially vigorous in pressing the Dominican government on behalf of their citizens. In late 1903 another revolution broke out, and by the next year the country was plunged into civil war. On 3 February 1904 the Dominican government requested an American guarantee for its independence and sovereignty in return for relaxed import duties and coaling and naval leases at Samaná and Manzanillo. The American government in return would pay the republic's foreign obligations and provide the government with arms and munitions to deal with the rebels.

Despite this offer Roosevelt continued to move cautiously, believing that a protectorate was unacceptable to the American public and that observers in the republic were exaggerating the danger from European intervention. Since the navy now had base sites in Cuba and Puerto Rico, Samaná and Manzanillo had less military value for the United States. In July 1904 an arbitral commission finally settled the special claims of the San Domingo Improvement Company, whereby the United States would appoint a financial agent to receive payments to be delivered to the company.

When the European governments learned of the award, they pressed even harder for resolution of their own claims. Italy, for instance, suggested that the United States assume responsibility for collecting on claims of Italian investors. By December 1904 Roosevelt concluded that the European governments were on the verge of ganging up on the republic for its failures to settle accounts, and the American minister in Santo Domingo was instructed to propose that the United States collect customs duties and divide the proceeds among the republic's creditors. The Dominican leaders were suspicious of American aims but daily voiced fears of impending European action. The protocol providing for the receivership was signed in January 1905. In February Roosevelt presented the protocol to the Senate, justifying it on the grounds that it would prevent aggravated European governments from violating the Monroe Doctrine.[37]

The second Venezuelan crisis and the Dominican customs receivership (which was maintained for several years by executive agreement, pending senatorial approval of a customs convention) represented no abrupt alteration in the European-American relationship in the Caribbean. European powers with traditional interests there had already committed themselves to accepting—in fact, they encouraged—American hegemony. The protectorate system that characterized American policy had already appeared in Cuba and Panama. But the Venezuelan and Dominican crises substantiated a basic tenet which governments on both sides of the Atlantic accepted: European powers could no longer afford to enter the Caribbean as equals of the United States. To allow European meddling with the financial affairs of unstable and improvident Caribbean governments was to risk military confrontation, to say nothing of possible violation of the Monroe Doctrine. The way to prevent such calamities was to accept the idea, as Roosevelt did in 1904, of "intervention by the United States to prevent European intervention."

Epilogue

In the twentieth century Americans became so accustomed to their role as both policeman and judge in the Gulf-Caribbean that they perhaps forgot much of the rivalry of earlier years. No longer would the United States accept a European power as an equal in the New World's Mediterranean. In the Gulf-Caribbean domain there was room for only one imperial power, and Americans had the example of late nineteenth-century European imperialism to emulate.[1] A generation of British leaders believed they saw their imperial philosophy accepted and applied by the United States in its Caribbean policies.[2]

In adopting some of Europe's imperial habits the United States assigned to Europe a secondary role in the Caribbean. The roots of such an attitude were in the colonial period when, as Max Savelle has noted in his monumental study of the diplomatic history of the American colonial world, the colonies developed some precise notions about their international interests. Exploitation of the European balance of power, the rejection of a European-controlled mercantilism, the determination to destroy any kind of European-established North American balance of power were powerful forces that shaped a distinctive attitude toward Europe before 1789.[3]

Moreover, the idea that Europe must be subordinate to the United States in the Gulf-Caribbean—a concept boldly asserted by Theodore Roosevelt—also had a long history. In Washington's administration, Thomas A. Bailey has argued, the United States was already a world power. It was able to capitalize on its geographical remoteness and the European balance of power.[4] It did not possess the military capability to prevent, let us say, French punitive measures against Mexico in 1838 or the tripartite intervention in Mexico in 1861–1862, but it exhibited a moral arrogance in lecturing European powers on their dealings with the smaller countries of the Gulf-Caribbean. For instance, William H. Seward did not condemn European creditors seeking to make Benito Juárez pay the debts of Mexico; he felt no reluctance in trying to arrange a loan to help Juárez out of his predicament (at the price of an American protectorate) or in informing Napoleon III that monarchy was inevitably doomed in a hemisphere committed to republicanism.

In its dealings with European powers in the Gulf-Caribbean the United States followed policies that were ingenious amalgams of idealism and expediency. From the history of the Spanish Main the American people learned the lesson that encroachment in the domain of a large empire often brought economic reward and territorial acquisition. The steady pressure against Spanish Florida was in fact a form of aggression largely sustained and defended by officials because it was politically, strategically, and economically expedient. Yet even where territorial control shaped the basic contours of policy—in Louisiana, Florida, and Texas—the American people could be exasperatingly moralistic in defending their expansionist tendencies. John Quincy Adams believed the Spanish should not control Florida because their resources for ruling the colony were woefully inadequate. James Oglethorpe and Andrew Jackson waged war against Spanish Florida because Spain, they contended, was unfit to rule there.

Not until the 1890s did the United States achieve the military capability necessary to enforce its prescriptive doctrines to any degree. The expansionism of that decade drew upon the traditional beliefs of democratic nationalism and moral superiority, and it blended these with economic and military assessments of the Gulf-Caribbean world. In the process of applying American economic and political tenets to presumably backward societies, the American people became unconsciously imperialistic. Basically the United States sought to aid the Caribbean republics in a search for stability by preventing internal disorders and financial crises. Political and financial order would not only obviate European punitive measures to collect debts, but it would also represent the successful transplanting of Anglo-Saxon concepts. It was no coincidence that the highwater mark of Caribbean imperialism occurred while the political philosophy of Progressivism reached its zenith in American domestic politics. The Progressives believed in pragmatic measures that assured honest elections and financial orderliness and in governments dedicated to progress through public works. The Caribbean thus served as a laboratory, for its history had been one of chronic disorder, mismanagement, and economic backwardness.[5] In such a laboratory, of course, there was no place for outside interference.

Bibliographical Essay

Aside from some occasional forays into unpublished Department of State material and the private papers of James Monroe, John Clayton, Hamilton Fish, Richard Olney, William McKinley, and other nineteenth-century policymakers, this study is based for the most part on published works. The following books proved most useful:

For the international history of the Gulf-Caribbean area before 1776 the reader should begin with J. H. Parry, *The Spanish Seaborne Empire* (New York, 1966), in the series The History of Human Society, edited by J. H. Plumb. In a similar tradition of scholarship appears Parry's *Establishment of European Hegemony, 1415–1715: Trade and Exploration in the Age of the Renaissance* (New York, 1961). Philip A. Means, *The Spanish Main: Focus of Envy* (New York, 1935), remains a standard work. For literary liveliness no one has surpassed Germán Arciniegas, *The Caribbean: Sea of the New World* (New York, 1946). On Hawkins and Drake see J. A. Williamson, *Sir John Hawkins: The Times and the Man* (Oxford, 1927), and Sir Julian Corbett, *Drake and the Tudor Navy*, 2 vols. (London, 1898). The most recent investigation of Drake's significance is Kenneth Andrews, *Drake's Voyages: A Re-assessment of Their Place in Elizabethan Maritime Expansion* (New York, 1968). Encyclopedic in its coverage is Max Savelle, *The Origins of American Diplomacy: The International History of Anglo-America, 1492–1763* (New York, 1967). The Anglo-Spanish rivalry is ventilated in J. Leitch Wright, Jr., *Anglo-Spanish Rivalry in North America* (Athens, Ga., 1971). A masterpiece of scholarship is Sir Richard Pares, *War and Trade in the West Indies, 1739–1763* (1936; reprint ed., London, 1963). For the international history of the American Revolution consult Samuel F. Bemis, *The Diplomacy of the American Revolution* (New York, 1935), and the more recent work, Richard W. Van Alstyne, *Empire and Independence: The International History of the American Revolution* (New York, 1965). The most recent general history of the Caribbean is Eric Williams, *From Columbus to Castro: The History of the Caribbean, 1492–1969* (London, 1970).

The history of the Louisiana Purchase and Florida acquisition has inspired a number of scholarly accounts. For the philosophical bases of expansionism, not only for the movement to acquire Louisiana and Florida but also for other expansionist projects in the nineteenth century, the ablest work is Albert K. Weinberg's *Manifest Destiny: A Study of Nationalist Expansionism in American History* (1935; reprint ed., Chicago, 1963). Its study of the interplay between thought and action in American continentalism constitutes a scholarly tour de force. Two studies focusing on the economic and population pressures of the frontier against Louisiana are Arthur Whitaker's *Spanish-American Frontier, 1783–1795: The Western Movement and the Spanish Retreat in the Mississippi Valley* (Boston, 1927), and his *Mississippi Question, 1795–1803: A Study in Trade, Politics and Diplomacy* (New York and London, 1934). Whitaker argues that frontier pressures constituted the significant elements in the American advance toward the Gulf coast. These two studies should be placed alongside Samuel Flagg Bemis, *Pinckney's Treaty: America's Advantage from Europe's Distress, 1783–1800* (1926; reprint ed., New Haven, Conn., 1960), a Pulitzer-prize winning study that emphasizes European diplomacy as the critical element in settling frontier difficulties with Spain in 1795. A very useful background study is Arthur Darling, *Our Rising Empire, 1763–1803* (New Haven, Conn., 1940). Somewhat more specialized and limited in their focus are E. W. Lyon, *Louisiana in French Diplomacy, 1759–1804* (Norman, Okla., 1934), and Abraham P. Nasatir, *Spanish War Vessels on the Mississippi, 1792–1796* (New Haven, Conn., 1968). Handy collections of primary materials are James A. Robertson, ed., *Louisiana under the Rule of Spain, France, and the United States,* 2 vols. (Cleveland, 1911), and Frederick J. Turner, ed., *Correspondence of the French Ministers to the United States, 1791–1797, American Historical Association Annual Report, 1903,* 2 vols. (Washington, D.C., 1904).

Numerous scholarly articles dealing with the Louisiana and Florida questions are listed in the footnotes. The published writings of Thomas Jefferson, James Madison, James Monroe, and John Quincy Adams contain a wealth of information about the European presence in Louisiana and Florida. One of the most convenient summaries of Florida's acquisition is Samuel Flagg Bemis's *John Quincy Adams and the Foundations of American Foreign Policy* (New York, 1949). Though occasionally adulatory, Bemis demonstrates how Adams ingeniously exploited the deteriorating Florida situation to convince his diplomatic counterpart that Spanish rule there should terminate as soon as possible. The standard works on Florida's absorption are Isaac J. Cox, *The West Florida Controversy* (Baltimore, 1918), and Philip C. Brooks, *Diplomacy and the Borderlands: The Adams-Onis Treaty of 1819* (Berkeley, Calif., 1939). Julius W. Pratt, *Expansionists of 1812* (New York, 1925), relates frontier designs on Florida to the coming of war with Great Britain in 1812. The Florida problem is viewed as part of the breakdown in Spanish colonialism in Charles C. Griffin, *The United States and the Disruption of the Spanish Empire, 1810–1822* (New York, 1937).,

Anyone working on inter-American problems from about 1810 to 1860 owes a great debt to William Ray Manning, who put together two of the handiest collections of documents in American diplomatic history: *Diplomatic Correspondence of the United States concerning the Independence of the Latin American Nations*, 3 vols. (New York, 1925), and *Diplomatic Correspondence of the United States: Inter-American Affairs, 1831–1860*, 12 vols. (Washington, D.C., 1932–1939). They also contain correspondence between the United States and Europe pertaining to Latin America.

Studies of the Monroe Doctrine abound. The best introductions are Dexter Perkins, *The Monroe Doctrine, 1823–1826* (Cambridge, Mass., 1927) and Bradford Perkins, *Castlereagh and Adams: England and the United States, 1812–1823* (Berkeley, Calif., 1964). The former is the first in a trilogy on the doctrine; the latter is the last in a trilogy on British-American relations from the Jay treaty to the Monroe Doctrine. Arthur P. Whitaker's *United States and the Independence of Latin America* (Baltimore, 1941) emphasizes the commercial aspects in United States policy. The problem of Haiti in United States foreign policy is discussed in Rayford Logan, *The Diplomatic Relations of the United States with Haiti, 1776–1891* (Chapel Hill, N.C., 1941). British policy is explained in Harold Temperley, *The Foreign Policy of Canning, 1822–1827: England, the Neo-Holy Alliance, and the New World* (1927; reprint ed., London,

1966). Much more needs to be done on the special place assigned to the Caribbean in the general formulation of a Latin American policy from about 1810 to 1826.

The United States–European diplomatic rivalry in the Texas question has been given less scholarly analysis than it deserves. Eugene Baker, *Mexico and Texas, 1821–1835* (1928; reprint ed., New York, 1965) stresses cultural conflict in the making of the Texan revolution. The French intrusion into the republic's affairs is dealt with by Eugene Maissin (James Shepard III, trans.), *The French in Mexico and Texas* (Salado, Tex., 1951). The ablest interpretation of the Franco-American diplomatic clashes of this era is Henry Blumenthal, *A Reappraisal of Franco-American Relations, 1830–1871* (Chapel Hill, N.C., 1959). Helpful studies from the Texan viewpoint are Joseph W. Schmitz, *Texan Statecraft, 1836–1845* (San Antonio, Tex., 1945) and Stanley Siegel, *A Political History of the Texas Republic* (Austin, Tex., 1956). E. D. Adams, *British Interests and Activities in Texas, 1848–1846* (Baltimore, 1910), though somewhat outdated, remains a standard account. Adams edited *British Diplomatic Correspondence concerning the Republic of Texas.* Charles G. Sellers, Jr., considers Polk's diplomatic dilemmas in the second volume of his biography, *James K. Polk: Continentalist, 1843–1846* (Princeton, N.J., 1966). See also the relevant chapters in Weinberg, *Manifest Destiny,* and two essential works by Frederick Merk: *Manifest Destiny and Mission in American History* (New York, 1963) and *The Monroe Doctrine and American Expansionism, 1843–1849* (New York, 1965).

London's interpretation of American policies during two decades is analyzed in Wilbur D. Jones, *The American Problem in British Diplomacy, 1841–1861* (London and Athens, Ga., 1974). United States interests in Central America in the 1840s and 1850s have appeared often in the works of Latin American scholars, both in the United States and in Latin America. Thomas Karnes, *The Failure of Union: Central America, 1824–1960* (Chapel Hill, N.C., 1961), sets the stage for the Anglo-American clash of the forties. Mario Rodríguez focuses on the rivalry by centering his attention on *A Palmerstonian Diplomat in Central America: Frederick Chatfield* (Tucson, Ariz., 1964). Mary W. Williams, *Anglo-American Isthmian Diplomacy,*

1815–1915 (Washington, D.C., 1916), and Gerstle Mack, *The Land Divided* (New York, 1944), are older but still useful studies. A very specialized and excellent study is R. A. Humphreys, *The Diplomatic History of British Honduras, 1638–1901* (London, 1961).

The French intervention in Mexico long ago began attracting scholarly attention. James M. Callahan produced *American Foreign Policy in Mexican Relations* (New York, 1932) and *Evolution of Seward's Mexican Policy* (Morgantown, W.Va., 1908). Carl H. Bock, *Prelude to Tragedy: The Negotiation and Breakdown of the Tripartite Convention of London, October 31, 1861* (Philadelphia, 1966), virtually exhausts the topic. Dexter Perkins concludes his second volume on the Monroe Doctrine with the French intervention and Maximilian. Ralph Roeder, *Juárez and his Mexico*, 2 vols. (New York, 1947), and Egon Corti, *Maximilian and Charlotte of Mexico*, 2 vols. (New York, 1928), assess the empire by focusing on two of the principal characters. For the French aspects, see Octave Aubry (Arthur Livingston, trans.), *The Second Empire* (Philadelphia, 1940), and Lynn Case, ed., *French Opinion on the United States and Mexico: Extracts from the Reports of the Procurers-Generaux* (New York, 1936). The reports are in French, but Case provides excellent introductions in English. Empress Eugénie and her role in the intervention are the subject of portions of Nancy Nichols Barker, *Distaff Diplomacy: The Empress Eugénie and the Foreign Policy of the Second Empire* (Austin, Tex., 1967). Seward's thinking is explored in Glyndon G. Van Deusen, *William Henry Seward* (New York, 1967).

Walter LaFeber's *New Empire: An Interpretation of American Expansion, 1860–1898* (Ithaca, N.Y., 1963), stresses the economic forces in foreign policy. Another path-breaking study, useful because it focuses on a neglected period of American diplomacy,. is David Pletcher, *The Awkward Years: American Foreign Policy under Garfield and Arthur* (Columbia, Mo., 1962). Allan Westcott, ed., *Mahan on Naval Warfare* (Boston, 1941), offers an introduction to Mahan's thinking. The Santo Domingo debacle is given detailed attention in Allan Nevins, *Hamilton Fish: The Inner History of the Grant Administration*, 2 vols. rev. ed. (New York, 1957). On the first Venezuelan crisis, see Ernest R. May, *Imperial Democracy: The Emergence of America as a Great Power* (New York, 1961); and J. A. S.

Grenville, *Lord Salisbury and Foreign Policy: The Close of the Nineteenth Century* (London, 1963), stresses cultural ties as the basis for the Anglo-American understanding. R. G. Neale considers the Anglo-American adjustment also in *Great Britain and United States Expansionism* (East Lansing, Mich., 1966). For the second Venezuelan crisis, a good survey is Howard K. Beale, *Theodore Roosevelt and the Rise of America to World Power* (Baltimore, 1956).

For other listings, scholarly and contemporaneous articles, and works in Spanish and French, consult the notes.

Notes

1 • The Southward Drive to the Gulf

1. Albert Weinberg, *Manifest Destiny: A Study of Nationalist Expansionism in American History* (1935; reprint ed., Chicago, 1963), pp. 24–25. See also Arthur P. Whitaker, *The Spanish-American Frontier, 1783–1795: The Western Movement and the Spanish Retreat in the Mississippi Valley* (1927; reprint ed., Boston, 1962); *The Mississippi Question, 1795–1803: A Study in Trade, Politics, and Diplomacy* (1934; reprint ed., Boston, 1962); Samuel Flagg Bemis, *Pinckney's Treaty: America's Advantage from Europe's Distresses* (1935; reprint ed., New Haven, Conn., 1960); and J. Leitch Wright, Jr., *Anglo-Spanish Rivalry in North America, 1492–1821* (Athens, Ga., 1971).

2. Whitaker, *Spanish-American Frontier*, pp. 4–5, 28, 47–48, 91.

3. Carondelet to Trudeau, 8 June 1792, in Lawrence Kinnaird, ed., *Spain in the Mississippi Valley, 1765–1794, American Historical Association Annual Report, 1945*, vol. 4, pt. 3 (Washington, D.C., 1946), p. 51; James Robertson, Brigadier General, Mero District, to Carondelet, 25 May 1792, in ibid., pp. 40–41; Carondelet to Luís de las Casas, 20 November 1792, in ibid., pp. 97–98.

4. Abraham Nasatir, *Spanish War Vessels on the Mississippi, 1792–1796* (New Haven, Conn., 1968), pp. 121–122, 143.

5. E. W. Lyon, *Louisiana in French Diplomacy* (Norman, Okla., 1934), pp. 66–67.

6. France, Ministre des Affaires Étrangères, Correspondance Politique, États-Unis, Supplement, Louisiane et Floride, vol. 7 (Photostat, Library of Congress Manuscripts Division); Ternant to Dumourier, 20 June 1792, in Frederick J. Turner, ed., *Correspondence of the French Ministers to the United States, 1791–1797, American Historical Association Annual Report, 1903*, vol. 2 (Washington, D.C., 1904), p. 136; Fauchet to Commissioners of Foreign Relations, 4 January 1795, in ibid., pp. 569–570.

7. W. G. Schaeffer, "The Delayed Cession of Spanish Santo Domingo to France, 1795–1801," *Hispanic American Historical Review* 29 (February 1949): 52–53; F. P. Renaut, *La question de la Louisiane, 1796–1806* (Paris, 1918), pp. 20, 23, 27.

8. Renaut, *Question de la Louisiane*, pp. 61–62, 68, 69; Lyon, *Louisiana in French Diplomacy*, pp. 104, 113–114.

9. Renaut, *Question de la Louisiane*, pp. 83, 86–87, 89, 90–91.

10. Ibid., p. 94.

11. J. Fred Rippy, *Rivalry of the United States and Great Britain over Latin America, 1808–1830* (Baltimore, 1929), pp. 23–24; Edward Thornton,

British legation, to Lord Robert Hawkesbury, January 1803, in James A. Robertson, ed., *Louisiana under the Rule of Spain, France, and the United States. 1785–1807*, 2 vols. (Cleveland, 1911), 1 : 17–18, 18–19.

12. Thomas Jefferson, "Considerations on Louisiana," in Robertson, *Louisiana*, 1 : 265–267.

13. Whitaker, *Mississippi Question*, pp. 102, 130, 150–151, 208; Arthur B. Darling, *Our Rising Empire, 1763–1803* (New Haven, Conn., 1940), passim.

14. *Moniteur de la Louisiane*, 3 December 1803, in France, Archives Nationales, Archives du Directoire Executif, series AFIV, carton 1681A (Microfilm, Library of Congress Manuscripts Division); Lyon, *Louisiana in French Diplomacy*, pp. 192, 195, 225, 231; Whitaker, *Mississippi Question*, p. 255; William N. Sloane, "The World Aspects of the Louisiana Purchase," *American Historical Review* 9 (April 1904): 513–514.

15. Philip C. Brooks, *Diplomacy and the Borderlands: The Adams-Onís Treaty of 1819* (Berkeley, Calif., 1939), pp. 2–3, 29.

16. Casa Irujo to Casa Calvo, 1 November 1803, in Robertson, *Louisiana under Spain*, 2 : 95; Vicente Folch (governor of W. Fla.), "Reflections on Louisiana," ibid., pp. 335–336, 339; Casa Irujo to Don Pedro Ceballos, 3 August 1803, ibid., 1 : 69–70.

17. Lawrence S. Kaplan, *Jefferson and France: An Essay on Politics and Political Ideas* (New Haven, Conn., 1967), pp. 126–127.

18. Isaac J. Cox, "The Pan American Policy of Jefferson and Wilkinson," *Mississippi Valley Historical Review* 1 (September 1914): 214–225, 231–232; idem, *West Florida Controversy* (Baltimore, 1918), p. 309.

19. Pedro Ceballos to Casa Calvo, 2 April 1804, in Robertson, *Louisiana under Spain*, 2 : 178–179; Herbert Fuller, *The Purchase of Florida* (1906; reprint ed., Gainesville, Fla., 1964), pp. 144–145; Albert Gallatin to Jefferson, 12 September 1805, in Henry Adams, ed., *The Writings of Albert Gallatin*, 3 vols. (New York, 1960), 1 : 242–243.

20. Cox, *West Florida Controversy*, pp. 667–668; Brooks, *Diplomacy of the Borderlands*, p. 35.

21. Secretary of State to John Armstrong, United States Minister to France, 2 November 1810, in William R. Manning, ed., *Diplomatic Correspondence of the United States concerning the Independence of the Latin American Nations*, 3 vols. (New York, 1925), 1 : 8; Secretary of State to William Pinkney, 22 January 1811, in ibid., pp. 10–11.

22. Julius W. Pratt, *Expansionists of 1812* (New York, 1925), p. 121.

23. Secretary of State to William Pinkney, 13 June 1810, in Manning, *Diplomatic...Latin American Nations*, 1 : 5–6.

24. The standard work on the "no-transfer" resolution is John A. Logan, *No Transfer: An American Security Principle* (New Haven, Conn., 1961). Wellesley to Foster, 28 January 1812, in Bernard Mayo, ed., *Instructions to the British Ministers to the United States, 1791–1812, American Historical As-*

sociation Annual Report, 1936, vol. 3 (Washington, D.C., 1941), pp. 345–346.

25. Brooks, *Diplomacy and the Borderlands*, pp. 32–33.

26. Monroe to the American Commissioners, 27 April 1813, in Adams, *Writings of Gallatin*, 1 : 539n; Gallatin to Monroe, 2, 8 May 1813, in ibid., pp. 539–540, 545; Pratt, *Expansionists of 1812*, pp. 111–112.

27. Charles C. Griffin, *The United States and the Disruption of the Spanish Empire, 1810–1822* (New York, 1937), pp. 40–41; Marshall Smelser, *The Democratic Republic, 1801–1815* (New York, 1968), p. 281.

28. Griffin, *United States and Disruption of Spanish Empire*, pp. 111–112; Monroe, Message to Congress, 2 December 1817, in Manning, *Diplomatic...Latin American Nations*, pp. 50–51; Allan Nevins, ed., *The Diary of John Quincy Adams, 1794–1845: American Political, Social, and Intellectual Life from Washington To Polk* (New York, 1929), p. 190; JQA to George W. Campbell, 28 June 1818, in Worthington Ford, ed., *The Writings of John Quincy Adams*, 7 vols. (New York, 1913–1917), 6 : 378–379.

29. Brooks, *Diplomacy and the Borderlands*, pp. 93–94, 140–141.

30. George Dangerfield, *The Era of Good Feelings* (New York, 1952), pp. 134–135; Samuel F. Bemis, *John Quincy Adams and the Foundations of American Diplomacy* (New York, 1949), pp. 314–315; Bradford Perkins, *Castlereagh and Adams: England and the United States, 1812–1823* (Berkeley, Calif., 1964), p. 288; JQA, 15 July 1818, in Nevins, *Diary of JQA*, p. 199; JQA to Onis, 23 July 1818, in Ford, *Writings of JQA*, 6 : 386–394.

31. Charles R. Vaughn to Viscount Castlereagh, 16 November 1815, in Sir Charles Webster, ed., *Britain and the Independence of Latin America, 1812–1830: Select Documents from the Foreign Office Archives* , 2 vols. (Oxford, 1938), 2 : 344; Perkins, *Castlereagh and Adams*, p. 284; Dangerfield, *Era of Good Feelings*, pp. 128–129; Griffin, *United States and Disruption of Spanish Empire*, pp. 82–83.

32. Samuel F. Bemis, *John Quincy Adams and American Foreign Policy* (New York, 1949), pp. 304–305; JQA to George W. Erving, 28 November 1818, in Ford, *Writings of JQA*, 6 : 487–488.

33. Griffin, *United States and Disruption of Spanish Empire*, pp. 161, 176–177.

34. Gallatin to JQA, 10 August 1818, in Manning, *Diplomatic...Latin American Nations*, 2 : 1384; Sir Charles Webster, *The Foreign Policy of Castlereagh, 1815–1822* (London, 1925), p. 448.

35. Dangerfield, *Era of Good Feelings*, pp. 152, 156. Spanish procrastination delayed ratification until 1821.

2 • The Era of the Monroe Doctrine

1. Felix Gilbert, *To the Farewell Address: Ideas of Early American Foreign Policy* (Princeton, N.J., 1961), p. 43.

2. Arthur P. Whitaker, *The United States and the Independence of Latin America* (Baltimore, 1941), passim.

3. Selden Rodman, *Haiti: The Black Republic* (New York, 1954), pp. 5–6; Rayford W. Logan, *Haiti and the Dominican Republic* (New York, 1968), p. 85.

4. William S. Robertson, *France and Latin American Independence* (Baltimore, 1939), pp. 442–443; Rayford Logan, *The Diplomatic Relations of the United States with Haiti, 1776–1891* (Chapel Hill, N.C., 1941), pp. 40–41; Sumner Welles, *Naboth's Vineyard: The Dominican Republic, 1844–1924*, 2 vols. (1928; reprint ed., Washington D.C., 1966), 1 : 14–15; Salvador de Madariaga, *The Fall of the Spanish American Empire* (1947; reprint ed., New York, 1963), p. 293.

5. Logan, *Haiti and the Dominican Republic*, pp. 88–89.

6. Hubert Cole, *Christophe: King of Haiti* (New York, 1967), p. 45; W. G. Schaeffer, "The Delayed Cession of Spanish Santo Domingo to France, 1795–1801," *Hispanic American Historical Review* 29 (February 1949): 46–47; Germán Arciniegas, *The Caribbean: Sea of the New World* (New York, 1946), p. 331.

7. Bradford Perkins, *The First Rapprochement: England and the United States, 1795–1805* (Philadelphia, 1955), pp. 106–111; John Adams to Timothy Pickering, Secretary of State, 17 April 1799; Adams to Benjamin Stoddert, Secretary of the Navy, 8 May 1799; in Charles F. Adams, ed., *The Works of John Adams*, 10 vols. (Boston, 1850–1856), 8 : 634–635, 642.

8. Carl L. Lokke, "Jefferson and the LeClerc Expedition," *American Historical Review* 33 (January 1928): 322–328; Schaeffer, "Delayed Cession of Spanish Santo Domingo," p. 68; Cole, *Christophe*, p. 77; Henry Adams, "Napoleon I et Saint Domingue," *Revue historique* 24 (1884): 92–94; Winthrop Jordan, *White Over Black: American Attitudes toward the Negro, 1550–1812* (Chapel Hill, N.C., 1968), p. 381.

9. Ralph Korngold, *Citizen Toussaint* (Boston, 1944), passim.

10. Adams, Diary, in Lyman H. Butterfield, ed., *The Adams Papers, Series I, Diaries, the Diary and Autobiography of John Adams*, 4 vols. (Cambridge, Mass., 1962), 3 : 328; Logan, *United States with Haiti*, pp. 16–17; John Adams to Robert Livingston, 23 June 1783, 17 July 1783, and 18 July 1783, in Adams, *Works of John Adams*, 8 : 74–75, 105, 107. In January 1806 Albert Gallatin wrote to Jefferson: "As relates to the West Indies..., it must be a permanent object of the United States policy to have the intercourse with them made as free as that of Europe" (Henry Adams, ed., *The Writings of Albert Gallatin*, 3 vols. [New York, 1960], 1 : 286).

11. J. H. Coatsworth, "American Trade with European Colonies in the Caribbean and South America, 1790–1812," *William and Mary Quarterly*, 3d ser. 24 (April 1967): 243–244.

12. George Dangerfield, *The Era of Good Feelings* (New York, 1952), p. 255; Henry Clay, Speech in Congress, 24 March 1818, in James F. Hop-

kins, ed., *The Papers of Henry Clay*, 4 vols. to date (Lexington, Ky., 1959–), 2 : 523–524. For a suggestive reinterpretation of economic forces in the making of a Latin American policy see William A. Williams, "The Age of Mercantilism: An Interpretation of the American Political Economy, 1763–1828," *William and Mary Quarterly* 15 (1958): 436–437.

13. Logan, *United States with Haiti*, p. 219.

14. Grenville to Liston, 19 January 1799, in Bernard Mayo, ed., *Instructions to the British Ministers to the United States, 1791–1812, American Historical Association Annual Report, 1936*, vol. 3 (Washington, D.C., 1941), pp. 169–170.

15. Ibid.

16. In the account on Cuba I have drawn heavily on material in my *Cuban Policy of the United States: A Brief History* (New York, 1968), pp. 4–14.

17. Richard Rush to John Quincy Adams, 17 January, 10 March, 17 April, and 10 October 1823, in Department of State, Dispatches from United States Ministers to Great Britain, 1791–1906 (Microfilm), vol. 28; Henry Addington to George Canning, 3 November, 1 December 1823, in Great Britain, Foreign Office, Dispatches from British Ministers in the United States (Photostat, Library of Congress Manuscripts Division), Foreign Office 5, vol. 177.

18. Canning to Rufus King, 7 August 1825, in William R. Manning, ed., *Diplomatic Correspondence of the United States concerning the Independence of the Latin American Nations*, 3 vols. (New York, 1925), 3 : 1558.

19. Viscount Granville to George Canning, 6 June 1825, in Sir Charles Webster, ed., *Britain and the Independence of Latin America, 1812–1830: Select Documents from the Foreign Office Archives*, 2 vols. (Oxford, 1938), 1 : 182–183; King to Clay, 9 August 1825, in Manning, *Diplomatic...Latin American Nations*, 3 : 1555; Dexter Perkins, *The Monroe Doctrine, 1823–1826* (Cambridge, Mass., 1927), pp. 200–201.

20. Clay to Alexander Everett, Minister to Spain, 27 April 1825, in Manning, *Diplomatic...Latin American Nations*, 1: 242–243.

21. Alexander Everett, Memorandum of Conversation with Spanish Secretary of State, 24 September 1825, in ibid., 3 : 2060–2062; Everett to Spanish Secretary of State, 10 October 1825, ibid., pp. 2063–2064.

22. Harold Temperley, *The Foreign Policy of Canning, 1822–1827: England, the Neo-Holy Alliance, and the New World* (1927; reprint ed., London, 1966), pp. 132, 154–155.

23. Ibid., pp. 173–174, 179; Canning to Edward Dawkins, 18 March 1826, in Webster, *Britain and the Independence of Latin America*, 1 : 404, 408–409; Francisco Cuevas Cancino, *Del congreso de Panamá a la conferencia de Caracas, 1826–1954*, 2 vols. (Caracas, 1955), 1 : 113–114.

24. Arthur Whitaker, *The Western Hemisphere Idea: Its Rise and Decline* (Ithaca, N. Y., 1954), pp. 43–44.

25. Gallatin to Clay, 10 November 1825, in Department of State, Rec-

ords of the Department of State Relating to the First Panama Congress, 1825–1827 (Microfilm); F. L. Reinhold, "New Research on the First Pan-American Congress Held at Panama in 1826," *Hispanic American Historical Review* 18 (August 1938): 355.

26. Clay to Anderson and Sergeant, 8 May 1826, in Panama Congress; Samuel Flagg Bemis, *John Quincy Adams and the Foundations of American Diplomacy* (New York, 1949), pp. 551, 556–557; James M. Callahan, *American Foreign Policy in Mexican Relations* (New York, 1932), p. 34.

27. Clay to Poinsett, 26 March 1825, in Manning, *Diplomatic...Latin American Nations*, 1 : 231; Perkins, *Monroe Doctrine*, pp. 203–204. France, too, feared Mexican-Colombian intentions. French Minister to the United States to the Minister of Foreign Affairs, 12 October 1824, in France, Ministre des Affaires Étrangères, Correspondance Politique, Etats-Unis, vol. 80 (Photostat, Library of Congress Manuscripts Division).

28. Poinsett to Clay, 15 June 1825, 1 February 1826, in Manning, *Diplomatic...Latin American Nations*, 3 : 1627, 1652; Gallatin to Clay, 16 December 1826, in ibid., pp. 1584–1585.

29. Alexander Everett, Memorandum, 7 January 1827, in ibid., pp. 2139–2140; Clay to Daniel Cook, 12 March 1827, in ibid., 1 : 282–283; Martin Van Buren to Cornelius P. Van Ness, Minister to Spain, 2 October 1829, in ibid., pp. 306–307.

30. On these points especially see J. Fred Rippy, *Rivalry of the United States and Great Britain over Latin America, 1808–1830* (Baltimore, 1929), pp. 304–305; Élie Halévy, *A History of the English People in the Nineteenth Century*, 6 vols. (1913; reprint ed., New York, 1961), vol. 2, *The Liberal Awakening*, p. 181; and Leonard Lawson, *The Relation of British Policy to the Declaration of the Monroe Doctrine* (New York, 1922), pp. 85, 103.

3 • The Balance of Power—Texas and Mexico

1. Clay to William Miller, chargé d'affaires, United Provinces of Central America, 22 April 1825, in William R. Manning, ed. *Diplomatic Correspondence of the United States concerning the Independence of the Latin American Nations*, 3 vols. (New York, 1925), 3 : 241.

2. Charles Salit, "Anglo-American Rivalry in Mexico, 1823–1830." *Revista de historia de América*, no. 16 (1943), pp. 68, 72, 82–84; J. Fred Rippy, *Latin America in World Politics: An Outline Survey* (New York, 1928), pp. 80–81.

3. Eugene C. Barker, *Mexico and Texas, 1821–1835* (1928; reprint ed., New York, 1965), pp. iv–v.

4. J. R. Poinsett to Henry Clay, 27 July 1825; Poinsett to Van Buren, 2 August 1829; Van Buren to Poinsett, 25 August 1829; in Carlos Bosch García, ed. and comp., *Material para la historia diplomática de México: México y los Estados Unidos, 1820–1848* (Mexico City, 1957), pp. 38–39, 101, 105. This collection is a convenient source for instructions and dispatches per-

taining to Mexican–United States relations; hereinafter cited as *Historia diplomática mexicana.*

5. "Informe presentado por el Secretario de Relaciones Exteriores en sesión secreta del Senado mexicano," 8 March 1830, in ibid., pp. 121–122; Barker, *Mexico and Texas*, pp. 56–57.

6. Barker, *Mexico and Texas*, pp. 29–31, 85–86.

7. Rafael F. Muñoz, *Santa Anna: el dictador resplandeciente* (Mexico City, 1945), pp. 222–227; Eugene Maissin (James Shepard III, trans.) *The French in Mexico and Texas* (Salado, Tex., 1951), pp. 34–35; Dexter Perkins, *The Monroe Doctrine, 1826–1867* (Baltimore, 1933), pp. 40–46.

8. Henry Blumenthal, *A Reappraisal of Franco-American Relations, 1830–1871* (Chapel Hill, N.C., 1959), pp. 35–37.

9. Maissin, *French in Mexico and Texas*, p. 147; Joseph W. Schmitz, *Texan Statecraft, 1836–1845* (San Antonio, Tex., 1941), pp. 78–79.

10. Stanley Siegel, *A Political History of the Texas Republic* (Austin, Tex., 1956), pp. 157–158; Blumenthal, *Reappraisal of Franco-American Relations*, pp. 38–39.

11. J. Fred Rippy, *Rivalry of the United States and Great Britain over Latin America, 1808–1830* (Baltimore, 1929), pp. 71, 91–92; E. D. Adams, *British Interests and Activities in Texas, 1838–1846* (Baltimore, 1910), pp. 226–227; Kenneth Bourne, *Britain and the Balance of Power in North America, 1815–1908* (Berkeley and Los Angeles, 1967), pp. 71, 75; G. L. Rives, "Mexican Diplomacy on the Eve of the War with the United States," *American Historical Review* 18 (January 1913): 275–276, 285.

12. Adams, *British Interests and Activities in Texas*, p. 53.

13. Crawford to Pakenham, 26 May 1837, in E. D. Adams, ed., *British Diplomatic Correspondence concerning the Republic of Texas* (Austin, Tex., 1918), pp. 12–13; Schmitz, *Texan Statecraft*, pp. 63–64, 129–130; Siegel, *Political History of the Texas Republic*, pp. 163–164.

14. Joseph Milton Nance, *Attack and Counterattack: The Texas-Mexican Frontier, 1842* (Austin, Tex., 1964), pp. 117–118, 130–131, 214.

15. A. P. Newton, "United States and Colonial Developments, 1815–1846," in A. W. Ward and G. P. Gooch eds., *The Cambridge History of British Foreign Policy*, 3 vols. (New York, 1922–1923), 2 : 255–256; Adams, *British Interests and Activities in Texas*, p. 79; Glenn Price, *Origins of the War with Mexico: The Polk-Stockton Intrigue* (Austin, Tex., 1967), pp. 135–136; Wilbur Jones, *Lord Aberdeen and the Americas* (Athens, Ga., 1958), pp. x, 83–84.

16. James Hook to Palmerston, 30 April 1841, in Adams, *British Diplomatic Correspondence*, p. 38; Frederick Merk, *The Monroe Doctrine and the American Expansionism, 1843–1849* (New York, 1966), pp. 10–18.

17. Siegel, *Political History of the Texas Republic*, p. 227.

18. Abel P. Upshur to W. L. Murphy, chargé d'affaires, Texas, 8 August 1843, Department of State, Instructions, Texas Republic.

19. Upshur to Murphy, 22 September 1843, ibid.; Upshur to Edward Everett, Minister to Great Britain, 28 September 1843, Department of State, Instructions, Great Britain.

20. Albert Weinberg, *Manifest Destiny: A Study of Nationalist Expansionism in American History* (1935; reprint ed., Chicago, 1963), pp. 109–110.

21. James Morton Callahan, *American Foreign Policy in Mexican Relations* (New York, 1967), pp. 115–116; Charles G. Sellers, Jr., *James K. Polk: Continentalist, 1843–1846* (Princeton, N.J., 1966), pp. 58–59; Calhoun to Pakenham, 18 April 1844, in William R. Manning, ed., *Diplomatic Correspondence of the United States: Inter-American Affairs, 1831–1860,* 12 vols. (Washington, D.C., 1932–1939), 7 : 18–19; Calhoun to T. A. Howard, chargé d'affaires, Texas, 18 June 1844, in Instructions, Texas. For public attitudes see also, "The Re-Annexation of Texas: In Its Influence on the Duration of Slavery," *United States Magazine and Democratic Review* 15 (July 1844): 16; and "Texas," *New Englander* 7 (July 1844): 453–454.

22. Adams, *British Interests and Activities in Texas,* pp. 174–175.

23. Robert J. Walker, "The Texas Question," *United States Magazine and Democratic Review,* n.s. 14 (April 1844): 423–430.

24. Callahan, *American Foreign Policy in Mexican Relations,* pp. 130–131.

25. Jonathan Tod to Walker, 18 December 1844, Walker Papers, Library of Congress Manuscripts Division; Aberdeen to Elliot, 23 January 1845, Adams, *British Diplomatic Correspondence,* pp. 429–430; Aberdeen to Lord Cowley, 7 January 1845; Aberdeen to Captain Elliot, Royal Navy, 23 January 1845; in Great Britain, Foreign Office 115, vol. 88, Instructions to British Ministers in the United States (Photostats, Library of Congress Manuscripts Division); Pakenham to Aberdeen, 29 January 1845, Foreign Office 5, vol. 424.

26. Siegel, *Political History of the Texas Republic,* pp. 253–254.

27. Carlos Bosch García, *Historia de relaciones entre México y los Estados Unidos, 1819–1848* (Mexico City, 1961), pp. 30–31, 265–266.

28. J. M. Castillo y Lanzas a su gobierno, 17 February 1836, in Bosch García, *Historia diplomática mexicana,* p. 212; M. E. Gorostiza, Contestación al memorandum de John Forsyth, 23 April 1836, ibid., pp. 221–222; Bosch García, *Historia de relaciones,* pp. 66–67.

29. Adams, *British Interests and Activities in Texas,* p. 23; Rives, "Mexican Diplomacy," pp. 278–279; Nance, *Attack and Counterattack,* p. 132.

30. Charles Bankhead to Aberdeen, 29 November 1844, in Great Britain, Foreign Office 115, vol. 88; Callahan, *American Foreign Policy in Mexican Relations,* pp. 122–123.

31. Major L. Wilson, "Manifest Destiny and Free Soil: The Triumph of Negative Liberalism in the 1840's," *Historian* 31 (November 1968): 39–40; Sellers, *Polk: Continentalist,* pp. 213–214, 232. For a detailed assessment of American expansion in this era see David Pletcher, *The Diplomacy of Annexation: Texas, Oregon, the Mexican War* (Columbia, Mo., 1973).

32. Perkins, *Monroe Doctrine, 1826–1867*, pp. 90–91; Allan Nevins, ed., *Polk: The Diary of a President, 1845–1849* (1929; reprint ed., New York, 1952), pp. 91–92.

33. Pakenham to Aberdeen, 25 June 1845, Foreign Office 5, vol. 426; Louis McLane to James Buchanan, 18, 26 September 1845, Dispatches, Great Britain.

34. Buchanan to Slidell, 10 November 1845, in Manning, *Inter-American Affairs*, 8 : 173.

35. Bosch García, *Historia de relaciones*, pp. 105–106; Pakenham to Aberdeen, 13 December 1845, Foreign Office 5, vol. 430.

36. Sellers, *Polk: Continentalist*, pp. 408–409; Pakenham to Aberdeen, 13 May 1846, Foreign Office 5, vol. 449.

37. Aberdeen to Charles Bankhead (Mexico), 1 June 1846, Foreign Office 115, vol. 91; McLane to Buchanan, 3 June 1846, Dispatches, Great Britain.

38. Perkins, *Monroe Doctrine, 1826–1867*, pp. 142–146.

39. Merk, *Monroe Doctrine and American Expansionism*, pp. 87–90.

40. Perkins, *Monroe Doctrine, 1826–1867*, pp. 147–148.

41. Merk, *Monroe Doctrine and American Expansionism*, pp. 165–170.

42. Ibid, pp. 194–207; Weinberg, *Manifest Destiny*, p. 182.

43. Perkins, *Monroe Doctrine, 1826–1867*, pp. 172–192.

4 • Central America and Cuba—Anglo-American Confrontation

1. Preston James, *Latin America* (New York, 1959), is a good introduction to the geography of the region. On the privateers, especially Drake, see Sir Julian Corbett, *Drake and the Tudor Navy*, 2 vols. (London, 1898), 1 : 118; J. A. Williamson, *The Age of Drake*, rev. ed. (London, 1946), pp. 118, 390; Philip A. Means, *The Spanish Main: Focus of Envy, 1492–1700* (New York, 1935), pp. 84–87; A. L. Rowse, *The Expansion of Elizabethan England* (New York, 1955), p. 180.

2. R. S. Platt, "Air Traverse of Central America," *Annals of the Association of American Geographers* 24 (1934): 38–39; Troy S. Floyd, *The Anglo-Spanish Struggle for Mosquitia* (Albuquerque, N.M., 1967), p. 1.

3. Thomas Karnes, *The Failure of Union: Central America, 1824–1960* (Chapel Hill, N.C., 1961), pp. 60–61; Mario Rodríguez, *A Palmerstonian Diplomat in Central America: Frederick Chatfield* (Tucson, Ariz., 1964), pp. 114–115; Robert A. Naylor, "The British Role in Central America prior to the Clayton-Bulwer Treaty of 1850," *Hispanic American Historical Review* 40 (August 1960): 370–371.

4. Karnes, *Failure of Union*, pp. 110–111.

5. Naylor, "British Role," pp. 364, 367, 369.

6. Dexter Perkins, *The Monroe Doctrine, 1826–1867* (Baltimore, 1933), pp. 16–17; Naylor, "British Role," passim.

7. Palmerston to Chatfield, 15 July 1840, quoted in Rodríguez, *Palmer-*

stonian Diplomat, p. 218; Sir Charles K. Webster, *The Foreign Policy of Palmerston, 1830–1841*, 2 vols. (London, 1951), 2 : 782–783.

8. Rodríguez, *Palmerstonian Diplomat*, pp. 53, 276–277, 282; Chatfield to Palmerston, 15 December 1849, in Foreign Office 115, vol. 106 (Photostat, Library of Congress Manuscripts Division); G. F. Hickson, "Palmerston and the Clayton-Bulwer Treaty," *Cambridge Historical Journal* 3, no. 3 (1931): 295–296.

9. Joseph B. Lockey, "Diplomatic Futility," *Hispanic American Historical Review* 10 (August 1930): 265.

10. "Atlantic and Pacific Canal," *Nile's Weekly Register* 31 (30 September 1826): 73; summary of 1826 commercial treaty with Central America, ibid., pp. 172–176.

11. J. B. Ferand, Consul in Panama, to Louis McLane, 21 October 1833, in Department of State, Consular Dispatches, Panama.

12. W. S. Robertson, "An Early Threat of Intervention by Force in South America," *Hispanic American Historical Review* 23 (November 1943): 630; E. T. Parks, *Colombia and the United States, 1765–1934* (Durham, N.C., 1935), pp. 194–195; William Nelson, Consul in Panama, to Abel P. Upshur, 18 January 1844, Consular Dispatches, Panama. Throughout this chapter I have used *Colombia* instead of *New Granada*.

13. Gerstle Mack, *The Land Divided* (New York, 1944), pp. 132–133; Mary W. Williams, *Anglo-American Isthmian Diplomacy, 1815–1915* (Washington, D.C., 1916), pp. 52–53; J. B. Lockey, "A Neglected Aspect of Isthmian Diplomacy," *American Historical Review* 41 (January 1936): 298–299, 305; Parks, *Colombia and the United States*, pp. 200–201.

14. Parks, *Colombia and the United States*, pp. 207–208, 214–215; Mack, *Land Divided*, pp. 134–135.

15. Richard W. Van Alstyne, "British Diplomacy and the Clayton-Bulwer Treaty, 1850–1860," *Journal of Modern History* 11 (June 1939): 151.

16. Chatfield to Palmerston, 28 June 1847, in Mark Van Aken, "British Policy Considerations in Central America before 1850," *Hispanic American Historical Review* 42 (February 1962): 57.

17. Rodríguez, *Palmerstonian Diplomat*, pp. 57, 72–73, 366.

18. Victor W. Von Hagen, "The Mosquito Coast of Honduras and Its Inhabitants," *Geographical Review* 30 (1940): 253; Richard W. Van Alstyne, "The Central American Policy of Lord Palmerston, 1846–1848," *Hispanic American Historical Review* 16 (1936): 344–346, 353–354.

19. Van Alstyne, "British Diplomacy," p. 149; Rodríguez, *Palmerstonian Diplomat*, p. 291.

20. William Nelson, Consul in Panama, to James Buchanan, 24 March 1848, Consular Dispatches, Panama; Clayton to George Bancroft, 2 May 1849, Clayton Manuscripts, vol. 4, Library of Congress Manuscripts Division; "British Aggression in Central America," *United States Magazine and Democratic Review*, n.s. 1 (January 1851): 14.

21. Williams, *Anglo-American Isthmian Diplomacy*, pp. 54–58; Buchanan to Hise, 3 June 1848, Instructions, Central America; Mack, *Land Divided*, pp. 183–184.

22. Williams, *Anglo-American Isthmian Diplomacy*, pp. 60–62; Charles L. Stansifer, "The Central American Career of E. George Squier," (Ph.D. diss., Tulane University, 1959), pp. 2, 19–20. See also Stansifer, "E. George Squier and the Honduras Interoceanic Railroad Project," *Hispanic American Historical Review* 46 (February 1966): 1–27, and "Ephraim George Squier," *Revista conservadora del pensamiento centroamericano* (November 1968): 3–64.

23. Clayton to Squier, 1 May 1849, Instructions, Central America; Clayton to George Bancroft, 30 April 1849, Clayton Manuscripts, vol. 4.

24. Stansifer, "E. George Squier," pp. 33–34, 40.

25. Ibid., pp. 47–49, 50–52, 55–59; Rodríguez, *Palmerstonian Diplomat*, pp. 302–303.

26. Mary W. Williams, ed., "Letters of E. George Squier to John M. Clayton, 1849–1850," *Hispanic American Historical Review* 1 (November 1918): 429–430.

27. Squier to Clayton, 12 September 1849, Clayton Manuscripts, vol. 6.

28. Williams, *Anglo-American Isthmian Diplomacy*, pp. 61–62, 64–66; Chatfield to Honduran Government, 2 November 1849, Great Britain, Foreign Office 115, vol. 106 (Photostat, Library of Congress Manuscripts Division); Squier to Chatfield, 2 November 1849, Squier Manuscripts, Library of Congress Manuscripts Division, box 3. Following the British departure from Tigre, Squier seized it while Chatfield increased the pressure on Nicaragua and Costa Rica. Mary W. Williams notes that the United States flag flew over the island "for many months,... regardless of the fact that the Honduras legislature had disavowed the treaty of cession" *(Anglo-American Isthmian Diplomacy*, pp. 115–116).

29. Squier to Clayton, 12 December 1849, Clayton Manuscripts, vol. 7; Clayton to Lawrence, 26 December 1849, ibid.

30. Clayton to Bulwer, 1 January 1850, ibid., vol. 8; Bulwer to Clayton, 3 January 1850, ibid.

31. Clayton to Lawrence, 13 December 1849, ibid., vol. 7; Clayton to W. C. Rives, 7, 26 January 1850, ibid., vol. 8.

32. Clayton to Lawrence, 31 March 1849, ibid., vol. 7.

33. Van Alstyne, "British Diplomacy," p. 152.

34. John Crampton to Palmerston, 1 October 1849, copy in Clayton Manuscripts, vol. 6; Clayton to Lawrence, 21 October 1849, ibid.; Lawrence to Clayton, 9 November 1849, ibid.

35. Van Alstyne, "British Diplomacy," p. 154; *New York Herald* clipping, in Great Britain, Foreign Office 5, vol. 500 (Photostat, Library of Congress Manuscripts Division).

36. Van Alstyne, "British Diplomacy," p. 157; Bulwer to Palmerston, 6

January 1850, Great Britain Foreign Office 5, vol. 511 (Photostat, Library of Congress Manuscripts Division); J. W. White (Canal Company official), to Bulwer, 18 January 1850, Clayton Manuscripts, vol. 8.

37. Clayton to Bulwer, 15 February 1850, Clayton Manuscripts, vol. 8; Bulwer to Clayton, 14 February 1850, ibid.; Clayton to Bulwer, 19 April 1850, ibid., vol. 9.

38. Hickson, "Palmerston and the Clayton-Bulwer Treaty," pp. 298–299; Van Alstyne, "British Diplomacy," pp. 152–154. In the Squier papers there is a manuscript on the Mosquito Question, in which the former diplomat unites the issue to the Monroe Doctrine.

39. R. A. Humphreys, *The Diplomatic History of British Honduras, 1638–1901* (London, 1961), p. 53; Van Alstyne, "British Diplomacy," p. 161; Rodríguez, *Palmerstonian Diplomat*, pp. 337–338.

40. Mack, *Land Divided*, pp. 191–192; Marcy to Solon Borland, 17 June 1853, Instructions, Central America; Louis N. Feipel, "The Navy and Filibustering in the Fifties," *United States Naval Institute Proceedings*, 44 (1918): 1220–1230, 1237; Perkins, *Monroe Doctrine, 1826–1867*, pp. 209–210.

41. Marcy to Buchanan, 6 August 1855, in William R. Manning, ed., *Diplomatic Correspondence of the United States: Inter-American Affairs, 1831–1860*, 12 vols. (Washington, D.C., 1932–1939), 8 : 118; Marcy to George M. Dallas, 26 July 1856, in ibid., pp. 143–144; Van Alstyne, "British Diplomacy," p. 178; Hickson, "Palmerston and the Clayton-Bulwer Treaty," pp. 301–303.

42. I have based this section primarily on material in my *Cuban Policy of the United States: A Brief History* (New York, 1968), pp. 21–52.

43. Stanley Urban, "The Africanization of Cuba Scare," *Hispanic American Historical Review* 37 (February 1957): 30–31; Philip Foner, *A History of Cuba*, 4 vols. (New York, 1967), 2 : 76; Crampton to Clarendon, 7 February 1853, in Richard W. Van Alstyne, ed., "Anglo-American Relations, 1853–1857," *American Historical Review* 42 (April 1937): 493–495; Graham to Clarendon, 24 October 1854, in ibid., pp. 497–498.

44. Marcy to Buchanan, 2 July 1853; Manning, *Inter-American Affairs*, 7 : 93–94.

45. Buchanan to Marcy, 31 March 1854, Marcy Manuscripts, Library of Congress Manuscripts Division.

5 • The French Intervention in Mexico

1. James Morton Callahan, *American Foreign Policy in Mexican Relations* (New York, 1967), p. 208.

2. J. Fred Rippy, *Latin America in World Politics: An Outline Survey* (New York, 1928), pp. 96–97; Callahan, *American Foreign Policy in Mexican Relations*, pp. 192, 200–201; William L. Marcy to John Forsyth, 16 August 1856, Department of State, Instructions, Mexico; Draft of Treaty, ibid.

3. Robert Toombs to W. W. Burwell, 13 March 1857, in Ulrich B. Phil-

lips, ed., *The Correspondence of Robert Toombs, Alexander Stephens, and Howell Cobb*, American Historical Association Annual Report, 1911, vol. 2 (Washington, D.C., 1913), p. 399. The concept of an American-ruled hemisphere from the Rio Grande to the Orinoco was ridiculed, however, by a future member of Lincoln's cabinet—Edward Bates, Diary, 20 April 1859, in Howard K. Beale, ed., *The Diary of Edward Bates, 1859–1866*, American Historical Association Annual Report, 1930, vol. 4 (Washington, D.C., 1933), p. 4.

4. Lewis Cass to Robert McLane, Instructions, Mexico.

5. Callahan, *American Foreign Policy in Mexican Relations*, pp. 263–264, 268–269.

6. Howard Wilson, "President Buchanan's Proposed Intervention in Mexico," *American Historical Review* 5 (July 1900): 691, 698; Callahan, *American Foreign Policy in Mexican Relations*, p. 271.

7. Agustín Cue Canovas, *El tratado McLane-Ocampo: Juárez, los Estados Unidos y Europa* (Mexico City, 1959), pp. 159–160; Ralph Roeder, *Juárez and His Mexico*, 2 vols., (New York, 1947), 1 : 224–225.

8. Henry Blumenthal, *A Reappraisal of Franco-American Relations, 1830–1871* (Chapel Hill, N.C., 1959), p. 45; Genaro Estrado, *Don Juan Prim y su labor diplomático en México* (Mexico City, 1928), pp. viii–ix; Christian Schefer (Xavier Ortíz Monasterio, trans.), *Los origenes de la intervención francesa en México, 1858–1862* (Mexico City, 1939), p. 22.

9. Roeder, *Juárez*, 1 : 279–280, 320; H. L. Hoskins, "French Views of the Monroe Doctrine and the Mexican Expedition," *Hispanic American Historical Review* 4 (November 1921): 679.

10. Schefer, *Los origenes*, p. 108; Egon Corti, *Maximilian and Charlotte of Mexico*, 2 vols. (New York, 1928), 1 : 113–114; William S. Robertson, "The Tripartite Treaty of London," *Hispanic American Historical Review* 20 (May 1940): 178, 188–189.

11. Lord John Russell to Sir Charles Wyke, 30 March 1861, in Great Britain, Foreign Office 115, vol. 286 (Photostat, Library of Congress Manuscripts Division); Wyke to Russell, 27 May 1861, ibid.; Russell to Cowley, 23 September 1861, ibid.

12. Col. Charles Blanchot, *Mémoires: l'intervention française au Mexique*, 3 vols. (Paris, 1911), 1 : 16; Wyke to Russell, 29 December 1861, in Great Britain, Foreign Office 115, vol. 286, Library of Congress Manuscripts Division.

13. Schefer, *Los origenes*, pp. 169–170; Russell to Sir John Crampton, 19 January 1862, Great Britain, Foreign Office 115, vol. 286; Kenneth Bourne, *Britain and the Balance of Power in North America, 1815–1908* (Berkeley and Los Angeles, 1967), pp. 255–256.

14. Schefer, *Los origenes*, pp. 99–100; Francisco Bulnes, *El verdadero Juárez y la verdad sobre la intervención y el Imperio* (Paris, 1904), p. 11.

15. Prim to Napoleon III, 17 March 1862, in Estrado, *Don Juan Prim*, pp. 107-108.

16. Roeder, *Juárez*, 2 : 422–423.

17. Callahan, *American Foreign Policy in Mexican Relations*, pp. 282–283; Seward to Thomas Corwin, 2 September 1861, Department of State, Instructions, Mexico.

18. Seward to Dayton, 3 March 1862, 31 March 1862, Instructions, France; Seward to Charles Francis Adams, 3 March 1862, quoted in Dexter Perkins, *The Monroe Doctrine, 1826–1867* (Baltimore, 1933), pp. 431–432; Alfred J. and Kathyrn A. Hanna, *Napoleon III and Mexico: American Triumph over Monarchy* (Chapel Hill, N.C., 1971), pp. 49–52.

19. Hanna and Hanna, *Napoleon III and Mexico*, pp. 5–6; Schefer, *Los origenes*, p. 29; Pierre de la Gorce, *Napoléon III et sa politique* (Paris, 1933), pp. 179–180; Blumenthal, *Reappraisal of Franco-American Relations*, p. 168.

20. Blumenthal, *Reappraisal of Franco-American Relations*, p. 168.

21. Perkins, *Monroe Doctrine, 1826–1867*, p. 415; Corti, *Maximilian and Charlotte*, 1 : 295–296.

22. Octave Aubry (Arthur Livingston, trans.), *The Second Empire* (Philadelphia, 1940), p. 290; Corti, *Maximilian and Charlotte*, 1 : 29; Schefer, *Los origenes*, pp. 33–34, 41.

23. Lynn Case, ed., *French Opinion on the United States and Mexico, 1860–1867: Extracts from the Reports of the Procurers-Generaux* (New York, 1936), pp. 311–313, 349; Roeder, *Juárez*, 2 : 453, 466–467; Napoleon III, Speech to the Legislative Session, 5 November 1863, in Dispatches, France.

24. Dayton, Memorandum, 9 April 1863, Dispatches, France.

25. Seward to Dayton, 21 June 1862, 8 May 1863, 26 September 1863, Instructions, France.

26. Corti, *Maximilian and Charlotte*, 1 : 352, 2 : 421–422; José L. Blasio (Robert Murray, trans.), *Maximilian, Emperor of Mexico; Memoirs of His Private Secretary* (New Haven, Conn., 1934), pp. 26–27.

27. Nancy Nichols Barker, *Distaff Diplomacy: The Empress Eugénie and the Foreign Policy of the Second Empire* (Austin, Tex., 1967), pp. 87–88, 129–130.

28. Dayton to Seward, 21 December 1863, 31 December 1863, 29 January 1864, 22 April 1864, Dispatches, France; Glyndon G. Van Deusen, *William Henry Seward* (New York, 1967), p. 369; Hanna and Hanna, *Napoleon III and Mexico*, pp. 118–119.

29. Marvin Goldwert, "Matías Romero and Congressional Opposition to Seward's Policy toward the French Intervention in Mexico," *Americas* 12 (1965): 22–23, 24–25, 32–33; Hanna and Hanna, *Napoleon III and Mexico*, pp. 122–123.

30. Corti, *Maximilian and Charlotte*, 2 : 484. On 13 March 1865, the *Memorial Diplomatique* editorialized on United States conditions: "An empty treasury, a country laid waste and a decimated population—are these not interior enemies with whom they shall also have to count?" (quoted in Dispatches, France).

31. John Bigelow to Seward, 14 February 1865, Dispatches, France.

32. Bigelow to Seward, 5 May 1865, 26 May 1865, ibid.

33. Hanna and Hanna, *Napoleon III and Mexico*, pp. 238–239; Roeder, *Juárez*, 2 : 601–602; Callahan, *American Foreign Policy in Mexican Relations*, p. 305. But many newspapers, especially in New England, urged a conciliatory policy toward France. See Perkins, *Monroe Doctrine, 1826–1867*, pp. 503–504.

34. Van Deusen, *Seward*, pp. 370, 487–488; Seward to Bigelow, 6 September 1865, Instructions, France.

35. Quoted in Goldwert, "Matías Romero," pp. 36–37; Clyde E. Duniway, "Reasons for the Withdrawal of the French from Mexico," *American Historical Association Annual Report, 1902*, vol. 1 (Washington, D.C., 1903), p. 326.

36. Translation of Debate in French Senate, 10 March 1865, 12 March 1865, Dispatches, France; Translation of Debate in Corps Legislatif, 10 April 1865, ibid.

37. Roeder, Juárez, 2 : 488, 537–538; Jack Dabbs, *The French Army in Mexico* (The Hague, 1964), pp. 275–276.

38. Napoleon III, Speech to Legislative Session, 22 January 1866; *Le Temps*, August 1866, in Dispatches, France.

39. Bigelow to Seward, 14 June 1866, ibid.; Duniway, "Reasons for the Withdrawal of the French," p. 322; Callahan, *American Foreign Policy in Mexican Relations*, p. 327.

40. Napoleon III, Speech to Senators and Deputies, 14 February 1867, Dispatches, France.

41. Blanchot, *Mémoires*, 3 : 399.

6 • The New Empire

1. Walter LaFeber, *The New Empire: An Interpretation of American Expansion, 1860–1898* (Ithaca, N.Y., 1963), pp. 3–4, 177–178. For comparisons of British, German, French, and American growth of this era see Élie Halévy, *A History of the English People in the Nineteenth Century*, vol. 5, *Imperialism and the Rise of Labor* (1913, reprint ed., New York, 1961), pp. 10–11.

2. Glyndon G. Van Deusen, *William Henry Seward* (New York, 1967), pp. 526–527; LaFeber, *New Empire*, pp. 27–28.

3. Dexter Perkins, *The Monroe Doctrine, 1867–1907* (Baltimore, 1937), pp. 22–23.

4. David Pletcher, *The Awkward Years: American Foreign Relations under Garfield and Arthur* (Columbia, Mo., 1962), pp. 284, 355–356; LaFeber, *New Empire*, pp. 48–49.

5. Harold and Margaret Sprout, *The Rise of American Naval Power, 1776–1918* (Princeton, N.J., 1942), pp. 175–176, 195.

6. Arthur Marder, *The Anatomy of British Sea Power: A History of British Naval Policy in the Pre-Dreadnought Era* (New York, 1940), p. 47.

7. Julius Pratt, *Expansionists of 1898: The Acquisition of Hawaii and the Spanish Islands* (Baltimore, 1936), pp. 222–223.

8. Mahan, "Influence of Sea Power on History," quoted in Allan Westcott, ed., *Mahan on Naval Warfare* (Boston, 1941), pp. 27–28.

9. Walter Herrick, *The American Naval Revolution* (Baton Rouge, La., 1966), pp. 10–11; Capt. W. D. Puleston, *Mahan: The Life and Work of Captain Alfred Thayer Mahan, USN* (New Haven, Conn., 1939), p. 129; LaFeber, *New Empire*, pp. 90–91.

10. Sumner Welles, *Naboth's Vineyard: The Dominican Republic, 1844–1924*, 2 vols. (1928; reprint ed., Washington, D.C., 1966), 1 : 140–141.

11. Rayford W. Logan, *Haiti and the Dominican Republic* (New York, 1968), pp. 37–38.

12. Welles, *Naboth's Vineyard*, 1 : 238–239; James Morton Callahan, *American Foreign Policy in Mexican Relations* (New York, 1967), p. 279; Francisco Cuevas Cancino, *Del congreso de Panamá a la conferencia de Caracas, 1826–1954*, 2 vols. (Caracas, 1955), 1 : 291.

13. Welles, *Naboth's Vineyard*, 1 : 324–325.

14. Ibid., 2 : 914–915; Allan Nevins, *Hamilton Fish: The Inner History of the Grant Administration*, 2 vols., rev. ed. (New York, 1967), 1 : 251; Melvin Knight, *The Americans in Santo Domingo* (New York, 1928), p. 7.

15. Nevins, *Hamilton Fish*, 1 : 318–319; Draft, Santo Domingo Annexation Message, 31 May 1870, in Grant Papers, series 3, Library of Congress Manuscripts Division; Robert Beisner, "Thirty Years Before Manila: E. L. Godkin, Carl Schurz, and Anti-Imperialism in the Gilded Age," *Historian* 30 (August 1968): 572–573; Charles Tansill, *The United States and Santo Domingo, 1789–1873* (Baltimore, 1938), pp. 432–433.

16. Halvadan Koht, "The Origin of Seward's Plan to Purchase the Danish West Indies," *American Historical Review* 50 (July 1945): 762–767; Charles Tansill, *The Purchase of the Danish West Indies* (Baltimore, 1932), pp. 7, 52–53, 59–60.

17. Tansill, *Purchase of the Danish West Indies*, pp. 78, 89–90, 151.

18. Ramiro Guerra y Sanchez, *Guerra de los Diez Años, 1868–1878*, 2 vols. (Havana, 1950), 1 : 166. For a general discussion see Lester D. Langley, *The Cuban Policy of the United States: A Brief History* (New York, 1968), chap. 3.

19. Nevins, *Hamilton Fish*, 1 : 180–181, 194–195.

20. Fish to William C. Bryant, 17 November 1873, in Fish Papers, Letterbooks, vol. 9, pp. 97–98. Library of Congress Manuscripts Division.

21. Charles Bartlett, "British Reaction to the Cuban Insurrection of 1868–1878," *Hispanic American Historical Review* 37 (1957): 312.

22. Gerstle Mack, *The Land Divided: A History of the Panama Canal and Other Isthmian Canal Projects* (New York, 1944), pp. 209–210; Pletcher, *Awkward Years*, pp. 23–24.

23. Pletcher, *Awkward Years*, pp. 7–8; LaFeber, *New Empire*, p. 43; Perkins, *Monroe Doctrine, 1867–1907*, pp. 65, 77–78.

24. Pletcher, *Awkward Years*, pp. 31–33; George Howe, "The Clayton-Bulwer Treaty," *American Historical Review* 42 (April 1937): 489; Mary W. Williams, *Anglo-American Isthmian Diplomacy, 1815–1915* (Washington, D.C., 1916), pp. 277–278.

25. Wayne Clegern, *British Honduras: Colonial Dead End, 1859–1900* (Baton Rouge, La., 1967), p. 163.

26. Thomas A. Bayard to E. J. Phelps, United States Legation, London, 23 November 1888, Department of State, *Foreign Relations, 1888*, pt. 1 (Washington, D.C., 1889), pp. 766–767.

27. Perkins, *Monroe Doctrine, 1867–1907*, p. 146; Bayard to Gresham, 2 May 1895, Department of State, Dispatches, Great Britain; *London Morning Post*, 3 May 1895, clipping in State Department files.

28. Nelson Blake, "Background of Cleveland's Venezuelan Policy: A Reinterpretation," *American Historical Review* 47 (January 1942): 263–264, 266; Perkins, *Monroe Doctrine, 1867–1907*, pp. 42–43. The Nicaraguan leader responsible for these nationalistic assertions was José Santos Zelaya, who later incurred the hostility of Theodore Roosevelt and William Howard Taft for his opposition to United States policies in Central America. For some insights into his career I am indebted to Charles L. Stansifer, who provided me with a copy of his paper, "José Santos Zelaya: An Interpretation," which was delivered at the Missouri Valley Conference of Collegiate Teachers of History, Omaha, March 1968.

29. Paul R. Fossum, "The Anglo-Venezuelan Boundary Dispute," *Hispanic American Historical Review* 8 (August 1928): 301–302; William Dawson, "Imperial Policy in the Old and New World, 1885–1899," in A. W. Ward and G. P. Gooch, eds., *Cambridge History of British Foreign Policy*, 3 vols. (New York, 1922–1923), 3 : 222–223; W. H. Gray, "American Diplomacy in Venezuela, 1835–1865," *Hispanic American Historical Review* 20 (November 1940): 553.

30. D. A. Graber, *Crisis Diplomacy: A History of U.S. Intervention Policies and Practices* (Washington, D.C., 1959), pp. 101–102; Pletcher, *Awkward Years*, pp. 128–129.

31. Gresham to Bayard, 1 December 1894, Instructions, Great Britain.

32. Ernest May, *Imperial Democracy: The Emergence of America as a Great Power* (New York, 1961), pp. 36–37.

33. Gresham to Bayard, 9 April 1895, Instructions, Great Britain.

34. LaFeber, *New Empire*, p. 256; Cleveland to Olney, 7 July 1895, Olney Papers, General Correspondence, vol. 28, Library of Congress Manuscripts Division.

35. Printed Copy, Olney to Bayard, 20 July 1895, Instructions, Great Britain; Alfred L. P. Dennis, *Adventures in American Diplomacy, 1896–1906* (New York, 1928), pp. 24–25. For a somewhat different view, see G. B.

Young, "Intervention under the Monroe Doctrine: The Olney Corollary," *Political Science Quarterly* 57 (June 1942): 262.

36. Bayard to Olney, 9 August 1895, Dispatches, Great Britain; Olney to Bayard, 8 October 1895, Instructions, Great Britain; *London Morning Post,* 11 October 1895, clipping in State Department files.

37. *Spectator,* 26 October 1895, clipping in State Department files.

38. Olney to Bayard, 20 November 1895, Olney Letterbooks, vol. 7, p. 314, Olney Papers, Library of Congress Manuscripts Division; Perkins, *Monroe Doctrine, 1867–1907,* pp. 172–173.

39. J. A. S. Grenville, *Lord Salisbury and Foreign Policy: The Close of the Nineteenth Century* (London, 1964), pp. 64–65.

40. Harold U. Faulkner, *Politics, Reform, and Expansion,* 1890–1900, paperback ed. (New York, 1963), pp. 215–216; "The President's Startling Message on Venezuela," *Literary Digest* 12 (28 December 1895): 241–245. Cleveland explored the reasons for his disagreement with his ambassador in London in Cleveland to Bayard, 29 December 1895, in Allan Nevins, ed., *Letters of Grover Cleveland, 1850–1908* (Boston and New York, 1933), pp. 417–418.

41. Bayard to Olney, 24 December 1895, Dispatches, Great Britain; May, *Imperial Democracy,* pp. 46–47; William L. Langer, *The Diplomacy of Imperialism, 1890–1902,* 2nd ed. (New York, 1960), p. 239; Resolution, 29 December 1895, State Department files.

42. Marder, *Anatomy of British Sea Power,* p. 255; A. E. Campbell, *Great Britain and the United States, 1895–1903* (London, 1960), pp. 29–30, 35–36; Grenville, *Lord Salisbury and Foreign Policy,* pp. 17–18, 67–68.

43. Perkins, *Monroe Doctrine, 1867–1907,* pp. 223–224; Olney to Bayard, 8 February 1896, Olney Letterbooks, vol. 7, p. 458, Olney Papers, Library of Congress Manuscripts Division; Joseph J. Matthews, "Informal Diplomacy in the Venezuelan Crisis of 1896," *Mississippi Valley Historical Review* 50 (September 1963): 195–212.

44. D. C. M. Platt, *Finance, Trade, and Politics in British Foreign Policy, 1815–1914* (Oxford, 1968), pp. 347–348; Halévy, *Imperialism and Rise of Labor,* pp. 42–43; Marder, *Anatomy of British Sea Power,* p. 257; Campbell, *Great Britain and the United States,* p. 45.

45. Young, "Olney Corollary," pp. 278–279; Olney to A. E. Keet, ed., *Forum,* 15 January 1897, Olney Letterbooks, vol. 9, p. 300, Olney Papers, Library of Congress Manuscripts Division.

46. For contrasting interpretations of the Venezuelan crisis see Blake, "Background of Cleveland's Venezuelan Policy," pp. 275–276; and Walter LaFeber, "The Background of Cleveland's Venezuelan Policy: A Reinterpretation," *American Historical Review* 66 (July 1961): 947–948; idem, *New Empire,* pp. 242–243, 280–281. Two essential works on the Anglo-American reconciliation are Charles Campbell, *Anglo-American Understanding, 1898–1903* (Baltimore, 1957), and Bradford Perkins, *The Great Rapproche-*

ment: England and the United States, 1898–1914 (New York, 1968). For late nineteenth century coverage, see also Milton Plesur, America's Outward Thrust: Approaches to Foreign Affairs, 1865–1900 (DeKalb, Ill., 1971), and Gerald G. Eggert, Richard Olney: Evolution of a Statesman (University Park, Pa., 1974).

7 • The Spanish-American War and After

1. Lester Langley, The Cuban Policy of the United States: A Brief History (New York, 1968), chap. 4. In this account I have made no effort to detail the Pacific issues in the coming of the war.

2. Jerónimo Becker, Historia de las relaciones exteriores de España durante el siglo xix, 3 vols. (Madrid, 1924–1926), 3 : 806, 856; Rafael Altamira y Crevea, Historia de España y la civilización española, 4th ed., 5 vols. (Barcelona, 1900–1911), vol. 5 by Don Pío Zabala y Lera, pt. 2, pp. 86–87.

3. Altamira, Historia de España p. 89; Becker, Historia, 3 : 864, 879–880. The quotation is from Octavio Gil Munilla, "Cuba, Problema Español, 1891–1898," Anuario de Estudios Americanos 9 (1953): 511–512. Translation mine.

4. Pascual Cervera (translation), The Spanish-American War (Washington, D.C., 1899), p. 25. Italics mine.

5. Stewart Woodford to McKinley, 20 October 1897, Dispatches, Spain; A. E. Campbell, Great Britain and the United States, 1895–1903 (London, 1960), p. 144; Orestes Ferrara (William Shea, trans.), The Last Spanish War (New York, 1937), pp. 75–76.

6. Reply of McKinley to representatives of Great Britain, Germany, France, Austria-Hungary, Russia, and Italy, 6 April 1898, in Speeches and Addresses of McKinley (New York, 1900), pp. 79–80; Alfred L. P. Dennis, Adventures in American Diplomacy, 1896–1906 (New York, 1928), p. 73.

7. Woodford to Sherman, 11 October 1897, Dispatches, Spain; L. M. Sears, "French Opinion of the Spanish-American War," Hispanic American Historical Review 7 (1927): 27–28; Jacques Crokaert, La Méditerranée Americaine: L'éxpansion des États-Unis dans la mer des Antilles (Paris, 1927), p. 213.

8. E. Malcolm Carroll, Germany and the Great Powers, 1866–1914: A Study in Public Opinion and Foreign Policy (New York, 1938), pp. 350–351, 411.

9. Lester B. Shippee, "Germany and the Spanish-American War," American Historical Review 30 (July 1925): 758–759, 763.

10. Sherman to Andrew White, 5 April 1898, Instructions, Germany.

11. William Day to White, 18 July 1898, ibid.; Andrew White, Autobiography, 2 vols. (New York, 1905), 2 : 168–169.

12. The Kaiser's letter is reprinted in Norman Rich and M. H. Fisher, eds., The Holstein Papers, vol. 4, Correspondence (Cambridge, 1963), p. 83.

13. *Times* (London), 23 August 1895, clipping in State Department files; Sherman to Hay, 30 June 1897, Instructions, Britain.

14. *London Daily Chronicle,* 26 March 1898, clipping in State Department files.

15. *Times* (London), 28 March 1898; clipping in State Department files.

16. Hay to Sherman, 1 April 1898, Dispatches, Britain.

17. J. A. S. Grenville, *Lord Salisbury and Foreign Policy: The Close of the Nineteenth Century* (London, 1964), p. 202; R. G. Neale, "British-American Relations during the Spanish-American War," *Historical Studies, Australia and New Zealand* 6 (November 1953): 81. The author has expanded on this subject in *Great Britain and United States Expansion* (East Lansing, Mich., 1966).

18. Denis Judd, *Balfour and the British Empire: A Study in Imperial Evolution, 1874–1932* (London, 1968), pp. 313–314; Geoffrey Seed, "British Reactions to American Imperialism Reflected in Journals of Opinion, 1898–1900," *Political Science Quarterly* 73 (June 1958): 258–259; Campbell, *Great Britain and the United States,* pp. 149–150; Charles Campbell, *Anglo-American Understanding, 1898–1903* (Baltimore, 1957), p. 26. On this point see also William L. Langer, *The Diplomacy of Imperialism, 1890–1902* (New York, 1960), pp. 490–491.

19. Walter R. Herrick, Jr., *The American Naval Revolution* (Baton Rouge, La., 1966), pp. 234–235; Day to Hay, 3 June 1898, Instructions, Britain.

20. Campbell, *Great Britain and the United States,* pp. 52-53; J. S. Ardagh, Director, Military Intelligence, Memorandum Respecting the Clayton-Bulwer treaty, 9 December 1898, quoted in Campbell, *Anglo-American Understanding,* pp. 353–356.

21. Wilfrid H. Callcott, *The Caribbean Policy of the United States, 1890–1920* (Baltimore, 1942), pp. 120–121; Campbell, *Anglo-American Understanding,* pp. 194–195; Howard K. Beale, *Theodore Roosevelt and the Rise of America to World Power* (1956; reprint ed., New York, 1970), pp. 102–103; Howard Hill, *Roosevelt and the Caribbean* (1927; reprint ed., New York, 1965), pp. 31–32.

22. Kenneth Bourne, *Britain and the Balance of Power in North America, 1815–1908* (Berkeley and Los Angeles, 1967), p. 348; Admiralty to Foreign Office, 5 January 1901, quoted in Campbell, *Anglo-American Understanding,* p. 360; Grenville, *Lord Salisbury and Foreign Policy,* pp. 385–386.

23. Campbell, *Anglo-American Understanding,* pp. 224–225; Dennis, *Adventures in American Diplomacy,* pp. 164–165; J. A. S. Grenville, "Great Britain and the Isthmian Canal, 1898–1901," *American Historical Review* 61 (October 1955): 51–52, 64–65, 66–67.

24. Campbell, *Anglo-American Understanding,* pp. 238–239; Grenville, *Lord Salisbury and Foreign Policy,* pp. 383–389.

25. P. F. Fenton, "Diplomatic Relations of the United States and Venezuela, 1880–1915," *Hispanic American Historical Review* 8 (1928): 333–334.

26. Mariano Picón-Salas, *Los días de Cipriano Castro,* 2nd ed. (Barquismeto, Venezuela, 1955), p. 9; Stephen Bonsal, *The American Mediterranean* (New York, 1913), pp. 183–184.

27. Chester Lloyd Jones, *Caribbean since 1900* (New York, 1935), pp. 219–220; Hill, *Roosevelt and the Caribbean,* pp. 109–110; Alfred Vagts, *Deutschland und die Vereinigten Staaten in der Weltpolitik,* 2 vols. (New York, 1935), 2 : 1525–1530. (Prof. Beverly Heckart, Central Washington State College, translated these pages from Vagts.) See also Dana G. Munro, *Intervention and Dollar Diplomacy in the Caribbean, 1900–1921* (Princeton, N.J., 1964), p. 67.

28. Campbell, *Anglo-American Understanding,* pp. 275–276.

29. Vagts, *Deutschland und die Vereinigten Staaten,* 2 : 1537–1541.

30. Callcott, *Caribbean Policy,* pp. 127–128; Dexter Perkins, *The Monroe Doctrine, 1867–1907* (Baltimore, 1937), pp. 332–333, 336–337.

31. Perkins, *Monroe Doctrine, 1867–1907,* pp. 387–388; Munro, *Intervention and Dollar Diplomacy,* pp. 70–71.

32. Hill, *Roosevelt and the Caribbean,* pp. 141–142; Jones, *Caribbean since 1900,* pp. 227–228; Dennis, *Adventures in American Diplomacy,* p. 289; Perkins, *Monroe Doctrine, 1867–1907,* p. 381; Élie Halévy, *A History of the English People in the Nineteenth Century,* vol. 5, *Imperialism and the Rise of Labor* (New York, 1961), p. 134.

33. Seward W. Livermore, "Theodore Roosevelt, The American Navy, and the Venezuelan Crisis of 1902–1903," *American Historical Review* 51 (April 1946): 456–457, 458–459, 459–460, 462–463, 465, 468–469.

34. Vagts, *Deutschland und die Vereinigten Staaten,* 2 : 1589–1590, 1592, 1593; Campbell, *Anglo-American Understanding,* pp. 291–292; Perkins, *Monroe Doctrine, 1867–1907,* pp. 355–356.

35. Beale, *Theodore Roosevelt,* pp. 340–369; Lloyd Jones, *Caribbean since 1900,* pp. 231–232. See also Vagts, *Deutschland und die Vereinigten Staaten,* 2 : 1602–1603, 1603–1604, 1606–1607.

36. Beale, *Theodore Roosevelt,* pp. 81–82, 101–102; Campbell, *Anglo-American Understanding,* pp. 283–284, 287–288; George Monger, *The End of Isolation: British Foreign Policy, 1900–1907* (London, 1963), pp. 106–107. On this matter see also Vagts, "Hopes and Fears of an American-German War, 1870–1915," *Political Science Quarterly* 54 (1939): 532–535; and D. C. M. Platt, "The Allied Coercion of Venezuela: A Reassessment," *Inter-American Economic Affairs* 15 (1962): 3–28.

37. Dana G. Munro, *Intervention and Dollar Diplomacy,* pp. 78–101; J. Fred Rippy, "The Initiation of the Customs Receivership in the Dominican Republic," *Hispanic American Historical Review* 17 (November 1937): 419–457.

The actual shooting of Heaureaux was committed by Ramón Cáceres, who became president in 1906.

Epilogue

1. Ernest R. May, *American Imperialism: A Speculative Essay* (New York, 1968), p. 164.

2. A. E. Campbell, *Great Britain and the United States, 1895–1903* (London, 1960), pp. 195–196.

3. Max Savelle, *The Origins of American Diplomacy: The International History of Anglo-America, 1492–1763* (New York, 1967), p. 157.

4. Thomas A. Bailey, "America's Emergence as a World Power: The Myth and the Verity," *Pacific Historical Review* 30 (February 1961), p. 3.

5. J. Fred Rippy, "Antecedents of the Roosevelt Corollary of the Monroe Doctrine," ibid. 9 (September 1940): 267–279; A. K. Weinberg, *Manifest Destiny* (1935; reprint ed., Chicago, 1963) p. 41; Dana G. Munro, *Intervention and Dollar Diplomacy in the Caribbean, 1900–1921* (Princeton, N.J., 1964), p. 65; William E. Leuchtenburg, "Progressivism and Imperialism: The Progressive Movement and American Foreign Policy, 1898–1916," *Mississippi Valley Historical Review* 39 (December 1952): 500.

Index